career CONNECTIONS

One Trade, Many Careers

Career Connections: One Trade, Many Careers CC00SSM

May 2023

ISBN: 978-0-615-94717-4

Send all inquiries to:

Carpenters International Training Fund

212 Carpenters Union Way, Las Vegas, NV 89119-4218

www.carpenters.org

Associate Membership ACTE

Career

CONNECTIONS

One Trade, Many Careers

CC00SSM

preface

The first priority of the Carpenters International Training Fund (CITF) is state-of-the art training—for the members of the United Brotherhood of Carpenters (UBC) and for the union contractors who employ them. With the *Career Connections* program, CITF brings the skill and experience of its members to high school students and pre-apprenticeship trainees.

The decision-making, goal setting, and employability skills presented in *Career Connections: One Trade, Many Careers* have long been known and are well-documented. Information on carpentry careers is illustrated with actual carpenters at work on jobsites.

The shop projects contained in *Career Connections: Project Book 1*, *Project Book 2*, and *Project Book 3* are designed to develop a progression of skills from basic (*Project Book 1*) to advanced (*Project Book 3*). Lead-Up Exercises allow students to practice skills that will be used in building projects and these Exercises build student confidence in their skills. Step-by-step procedures for each project are supported by drawings and photos illustrating critical steps in the process.

CITF supports this instructional system with the active participation of its instructor-members located across the United States in more than 120 UBC Training Centers. Carpentry programs will have access to these outreach programs for guidance and technical assistance.

A Cautionary Note

The tasks and procedures in this program have been created to teach one or more acceptable and recognized methods of performing specific tasks. These procedures are not meant to be, nor should they be considered, an absolute or complete presentation of the procedures and safety measures related to the tasks.

In the real world of construction, work processes and government regulations can and do change, and it is the employer's responsibility to provide workers with the most recent technical and safety information regarding these processes. Guidelines and instructions presented in this program are not meant to supersede manufacturers' instructions or contractors' jobsite procedures; nor are they meant to replace any current local, state, provincial, or federal safety rules and regulations.

It is essential that everyone always follow all current local, state, provincial, or federal safety rules, regulations, and guidelines in performing any of these tasks.

No statements made in this program should give the impression that the Carpenters International Training Fund or the United Brotherhood of Carpenters and Joiners of America, their affiliates, representatives, or employees have assumed any part of the employer's legal responsibility to provide a "safe and healthful workplace," as mandated by the Occupational Safety and Health Act of 1970.

acknowledgments

The preparation of this program would not have been possible without the technical contributions and cooperative efforts of a wide range of individuals and groups associated with the United Brotherhood of Carpenters (UBC).

Let us start with the members. Without their commitment to excellence, their understanding of the importance of training, and their continued contributions and support, this program would be meaningless. It is their contributions that make this program possible, and this program serves their interests as well as the interests of future workers in the industry.

We would like to acknowledge the instructors and JATCs throughout the United States and Canada who helped develop and review this program. We also recognize the contributions of the members of the Carpenters International Training Advisory Group. Finally, we recognize the ongoing efforts of the staff at the Carpenters International Training Fund (CITF). They have been vital to keeping the development of the program on track and they continue to be key to a successful implementation of the program.

In particular we owe thanks to the following subject matter experts for this program and the Training Programs they represent, which generously allowed them to participate, and the CITF staff who guided and reviewed material.

Thomas Barrett, PhD
Mid-Atlantic Regional Council Joint School of Carpentry, Washington, DC

Paul Bowes
North Texas Carpenters and Millwright Training Center, Arlington, Texas

David Lawson
Senior Technical Coordinator, CITF, Las Vegas, Nevada

Lee Libert
CJATC of Greater Pennsylvania, Pittsburgh, Pennsylvania

Michael Maguire
Chicago Regional Council of Carpenters Training Center, Elk Grove, Illinois

Bill McKenna
Washington/Idaho Carpenters Training Program, Kent, Washington

Craig Ramey
Carpenters Training Committee for Northern California, Pleasanton, California

Dan Russell
Washington/Idaho Carpenters Training Program, Kent, Washington

Dale Shoemaker
Senior Technical Coordinator, CITF, Las Vegas, Nevada

Gary A. Stelzer
Carpenters Joint Apprenticeship Program (CJAP), St. Louis, Missouri

Robert W. Swegle,
Mid-Central Illinois Regional Council of Carpenters-JATC, Pekin, Illinois

Jim Vodicka
Technical Coordinator, CITF, Las Vegas, Nevada

Special Thanks to the instructors and apprentices who validated the procedures in this program by building each one of the projects contained in the *Project Books*.

Douglas Lid, *Director;* **Vincent Sticca,** *Assistant Director;* **Michael Maguire,** *Instructor; and the apprentices of the Chicago Regional Council of Carpenters Training Center, Elk Grove, Illinois*

Mark Fuchs, *Program Coordinator;* **Gary Stelzer,** *Retired Coordinator; and the apprentices of Nelson-Mulligan Carpenters Training Center, St. Louis, Missouri*

Louis Russo, *Instructor, and the apprentices of the Southern Nevada Carpenters and Millwrights Training Center, Las Vegas, Nevada*

Vincent Banderman, *Instructor, St. Louis Carpenters Joint Apprenticeship Program, St. Louis, Missouri*

Richard Emerson, *Instructor, Southwest Carpenters Training Center, Reno, Nevada*

James Gault, *Instructor, Detroit Carpenters Joint Apprenticeship School, Detroit, Michigan*

Daniel Hughes, *Instructor, Chicago Regional Council of Carpenters, Chicago, Illinois*

Timothy Moriarty, *Instructor, Connecticut Carpenters Apprentice Training Center, Yalesville, Connecticut*

One Trade, Many Careers

contents

part 1 My World

part 2 The World of Work

part 3 The World of Construction

to the student

A good life—what does that mean and how do you get it?

A life that has meaningful work, work that makes you proud—what does that mean and how do you get it?

Career Connections: One Trade, Many Careers offers you some ways to understand yourself, and some ways to evaluate all the choices available to you. At the heart of the book is the understanding that you want work that really interests and engages you, work that offers you a variety of experiences, work that offers you opportunities to grow by increasing your skills and earning power.

The Carpenters International Training Fund is pleased to make available to you the experience and skills of its members in the Career Connections program. In all of the books in the Career Connections program—One Trade, Many Careers; Project Book 1; Project Book 2; and Project Book 3—you will get a good idea of life as a skilled and well trained worker: what a jobsite is like, what the working conditions are like, what challenges and satisfactions go along with doing the job. You will have the opportunity to explore yourself—your interests and preferences—and to explore the craft—by learning and practicing the skills you will use as a professional carpenter.

We hope that this program will play a role in bringing you closer to making the connection between your present and your future.

Royce Peters
Executive Director
Carpenters International Training Fund

inside the student edition

Your textbook *Career Connections: One Trade Many Careers* is organized to help you learn more about yourself, the workplace, and careers in construction.

Each **PART** focuses on one aspect of the big picture and how you fit into it.

PART 1

My World

You have a bright future ahead, and what shape this future takes is up to you.

2 CAREER CONNECTIONS: One Trade, Many Careers

You have a bright future ahead, and what shape this future takes is up to you. Where will you be and what will you be doing five, ten, or even twenty years from now? Will you be married and have a family? Will you drive a car you like and own a beautiful home in a nice neighborhood? Will you have a job you enjoy and that pays well? Will you be satisfied with your life? Will you be happy? No one can say for sure what tomorrow may bring, but one thing is certain: the decisions you make today will play a big role in the future you create.

Many of us don't think much about the future. We drift along one year to the next convinced that good things will come to us in time. For some, this approach may work well. But for most of us, a good life doesn't just happen. A good life has to be built from the ground up.

A rewarding and satisfying life has a structure much like that of a house. It has a solid foundation that is grounded in your personal values, knowledge, and abilities. It has strong walls consisting of a rewarding home life and interesting work that provides a steady income. And it has a secure roof consisting of savings, health insurance, employment protection, and other benefits designed to reduce some of the uncertainty of the future. For most people, these things—abilities, values, education, work life, home life, and security—are the necessary building blocks of a fulfilling life.

Practically everyone would like to live a life much like the one just described. Will you be able to build a life like that for yourself? Of course you will! But building such a life will take careful planning, hard work, and commitment. Like a carpenter who builds a house, you will need to start with a good set of plans. This book, *Career Connections: One Trade, Many Careers*, can help you with the planning. Think of this book as a blueprint. And, just like a carpenter, in order to build from a blueprint, you will need the right tools. These tools include personal strengths, people skills, and talents. You probably have most of those tools already. But don't just assume that you do. As you read further, take the opportunity to identify which tools you have and which ones you may still need. You will want to be sure you have a full toolbox so you will have what you need to build your own successful and rewarding career.

PART ONE *My World* 3

Each **CHAPTER** gives you the tools you need to move ahead in your career.

CHAPTER 1

This may seem like an odd question to ask, but who are you anyway? Obviously, you are far more than a name. What are your values, interests, and attitudes? How well developed are your people skills? Do you make friends easily? Do you earn the confidence of teachers, employers, parents, and peers? Do you influence the people around you? Are you a team player? Do you make personal goals? How well defined is your vision of your own future? By reading on, you may learn some important things about who you are and what you may want in your future.

Who Am I?

What are your values, interests, and attitudes?

What You Now Know
- Your likes and dislikes
- How to interact with people
- The type of life you want for yourself and your family

What You Will Know
- The importance of a value system
- How attitudes influence your thoughts and actions
- The role people skills play in a successful career
- How to establish and achieve goals
- The important role goals play in achieving your dreams

CHAPTER 1 Who Am I? 5

What You Now Know points out what you've already got under your belt.

What You Will Know shows what you'll learn in the chapter.

sections

each chapter is divided into Sections that focus on specific topics

Easy-to-read text and descriptive photos communicate the chapter topics clearly.

1 What Is a Construction Site?

A construction site is any place where a structure is being built or remodeled. It may begin as an empty field, a vacant lot on a city or suburban block, a few acres of forest, or someday even in outer space. A construction site may be alive with workers and crammed with materials and equipment, or it may be a relatively quiet and peaceful place. The sights and sounds of a construction site are determined by the type and size of the project, the stage of the construction process, and how much work is being done at the time.

Can you see yourself one day working on a construction site?

CRITICAL THINKING How would you recognize a construction site? What activities on a construction site do you find interesting? Can you see yourself one day working on a construction site?

STAGES OF CONSTRUCTION

A construction site may seem like a chaotic place with workers and machines coming and going. But actually, construction is an orderly process. All structures are built in carefully planned stages. Usually, one part of the process must be complete, or almost complete, before workers move to the next part of the process. The construction process will differ from project to project, but most structures are built in the following basic stages:

* **Site Preparation** Before construction can begin, the site must be properly prepared. Any trees, shrubs, or existing structures that may interfere with the construction process must be cleared away, and then the ground is prepared. This stage of the construction process is sometimes called **clearing and grading**.
* **Establishing the Foundation** The ground may seem hard if you trip and fall on it, but natural soils and rock formations are not firm enough to support modern buildings. To keep them from sinking into the ground and eventually toppling over, buildings are placed on top of a solid **footing** made of reinforced concrete. The footing is the part of the foundation that bears on the prepared soil. The foundation above the footing is also made of reinforced concrete, or concrete block, or a combination of these materials. In many cases the foundation is further supported by steel, wood, or concrete pile driven deep into the ground.

154 CAREER CONNECTIONS: One Trade, Many Careers

CHAPTER 8 What Happens on a Construction Site? 155

descriptive photos

shout out!

Derek Stump of South Bend, Indiana, has made three important decisions in his life. The first one was in high school, when he got his Dodge Ram pick-up truck. The second decision was to customize the truck and race it competitively. With 360 horsepower at the wheels and 866 foot pounds of torque, Stump became the defending national champion in Street Class with the Diesel Hot Rod Association. To earn enough money to support his love of racing, Stump made a career decision when he got out of high school: to become a union carpenter. "I'm a hands-on person, and I was always building stuff when I was growing up. In carpentry, you really feel like you've accomplished something once it's all done. It makes you feel good." Today, Stump is content with his career and lifestyle decisions. "I'm single. I own my own house. I have a truck I love. What more can I ask for?"

framing your future

First Lady Eleanor Roosevelt wrote in a letter to a friend, "Somewhere along the line of development we discover what we really are, and then we make our real decision for which we are responsible. Make that decision primarily for yourself because you can never really live anyone else's life, not even your own child's."

32 CAREER CONNECTIONS: One Trade, Many Careers

These and other decisions can be hard to make. The most difficult thing about making decisions is that you can't be absolutely certain you are making the right ones. Making a decision requires what is sometimes referred to as a "judgment call," and our judgment can mislead us. Maybe you were the one who picked the movie that turned out to be terribly boring. That may have been disappointing and perhaps even a little embarrassing, but it's hardly a disaster. It's just a decision you made that didn't work out as well as you had hoped. Everyone makes the wrong decision sometimes, and the results can be far worse than having to sit through a bad movie. That's why people occasionally get anxious when faced with a key decision.

The best way to ensure that you reach your own goals is to be in charge of your own decision making.

Shout Out profiles people you can relate to in construction.

features

features in each chapter provide real-world examples, information, and ideas you can relate to.

Framing Your Future provides useful tips for your career path.

framing your future

There are over 450,000 active apprentices in over 850 apprenticable occupations in the United States. To find out more about these occupations and apprenticeship programs, go to the Apprenticeship website of the U.S. Department of Labor, Employment & Training Administration at www.doleta.gov/oa.

Carpentry is just one of hundreds of technical careers that can begin with an apprenticeship. Most apprenticeship programs require applicants to have either a high school diploma or GED. Some apprenticeship programs may prefer applicants with junior college or college backgrounds. If you think you might be interested in an apprenticeship, it is not too early to find out about the requirements. If you are still going to school, you may want to take courses that will better prepare you for the apprenticeship program. For example, if you want a career and an apprenticeship in carpentry, you might want to take math courses, as well as courses such as computer aided design (CAD) and carpentry.

CRITICAL THINKING How do you think an apprenticeship program would fit into your career plans? Do you know if apprenticeship programs exist for your career choice? How might you find out?

Being able to learn new things is an essential element in advancing your career.

Learning Is a Lifelong Process You may think of your education as something you get in school or at college. Once you have earned a diploma or degree, your education is finished. Of course, this couldn't be further from the truth. You learned things long before you ever went to school and you will continue to learn things long after you are out of school. In other words, learning is a lifelong process.

Learning at work will be vitally important. You will have to learn tasks at work that you have probably never done before. You will have to learn about unfamiliar procedures and processes. You will have to learn unfamiliar tools, equipment, and materials that you may be required to use. You will also have to learn about an unfamiliar worksite and about how to interact with your new coworkers and supervisors. No wonder people feel very stressed when they start a new job. There is so much to learn!

Even once you have become an old hand at work, learning will still be important. You will want to learn about new materials and techniques as they are introduced to improve efficiency. You will want to learn about any new equipment that is put into service and about any safety hazards that may arise. You may need to learn how to work with new team members, coworkers, and supervisors. You may even want to learn how to do your job so well that you would be considered for a promotion to a better job. Being able to learn new things is an essential element in advancing your career. The more knowledge and skills you acquire, the more responsibility you will be ready to handle.

CRITICAL THINKING Do you like to learn new things or do you do so reluctantly? How might your willingness to learn affect your chosen career path?

104 CAREER CONNECTIONS: One Trade, Many Careers

real-world examples

ideas you can relate to

3 Skills Needed on a Construction Site

Construction work requires a wide range of skills. The personal skills needed on a construction site are the same as those required for any other type of employment. Construction workers must be able to listen carefully and speak clearly. They must be able to respond well to supervision and work with others as part of an effective team. They must be able to manage time, make decisions, and solve problems. They must be reliable, on time, and ready to do their best work every day. They should know how to think critically, that is, to ask the right questions and to recognize meaningful answers. Every worker should also have well developed basic skills such as reading, writing, and math.

Construction workers must have the hands-on skills needed to use tools that are required for the job. Reading and interpreting prints, using a computer, and executing a complex construction process are required technical skills. When workers step onto a construction site, they must bring all of these skills with them.

Experienced construction workers know how to safely and efficiently use many different hand tools and power tools. They know how to safely and efficiently use wood, metal, drywall, concrete, and many other materials. And they know how to make proper use of technical processes such as forming a level foundation, installing a staircase, or stretching a carpet.

CRITICAL THINKING What are the three kinds of skills needed by a construction worker?

nailing it!

Using the right tools for the job is critical on a construction site. And knowing how to identify tools and materials is equally important. Skilled tradespeople know which power tool or hand tool is needed and when. They can recognize one grade of material from another. They know one drill bit from another. They know the difference between a nut, bolt, screw, spacer, rivet, and clip and the tools needed for driving them. Do you know the nuts and bolts of building materials and tools, and is it something you want to learn?

CHAPTER 8 What Happens on a Construction Site? 161

Nailing It describes mastering certain skills.

features

make yourself **more valuable** in the workplace

iron worker

The outer shells or exteriors of most large buildings do little to support their weight. In fact, most of the siding materials you see on the outside of these buildings are attached to a sturdy internal framework of steel. The frameworks are put in place by iron workers. An **iron worker** is a skilled worker who bolts and welds steel beams and girders and places the network of steel that reinforces concrete walls and supports. Iron workers work on roads, bridges, dams, sports complexes, high rises, and large structures of all types. They often work at great heights. Iron workers also must be able to direct the operators of heavy equipment.

painter
wallpaper hanger
drywall finisher

The interior walls of buildings and homes would look very plain and unattractive without the benefit of paint, wallpaper, and other finishes. The basic job of a painter and a wallpaper hanger is probably obvious without much further explanation. On the other hand, you may not be as familiar with the work of a **drywall finisher**. Once sheets of drywall have been attached to the interior walls and ceilings of a building or house, it is the job of drywall finishers to make all the individual sheets of drywall look like a continuous, smooth surface. Once this is done, drywall finishers often add decorative textures to make the surfaces more pleasing to the eye and also to hide surface imperfections. Most of the work of drywall finishers is done using paper tape and a plaster-like material called joint compound.

As for painters, they skillfully apply paint to the interiors of buildings and houses. They also paint the outside of certain buildings, homes, and structures such as bridges and water tanks. To do these jobs properly, painters must know the characteristics of a variety of paints and know how to apply each one. They must also be very detailed oriented and possess a strong sense of color and design. These characteristics also apply to wallpaper hangers, who must know how to select and apply a variety of adhesives and wallpapers.

building a better u

"Doing a great job is more than showing up and working a day's pay just to get better pay; it's when all the training and experience you've had falls into place. Pride in workmanship is also what many wish for and never achieve." Entrepreneur David A. Goldsmith points out that no matter what your occupation is, taking pride in what you do is what really counts.

CHAPTER 7 Construction Trades, Part Two 147

Building a Better You tells you how to make yourself more valuable in the workplace.

how

4 What Is a Pile Driver?

Have you ever gone boating, tied the boat to a dock, and wondered what the dock was connected to under the water? Maybe you have looked at a tall skyscraper and wondered why it doesn't sink into the ground. Or perhaps you wondered what could possibly hold up a large bridge that supports hundreds of cars and trucks. The answer to all these questions lies with the pile driver.

Skyscrapers, sports stadiums, bridges, dams, and other large structures don't just sit on the ground or on an unsupported concrete foundation. If they did, they would slowly settle into the earth and eventually topple over. Many types of structures and the foundations on which they rest must be supported by sturdy concrete, wood, or metal shafts, called **pile**, which are driven deep into the ground. The skilled worker who installs the pile is called a **pile driver**.

how i see myself

Brent McLain has been a commercial diver in San Francisco for five years. A day's work might include resisting a 5-knot current while dragging 200 feet of hose, using power tools underwater in total darkness, and fending off curious harbor seals. McLain helps maintain pier pile, salvages wrecks, and assists officers with homeland security. Are you up for the challenge and adventure of an underwater pile driver?

CHAPTER 7 Construction Trades, Part Two 141

How I See Myself gives you food for thought about your career potential.

food for thought

chapter check

allows you to review what you learned and then apply the concepts in practical ways.

expand on what you have learned

These Important Words were introduced in the chapter and are redefined here.

On the Trail Of lets you expand on what you learned in the chapter.

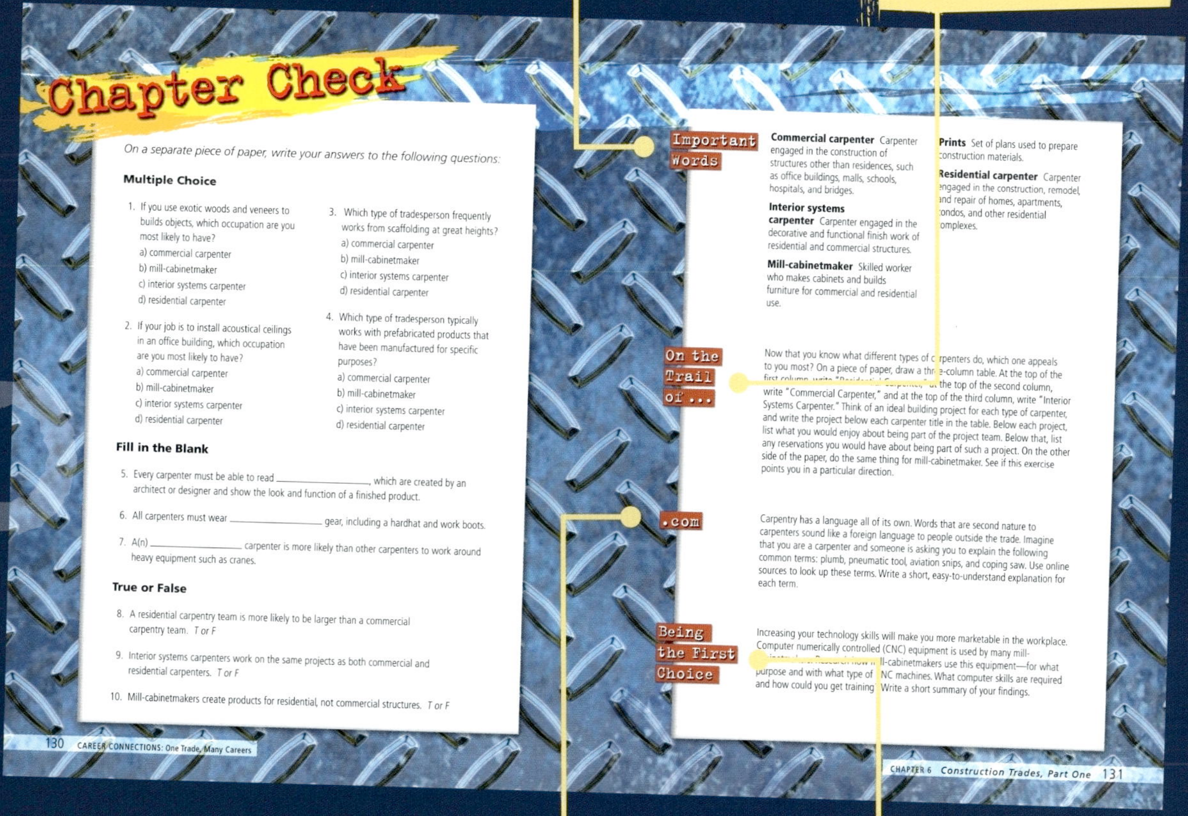

Chapter Check

On a separate piece of paper, write your answers to the following questions:

Multiple Choice

1. If you use exotic woods and veneers to builds objects, which occupation are you most likely to have?
   a) commercial carpenter
   b) mill-cabinetmaker
   c) interior systems carpenter
   d) residential carpenter
2. If your job is to install acoustical ceilings in an office building, which occupation are you most likely to have?
   a) commercial carpenter
   b) mill-cabinetmaker
   c) interior systems carpenter
   d) residential carpenter
3. Which type of tradesperson frequently works from scaffolding at great heights?
   a) commercial carpenter
   b) mill-cabinetmaker
   c) interior systems carpenter
   d) residential carpenter
4. Which type of tradesperson typically works with prefabricated products that have been manufactured for specific purposes?
   a) commercial carpenter
   b) mill-cabinetmaker
   c) interior systems carpenter
   d) residential carpenter

Fill in the Blank

5. Every carpenter must be able to read ________, which are created by an architect or designer and show the look and function of a finished product.
6. All carpenters must wear ________ gear, including a hardhat and work boots.
7. A(n) ________ carpenter is more likely than other carpenters to work around heavy equipment such as cranes.

True or False

8. A residential carpentry team is more likely to be larger than a commercial carpentry team. *T or F*
9. Interior systems carpenters work on the same projects as both commercial and residential carpenters. *T or F*
10. Mill-cabinetmakers create products for residential, not commercial structures. *T or F*

130 CAREER CONNECTIONS: One Trade, Many Careers

Important Words

Commercial carpenter Carpenter engaged in the construction of structures other than residences, such as office buildings, malls, schools, hospitals, and bridges.

Interior systems carpenter Carpenter engaged in the decorative and functional finish work of residential and commercial structures.

Mill-cabinetmaker Skilled worker who makes cabinets and builds furniture for commercial and residential use.

Prints Set of plans used to prepare construction materials.

Residential carpenter Carpenter engaged in the construction, remodel, and repair of homes, apartments, condos, and other residential complexes.

On the Trail of ...

Now that you know what different types of carpenters do, which one appeals to you most? On a piece of paper, draw a three-column table. At the top of the first column, write [illegible] at the top of the second column, write "Commercial Carpenter," and at the top of the third column, write "Interior Systems Carpenter." Think of an ideal building project for each type of carpenter, and write the project below each carpenter title in the table. Below each project, list what you would enjoy about being part of the project team. Below that, list any reservations you would have about being part of such a project. On the other side of the paper, do the same thing for mill-cabinetmaker. See if this exercise points you in a particular direction.

.com

Carpentry has a language all of its own. Words that are second nature to carpenters sound like a foreign language to people outside the trade. Imagine that you are a carpenter and someone is asking you to explain the following common terms: plumb, pneumatic tool, aviation snips, and coping saw. Use online sources to look up these terms. Write a short, easy-to-understand explanation for each term.

Being the First Choice

Increasing your technology skills will make you more marketable in the workplace. Computer numerically controlled (CNC) equipment is used by many mill- [illegible] ll-cabinetmakers use this equipment—for what purpose and with what type of CNC machines. What computer skills are required and how could you get training? Write a short summary of your findings.

CHAPTER 6 *Construction Trades, Part One* 131

.com is an opportunity to do some Internet research on a chapter topic.

Being the First Choice allows you to develop skills that will make employers want to hire you.

opportunity to do some Internet research

as you begin

Career Connections One Trade, Many Careers

You're about to embark on a new adventure—the next stage of your life. Everything you've learned and experienced up to this point has created a foundation. The next step is to use that foundation to build your future. What kind of future do you want to create? This book will help you answer that question as you transition from school into the workplace.

PART ONE: My World

The first part of this book will help you learn more about you. Self-knowledge is the key to understanding what will make you happy and successful in the future.

Chapter 1: Who Am I?

What are your likes and dislikes? What is important to you? How do you interact with others? In this chapter, you begin to identify your personal characteristics in preparation for finding your ideal fit in the workplace.

Chapter 2: What's in My Toolbox?

You already have a set of personal tools that you've used for learning. This chapter shows you how to use these tools to make a decision about your future.

PART TWO: The World of Work

With self-knowledge now under your belt, you're ready to look at the opportunities out there in the workplace.

Chapter 3: The Modern Workplace

What is work and why do people do it? This chapter explores how work can enrich your life and describes the dynamics of our changing workplace.

Chapter 4: What Basic Skills and Personal Qualities Do I Need?

What skills do you already have that employers want? This chapter shows how your reading, writing, and thinking skills will help you achieve success in the workplace. It also shows how the qualities that make you a good person will make you a good worker.

Chapter 5: Choosing a Career That Is Right for You

You have the power to shape your life by choosing a career that matches your interests and personal characteristics. This chapter shows you how to make this choice and reach your fullest potential.

PART THREE: The World of Construction

The title of this book, "One Trade, Many Careers," refers to the carpentry trade, and the many careers within that trade. Under the umbrella of carpentry, there are a variety of crafts that require specific skills. This portion of the book will help you explore all of these diverse career options.

Chapter 6: Constriction Trades, Part One

Building new structures and maintaining existing ones requires the contribution of professionals with different skills. This chapter begins exploring the carpentry trade by explaining the role of carpenters and mill-cabinetmakers.

Chapter 7: Construction Trades, Part Two

This chapter describes some of the specific crafts within the carpentry trade, including floor layer, lather, millwright, and pile driver. It also introduces 13 more construction occupations, from boilermaker to sheet metal worker.

Chapter 8: What Happens on a Construction Site?

The workplace is where people work together to achieve a common purpose. For carpenters and other construction occupations, the workplace is a construction site. This chapter describes the sights, sounds, and activities of a construction site.

Chapter 9: Is a Career in Construction Right for You?

This chapter helps you narrow down your career options and choose on occupation that you enjoy. Using your abilities and mastering new skills on the job will give you a sense of purpose and personal pride, for many years to come.

PART 1

My World

You have a bright future ahead, and what shape this future takes is up to you.

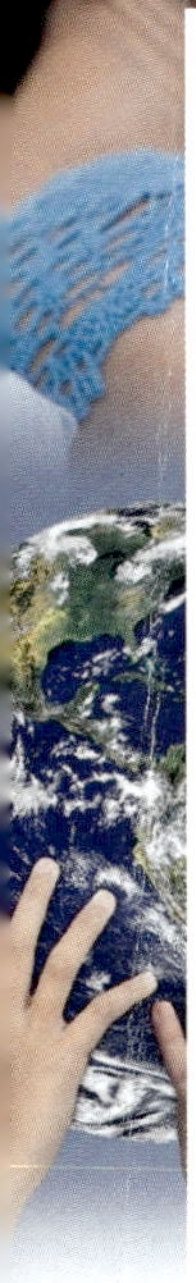

You have a bright future ahead, and what shape this future takes is up to you. Where will you be and what will you be doing five, ten, or even twenty years from now? Will you be married and have a family? Will you drive a car you like and own a beautiful home in a nice neighborhood? Will you have a job you enjoy and that pays well? Will you be satisfied with your life? Will you be happy? No one can say for sure what tomorrow may bring, but one thing is certain: the decisions you make today will play a big role in the future you create.

Many of us don't think much about the future. We drift along one year to the next convinced that good things will come to us in time. For some, this approach may work well. But for most of us, a good life doesn't just happen. A good life has to be built from the ground up.

A rewarding and satisfying life has a structure much like that of a house. It has a solid foundation that is grounded in your personal values, knowledge, and abilities. It has strong walls consisting of a rewarding home life and interesting work that provides a steady income. And it has a secure roof consisting of savings, health insurance, employment protection, and other benefits designed to reduce some of the uncertainty of the future. For most people, these things—abilities, values, education, work life, home life, and security—are the necessary building blocks of a fulfilling life.

Practically everyone would like to live a life much like the one just described. Will you be able to build a life like that for yourself? Of course you will! But building such a life will take careful planning, hard work, and commitment. Like a carpenter who builds a house, you will need to start with a good set of plans. This book, *Career Connections: One Trade, Many Careers,* can help you with the planning. Think of this book as a blueprint. And, just like a carpenter, in order to build from a blueprint, you will need the right tools. These tools include personal strengths, people skills, and talents. You probably have most of those tools already. But don't just assume that you do. As you read further, take the opportunity to identify which tools you have and which ones you may still need. You will want to be sure you have a full toolbox so you will have what you need to build your own successful and rewarding career.

CHAPTER 1

Who

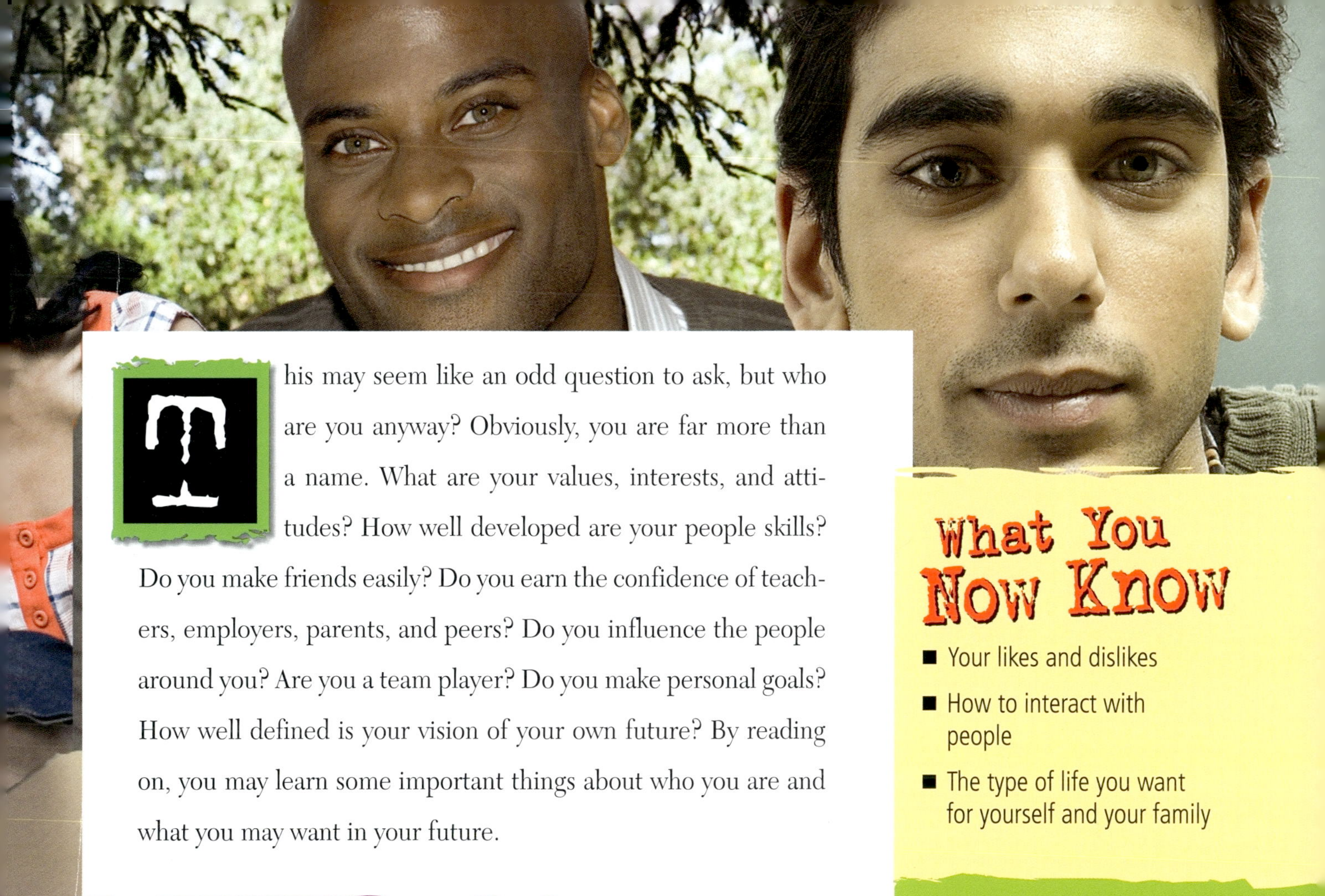

This may seem like an odd question to ask, but who are you anyway? Obviously, you are far more than a name. What are your values, interests, and attitudes? How well developed are your people skills? Do you make friends easily? Do you earn the confidence of teachers, employers, parents, and peers? Do you influence the people around you? Are you a team player? Do you make personal goals? How well defined is your vision of your own future? By reading on, you may learn some important things about who you are and what you may want in your future.

Am I?

What are your values, interests, and attitudes?

What You Now Know

- Your likes and dislikes
- How to interact with people
- The type of life you want for yourself and your family

What You Will Know

- The importance of a value system
- How attitudes influence your thoughts and actions
- The role people skills play in a successful career
- How to establish and achieve goals
- The important role goals play in achieving your dreams

1 Values

Some beliefs are far more important than others. You may have a favorite sports team and are convinced that they are better than all the other teams. Or you may think that a particular singer is especially talented. Both of these beliefs are just opinions. It's very possible that you will change your mind about these things from one day to the next. For example, your favorite sports team might start losing, and before the season is over you may like another team better. The singer you liked so much may start singing in a style you find less appealing, and now you listen to someone else. Opinions can change, and often change as you change. Values however, typically do not change so easily.

how i see myself

When you have strong opinions, do you express them? The poet Ralph Waldo Emerson said, "People do not seem to realize that their opinion of the world is also a confession of character." What do your opinions reveal about you?

A **value** is an idea or belief that has great importance. Once a value is established, it tends to stick with you for a lifetime. Let's say that you believe a person can achieve anything with hard work, or that it is a citizen's duty to vote. These are unlikely to be passing opinions. They are more likely to be values that you think are important. Regardless of what values you have, they become a vital part of who you are as a person.

An **opinion** is a view or attitude about a particular subject. An opinion usually refers to a specific thing such as the worthiness of a particular political candidate or whether it's more fun to see a comedy than an action film at the movies. People often feel very strongly about their opinions, and for this reason may confuse them with their values. Unfortunately, it's not always easy to tell the difference between these two beliefs. To tell values and opinions apart, ask yourself the following questions.

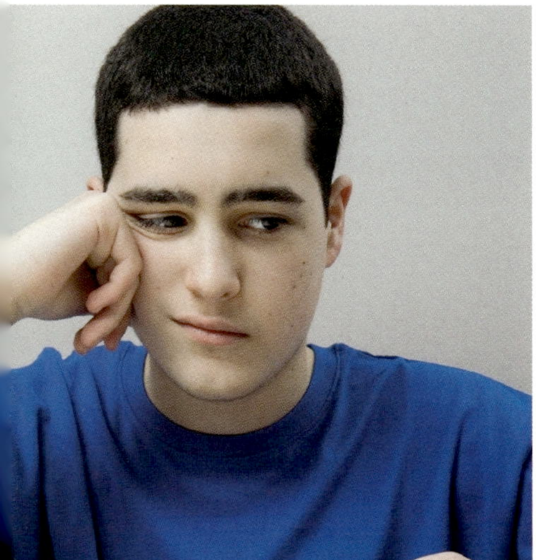

- Is the belief general in nature?
- Do you feel very strongly about this belief?
- Have you felt that way for a long time?
- Do you think that years from now you will feel the same way?
- Do you consider the belief to be a part of you and closely linked to who you are as a person?

If you answered "yes" to at least four of the five questions above, then you have probably just identified one of your personal values. If you answered "no" to two or more of the questions, then the belief is probably just an opinion.

It is important to have opinions and to share them with others when it is appropriate. However, opinions cannot guide you through life. Values, on the other hand, can help you make key decisions during moments of uncertainty. They can help you get through troubled times and can assist you in planning your future.

CRITICAL THINKING Make a list of two or three beliefs that you consider important and ask the questions listed on the previous page for each. Which of your beliefs are values and which are opinions?

Where Do Values Come From? Your values have most likely come from a variety of sources. You may have developed some of your values at school or at church. However, most of your values were probably learned at home from the members of your own family. In fact, many of your most important values began to develop during early childhood and were already in place by the time you started school. So, you probably developed many of your values long before you really knew what values were.

Throughout your life you have been constructing and even modifying your values. You may find yourself in situations that bring certain values to the surface and even cause you to question them. Let's say, for example, that a friend asks you to help him cheat on a test. How you answer your friend would depend on your values about honesty and fairness. If these values were strong you would probably say no. But now let's say that if your friend fails the test, he would fail the class and would not graduate. Are your values still strong enough to say no? Situations like this test your values and make them stronger. But some situations can also cause you to rethink and even change your values.

Identifying Your Values You may not be able to sit down and make a list of every one of your key values, but if you tried, you could probably identify many of them. Being able to identify your own personal values can be a big help in understanding who you are. For example, you may feel uncomfortable going to movies that are particularly violent in nature. This

shout out!

When people donate time and effort to help others, what does it say about their values? Two years after Hurricane Katrina, none of the city's 22 destroyed or damaged firehouses had been rebuilt—until the New York City members of the United Brotherhood of Carpenters and Joiners of America, in partnership with the Leary Firefighters Foundation, stepped in. Over the course of eight months, the carpenters volunteered their time, skill, and expertise to construct seven new firehouses. Their contribution is valued at over $500,000 in labor and materials. They used their vacation time and paid their own airfare to help rescue the rescue workers and restore confidence to the City of New Orleans.

feeling of discomfort may be rooted in values such as a respect for life or a concern for the well being of other people.

Identifying your values can also help you in building the life you desire. This is because your values, even if you are unaware of them, have a big influence on the decisions you make. For example, your values influence your decisions about what church to attend or what people you choose as friends. And, as you will soon learn, your values will also influence your future career decisions.

The ability to identify your values can also help you recognize the values of others. This skill can be useful in resolving conflicts. Recognizing the differences between your own values and the values held by other people can make it easier to see what may lie beneath a disagreement. Understanding and respecting the values of others can help resolve or even avoid such conflicts. After all, other people are entitled to their values—even if they don't match your own.

CRITICAL THINKING Which of your values do you consider most important in defining who you are in your personal life? Which do you think are important when considering a career? Do your friends know and respect your values? Does someone close to you have values that don't match yours?

Values and Your Career Identifying your values can be especially helpful in selecting a career that is right for you. This is because values can have an important influence on how you feel about your work. For instance, you may believe that nature is sacred and that it is everyone's duty to protect the environment. This value might make it difficult for you to work in an industry that you think is damaging the environment. Other values may also affect your career choices. Consider your values related to money, family and friends, security, and job satisfaction.

...values can be especially helpful in selecting a career that is right for you

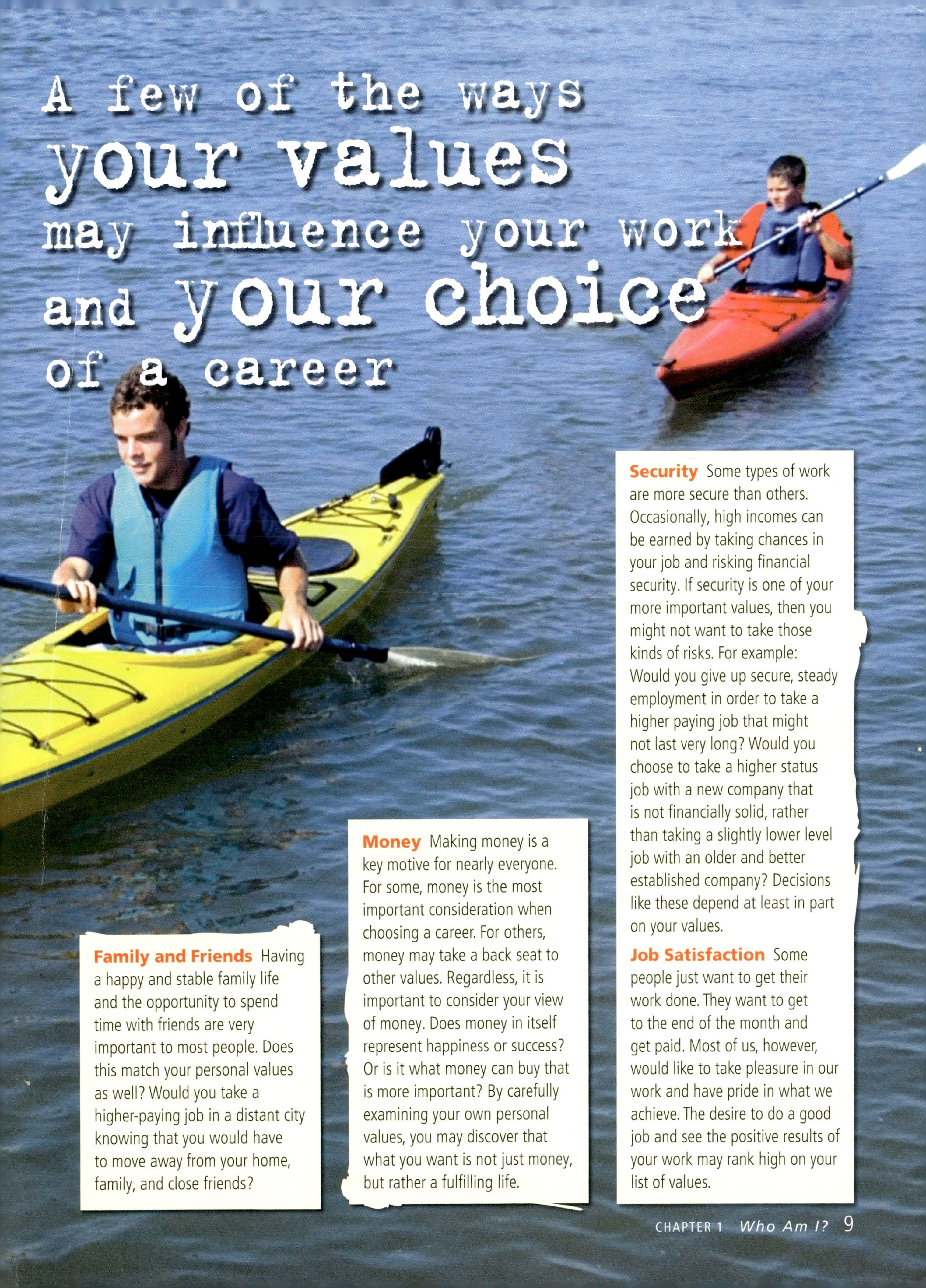

A few of the ways **your values** may influence your work and **your choice** of a career

Family and Friends Having a happy and stable family life and the opportunity to spend time with friends are very important to most people. Does this match your personal values as well? Would you take a higher-paying job in a distant city knowing that you would have to move away from your home, family, and close friends?

Money Making money is a key motive for nearly everyone. For some, money is the most important consideration when choosing a career. For others, money may take a back seat to other values. Regardless, it is important to consider your view of money. Does money in itself represent happiness or success? Or is it what money can buy that is more important? By carefully examining your own personal values, you may discover that what you want is not just money, but rather a fulfilling life.

Security Some types of work are more secure than others. Occasionally, high incomes can be earned by taking chances in your job and risking financial security. If security is one of your more important values, then you might not want to take those kinds of risks. For example: Would you give up secure, steady employment in order to take a higher paying job that might not last very long? Would you choose to take a higher status job with a new company that is not financially solid, rather than taking a slightly lower level job with an older and better established company? Decisions like these depend at least in part on your values.

Job Satisfaction Some people just want to get their work done. They want to get to the end of the month and get paid. Most of us, however, would like to take pleasure in our work and have pride in what we achieve. The desire to do a good job and see the positive results of your work may rank high on your list of values.

2 Attitudes

Although values influence your feelings about a great many things, they are not always obvious to you or to others. Attitudes, on the other hand, are easier to detect. An attitude is the way in which you think, feel, and act. Attitudes can be seen as positive or negative and everybody has them. Attitudes show up in your personality and they dictate, in part, your behaviors and actions. And, it is from your behaviors and actions that other people interpret your attitude.

Attitudes are often expressed in the form of strongly stated opinions or emotionally charged remarks. In most cases, these involve positive or negative judgments about situations or people. For example, you might say "I can't stand people who talk at the movies while others are trying to enjoy the film." This blunt statement makes your negative attitude toward such people very clear. However, you might also say "I really like people who are open to new ideas." This is an example of a positive attitude that identifies you as someone who appreciates open-minded people.

Fortunately, you have some control over your attitudes. You can change the way you think about and act toward other people. You may also be able to change the way you feel about them. Let's say a coworker seems cool or unfriendly toward you. It may be hard to avoid developing a negative attitude toward this person. However, if you maintain a positive attitude this person may respond to you by becoming more positive. Your attitude may positively affect his or her attitude! As a result, working together on a project with this person will become more pleasant and rewarding.

It is hard to overstate the importance of a positive attitude. Thinking positively often generates positive actions which get positive results. Thinking negatively does just the opposite. Keeping a positive attitude will go a long way in helping you achieve your life and career goals.

framing your future

Studies have shown that more people get jobs *not* because of their résumés, skills, experience, or education, but because of their positive attitude. People simply like people who have a positive attitude, and employers hire people they like.

building a better u

Are positive and negative thinking contagious? There's no scientific evidence to support it, but it feels good to be around positive people. Enthusiasm rubs off one person and onto another person, and laughter is infectious. Similarly, it feels bad to be around negative people. Work on developing the power of positive thinking by thinking good thoughts and using positive words such as "I can." Surround yourself with enthusiastic people and when possible, avoid people with negative attitudes.

CRITICAL THINKING Make a list of your positive and negative attitudes. Which list is longer? Have any of these attitudes ever been pointed out to you by another person? Which of these attitudes might affect your future career, and in what way?

Prejudices Attitudes may be closely linked to personal values, but this is not always the case. Sometimes attitudes can directly contradict our most fundamental values. For example, it is probably safe to say that most Americans hold dear the notion of equality. After all, equality is expressed directly in our nation's Declaration of Independence: "We hold these truths to be self-evident that all men are created equal..." Yet many of the same Americans who firmly believe those words find that they feel uncomfortable around people of a different race or religion. They may have unrealistic beliefs that people who don't speak English well are not intelligent or people who are very religious think they are better than others. Such beliefs and ideas are prejudices.

A prejudice is an attitude that has no reasonable or justified basis in fact. Prejudices are by their very nature untrue and unfair. They can injure both the person the prejudice is directed against as well as the person holding the prejudice. Prejudices are dangerous. They can end friendships before they even get started, and they can cause all kinds of bad feelings and problems in the workplace. Prejudices can even damage or put an end to promising careers.

Keep in mind that prejudice is not limited to the people you may think of as small minded or hard hearted. Practically everyone is prejudiced in one way or another. While some of these prejudices may be viewed as relatively harmless, none of them are actually good for us.

Unfortunately, it can be very difficult to let go of a prejudice you have had for a long time. The first step is to recognize it as an extremely negative attitude. This may take some courage, particularly if you have friends or family who share this negative attitude. However, your courage and determination to face your own negative attitude may make it safer and easier for others to do the same. In the end, you may find yourself with better relationships than you ever thought possible.

how i see myself

American author E.B. White wrote: "Prejudice is a great time saver. You can form opinions without having to get the facts." When have you taken this shortcut to form an opinion?

CRITICAL THINKING Do you have any prejudices? What effects do you think they have had on you and on others? What are some things you could do to let go of any prejudices you might have? When have you ever felt prejudice from other people? What can you learn from other people's prejudices about your own?

3 People Skills

Getting along with other people is very helpful in becoming successful in life. Generally speaking, successful people know how to deal effectively with others. They form friendships readily, communicate well, and know how to work cooperatively with others to get things done. In most cases, when people work together in a friendly and efficient way, everybody wins. The ability to work well with others requires a variety of people skills.

In one sense, people skills are like any other skills. That is, you are not born with them. You are no more born with the skill to communicate well than you are born with the skill to play a musical instrument, paint a picture, or catch or throw a ball. All of these skills must be learned. Many of the basic people skills, such as the ability to carry on a conversation, are learned at a very early age from parents, siblings, or childhood friends. Other important people skills, such as the ability to listen and work as a team, may be learned in the classroom, in a band, on a sports team, or on a job.

Your people skills may be the most useful items in your personal toolbox. They can serve you well not just at work but also at home and in your social life. You will want to include the following people skills in your toolbox:

- Listening carefully
- Showing concern for others
- Avoiding gossip or harming others with loose talk
- Being a good teammate
- Earning the confidence of others
- Being persuasive
- Keeping an open mind
- Handling criticism well
- Keeping confidential information confidential
- Winning and losing well

These are only some of the many people skills that will help make y successful in your life. As your read these you may think of others that w be equally important to you.

building a better u

An important people skill is being able to talk to all kinds of people, of all ages. Not over the phone, not by texting, but face to face. Practice making conversation with an elderly neighbor, a toddler, a store clerk, a librarian. Say the person's name during the conversation. "A person's name is to that person the sweetest and most important sound in any language," said Dale Carnegie in his famous 1936 book *How To Win Friends and Influence People.* Repeating the name will also help you remember the name of a person you just met.

avoid gossip

Listening Carefully

Much of what you have learned in life has come from others speaking to you. Obviously, you can't learn anything from someone if you are not listening. Careful listening is especially important when you receive a set of instructions on how to carry out a task. How well you complete the task will depend largely on how well you listened to the instructions. Listening skills are vital in the workplace. Careful listening is also important in social relationships. Listening to people shows that you respect them and that you care about what they have to say. Interrupting people, on the other hand, may be regarded by them as a sign of disrespect or that you don't value their contribution.

Showing Concern for Others

A good way to earn the respect and confidence of the people around you is to show concern for them even if they are not close friends. People show concern for others every day when they say "Hi! How's it going?" However, there are more meaningful and memorable ways to show that you care about other people. For instance, congratulating classmates or coworkers on something they did successfully shows that you care about their success. Similarly, if a friend or coworker has an illness or gets bad news, a simple "I'm sorry to hear that" may be all it takes to demonstrate your genuine concern. Of course, there are many ways to show your concern. Lending a helping hand, sending a card, or going to visit might be even better ways to show your concern.

Being Careful When Talking About Others

Words can hurt people even when no harm is intended. Since it's impossible to know what another person is thinking or feeling, even an innocent remark about a person's looks, personality, ability, or circumstances may be hurtful. Also, it is a good idea to always assume that even things said about a person in private will find their way to the person being talked about. When it comes to talking negatively about someone, you are almost always better off just not doing it. Just the opposite is true when you have positive things to say. The more you share positive insights about people, the more people will like being associated with you. When this happens, the person is usually grateful.

Being a Team Player

If you have ever played on a sports team, played in a band, sung in a choir, or participated in some other group activity, then you probably have had experience working as part of a team. Even though many teams exist to win a game or some other competition, the experience of a team member is more about being in service to the team. Yes, there may be opposing views and disagreements, but good team players put aside individual differences in order to work out the best solutions for the entire team. Individual recognition is secondary to making the entire team successful. When the entire team is successful, that is when all the team members are successful.

Earning the Confidence of Others

Earning the confidence of others is a people skill that cannot be overemphasized in the world of work. Your success in a job may largely be determined by your ability to earn the confidence of your employer, supervisors, and coworkers. It would be very hard to become an effective member of a team unless the other teammates have confidence in you and your abilities. However, earning the confidence of others does not come easy. It has to be earned by demonstrating your competence, hard work, and your ability to use various people skills such as listening well and showing concern for others. The confidence you earn from others is also fragile. It can be quickly destroyed by failing to be honest or reliable.

Solving the

Persuading Others

The ability to persuade others can be a very valuable people skill in the workplace. If you think of a faster way of doing something, persuading others to do it the same way shows initiative and teamwork. On the other hand, if your idea of persuading others is to argue with them until they give in, you will have a negative effect on the people around you. People are almost never persuaded by arguments. In fact, getting into an argument with someone—no matter how certain you may be about your point of view—is one of the quickest ways to lose that person's confidence and friendship.

Most people are persuaded by examples, not by words. Merely asking someone to wear a hard hat because it is safer is not especially persuasive. Pointing out overhead hazards and showing the person how a hard hat can prevent a serious and even life-threatening injury would be much more convincing.

Keeping an Open Mind

An open mind is a mind that is receptive to new ideas, new experiences, and new ways of doing things. The modern workplace requires that workers are open to new ideas and methods that may produce positive results. Of course, not all ideas are valuable, just as not all statements are true. It is important to evaluate new ideas from your own perspective, background, and experiences. In other words, you will want to scrutinize any idea that is new to you. But you should also try to give every idea a fair evaluation, without a negative attitude. Many good ideas did not seem like good ideas at first. They were not viewed as good ideas until they were given a fair chance by people with open minds.

Handling Criticism

Nobody likes to be criticized. It is difficult to hear criticism and even more difficult to respond to it well. Most people take criticism very personally. Criticism can damage a person's pride and hurt his or her feelings. This damaged pride and hurt feelings may even get in the way of the person changing the behavior that brought about the criticism in the first place. Although it's never easy to be on the receiving end of criticism, it does help to remember that the criticism is not directed to you as a person. It is most often a criticism of an action or a failure to act. By having the right attitude, you can learn a great deal from the criticism you receive. After all, no matter how good you are at something, there is always room for growth.

If you are ever the person responsible for evaluating and criticizing the work of someone else, it is essential to focus on the positive. Solving the problem or correcting the situation is what matters most. There is little value in focusing on blame. If someone has done something incorrectly, it is much more helpful to describe or demonstrate the solution rather than to blame the person for making a mistake.

Keeping Information Confidential

It's often hard for friends to trust someone who can't keep a secret. Likewise, it is hard for coworkers and employers to trust someone who can't keep information confidential. You have probably shared with a friend some information that you don't want anyone else to know. This information was probably not a big secret that would cause a catastrophe if revealed. More than likely, the information was just something that for one reason or another was best kept within a small circle of people. This is normally the case in the workplace. You could be given information that shouldn't be discussed with anyone who doesn't know about it already. This confidential information could come from your employer, supervisor, or a coworker. Regardless of who asked for the information to remain confidential, sharing this information with others is a sure way to lose the confidence of the person who asked you to keep the information confidential.

Finding Ways for Everybody to Win

Many conflicts in life and at work do not have to end with a win or a loss. In most cases, conflicts can be resolved in ways that are acceptable to everyone involved. Successful people often try to promote what are sometimes referred to as "win-win" situations. To achieve a win-win situation, everyone needs to understand that compromises must be made to arrive at the best solution. An example of a win-win situation is when you ask to use the family car from 6 p.m. until midnight but agree to stay home for dinner until 8 p.m. to satisfy your parents. You win by getting the car until midnight, while your parents win by having your company for dinner.

CRITICAL THINKING What are your most effective people skills? What do your friends say about the way you interact with other people? Are there any areas where your people skills are weak or could use some work?

how i see myself

Comedian Jerry Seinfeld, in his popular sitcom, said he was putting something he heard "in the vault" that he promised to keep confidential. While the Seinfeld characters might not have been very good at keeping secrets, are you? Can the people in your life count on you to keep what they tell you "in the vault"? How can you build their confidence and trust?

4 Goals

What do you want to accomplish with your life? You might want to make lots of money, drive a nice car, own your own home, or have a big family. Maybe you want to set a record as an athlete, write a book, or learn to play the guitar. Or you may want to improve the lives of needy people or help clean up the environment. All of these are examples of goals. A goal is something we want to attain or achieve in our life.

Some goals, such as having kids and putting them through school, are general and long term in nature. Others goals, such as winning a race or learning to play the guitar, are more specific and short term. However, short-term goals are very often part of long-term goals. For example, learning to play the guitar may be a short-term goal along the road to accomplishing the long-term goal of becoming a musician in a band.

Most good things don't happen by accident. To get what you want, you will want to establish clear goals and then work hard to achieve them. Obviously, if you don't know what you want, it is unlikely you will achieve it. Even if you do know what you want but you don't set goals for yourself to achieve it, you are unlikely to make much progress. You may have noticed that people who set both short-term goals and long-term goals for themselves seem to get a lot more done. In fact, goal setting is one of the most common and recognizable behaviors of successful people.

...establish clear goals and then work hard to achieve them.

When setting personal goals, it is a good idea to make sure they are things that you really want to achieve. Sometimes, parents, teachers, or friends suggest goals that may not really fit your personal aspirations or objectives. You must decide for yourself what is right for you. After all, it's your life. But, remember, deciding what you want is not the same thing as setting goals to achieve it. You will want to do both if you expect to get what you want. Follow these steps to start your own process of setting goals for your future.

What you Want?

✱ Decide what you want First ask yourself what you want. Be sure it is, in fact, what you want and not what others want for you. These kinds of decisions will probably point to long-term goals. Make sure these goals are in line with your interests and aspirations.

✱ Set realistic goals Make sure the goals you set for yourself are realistic and achievable. For instance, if you are 5 ft. tall, you probably won't be able to achieve a goal of being the starting center for the Boston Celtics. For all but the tallest and most talented, such a goal is unrealistic and could waste valuable time and energy. Instead, you might want to focus on a more realistic goal such as becoming a basketball coach or a sports writer.

✱ Make sure your goals are consistent with your values
Take time to understand your goals and what achieving them will mean for you personally and for others. In other words, think of how your goals line up with your values. For example, let's say you have the goal of joining a successful rock band. To be successful, most bands must tour. This means you would have to travel constantly and spend a great deal of time in the company of strangers. How does this match your values? If you place high value on the familiarity and security of your home town or the company of friends and family, then being a member of a rock band may not be very satisfying to you.

✱ Consider costs and rewards Is it worth the trouble? This is a good question to ask when setting your goals. For some goals, the reward might not be worth the cost in work, time, and money. Be sure to take the time to consider the costs and rewards of your goals. A good business person would never intentionally buy a company that did not have the potential to earn more than its purchase price. You may want to take that same approach to selecting goals for yourself.

* **Write your goals down** It may help to write down your goals and keep them in a notebook or some other place where you can refer to them from time to time. By writing down your goals, you will be strengthening your commitment to reaching them. Review your goals periodically to keep them fresh in your mind and to reinforce your commitment to them.

* **Develop a plan for reaching short-term goals** Suppose that one of your goals is to learn to play the guitar. This is certainly a reasonable goal, but not one that could be reached with a single giant step. This goal, like so many others, can only be reached one step at a time. And, to organize all these steps, you need a plan. For example, a plan for learning to play the guitar might include the following steps:

  1. Purchase a guitar suitable for beginners.
  2. Learn the basic chords.
  3. Learn more difficult chords.
  4. Learn to make chord changes.
  5. Learn to play a few simple songs.
  6. Begin learning a more difficult piece.
  7. Keep practicing and build a growing selection of songs.
  8. Practice performing songs for others.

* **Develop a plan for reaching long-term goals** Planning is especially important for reaching long-term goals. Long-term goals are much less intimidating and difficult if they are broken down into smaller short-term goals. For example, if your long-term goal were to become an expert cabinet maker, then becoming familiar with woodworking tools would be a sensible short-term goal. Another short-term goal would be to become familiar with the kinds of wood used in cabinetmaking. These and any other short-term goals should be included in the plan. The completed plan will be like a ladder, with each rung representing an important short-term goal. By completing each goal, you not only get the satisfaction of achieving the immediate goal, you get the satisfaction of knowing you are one step closer to reaching your ultimate goal.

* **Develop timelines** Each goal in your plan should have a clear objective so that you can measure your progress. Whenever possible, both long-term and short-term goals should also be matched to some sort of schedule or timeline. For example, if learning to play the guitar is your goal, you might allow yourself three weeks for learning five basic guitar chords and three more weeks to learn five additional chords. If you don't complete these smaller tasks on schedule, it won't mean you have failed. It just means that you have to create a more realistic schedule and try again. While a timeline may not always be possible, open-ended goals without any timelines are less likely to be achieved than those matched to a schedule.

Setting well-defined goals and establishing reasonable timelines for achieving them are skills just like throwing or catching a ball. You get better at these things with practice. You may want to practice your goal-setting skills by establishing and working toward one or more of your smaller short-term goals. Write down the goal, develop a plan for achieving it, stick to your timelines, and then take pleasure in the accomplishment. The more often you repeat this process, the more likely you will be able to create the future that you want.

CRITICAL THINKING What are two of your long-term goals? What long-term goal do you have for your career? What short-term goals will get you to your long-term career goal? What are your timelines for reaching these goals? Are your goals realistic and what you really want?

5 Vision

Planning for the future takes the ability to imagine what the future might be like. This ability is often called vision. Having vision doesn't mean you can see into the future. Nobody can do that. It simply means you have a good imagination and a good sense of how things might work out in the future. Maybe you are a person who can look at a set of plans and a pile of lumber and other materials and see them as a sturdy table or a decorative cabinet. This is one example of vision. Another example of vision is the ability to imagine yourself on a particular career path.

Now would be a good time for you to start looking ahead into your own future. Ask yourself what your life will be like a few years or even decades from now. You will be using your own imagination and vision in answering this question. Now imagine that you have chosen a particular career, for instance, a career in construction. Again, ask yourself what your life would be like in a few years or in a few decades. Your vision around your future career may not be very clear at this point. But don't worry. *Career Connections: One Trade, Many Careers* is intended to help you clarify your vision about construction careers and the many rewards they can offer.

Chapter Check

On a separate piece of paper, write your answers to the following questions:

Multiple Choice

1. Which of the following is the belief that a person can achieve anything with hard work?
   a) value
   b) opinion
   c) attitude
   d) judgment

2. Which of the following is the first step in the process of setting goals?
   a) develop timelines
   b) decide what you want
   c) consider costs and rewards
   d) develop a plan for reaching short-term goals

3. Which of the following is, by its very definition, untrue and unfair?
   a) opinion
   b) criticism
   c) attitude
   d) prejudice

4. Which of the following is not a people skill?
   a) listening carefully
   b) being persuasive
   c) being critical
   d) winning and losing well

Fill in the Blank

5. A belief that is closely linked to who you are as a person is a(n) ____________ .

6. A(n) ____________ player puts his or her differences aside for the best interests of the group.

7. Rather than being open-ended, a goal should be set with a reasonable ____________ for achieving it.

True or False

8. Your goals should be consistent with your values. *T or F*

9. Having vision means being able to see into the future. *T or F*

10. Values can guide you to make key decisions during moments of uncertainty. *T or F*

Important Words

Attitude The way a person thinks, feels, and acts.

Goal Something you want to attain or achieve.

Long-term goal A goal that might take a year or more to achieve.

Opinion A view or attitude about a particular subject.

Prejudice An attitude that has no reasonable or justified basis in fact.

Short-term goal A goal that might take a few months to achieve.

Value An idea or belief that has great importance to a person.

Vision The ability to imagine what the future might be like.

On the Trail of ...

One way to uncover your dreams and visualize your future is to create a "vision board," also called a "dream board." A vision board is a collage of words and pictures that describe what you want in your life. Go through magazines and newspapers and search for images and words that represent your dreams. Cut out the images and words and glue them on a piece of cardboard. Bring in your vision board to discuss in class. Explain how the items on your board tie into short- and long-term goals. Keep your vision board in a prominent place where you can view it daily and focus your attention on it. Who knows, maybe the things on your vision board will begin to show up in your life, sooner than later.

.com

With one of your long-term goals in mind, think of a person who has achieved the same goal successfully. Use the Internet to research this person. How did he or she decide to pursue this goal? How long did it take to reach it? What obstacles or challenges were encountered along the way? Write a short report on your findings.

Being the First Choice

Listening and speaking are two of the basic skills you'll need to get a job and be successful in the workplace. Team up with another student to practice these skills. One student speaks while the other student listens. In a one-minute speech, the speaker describes one of his or her short-term goals to the listener. The listener pays careful attention. At the end of the speech, the listener repeats back to the speaker a summary of the goal described. The speaker and listener can then switch roles. How do you rate each other's performance as speaker and listener?

CHAPTER 2

What's in My

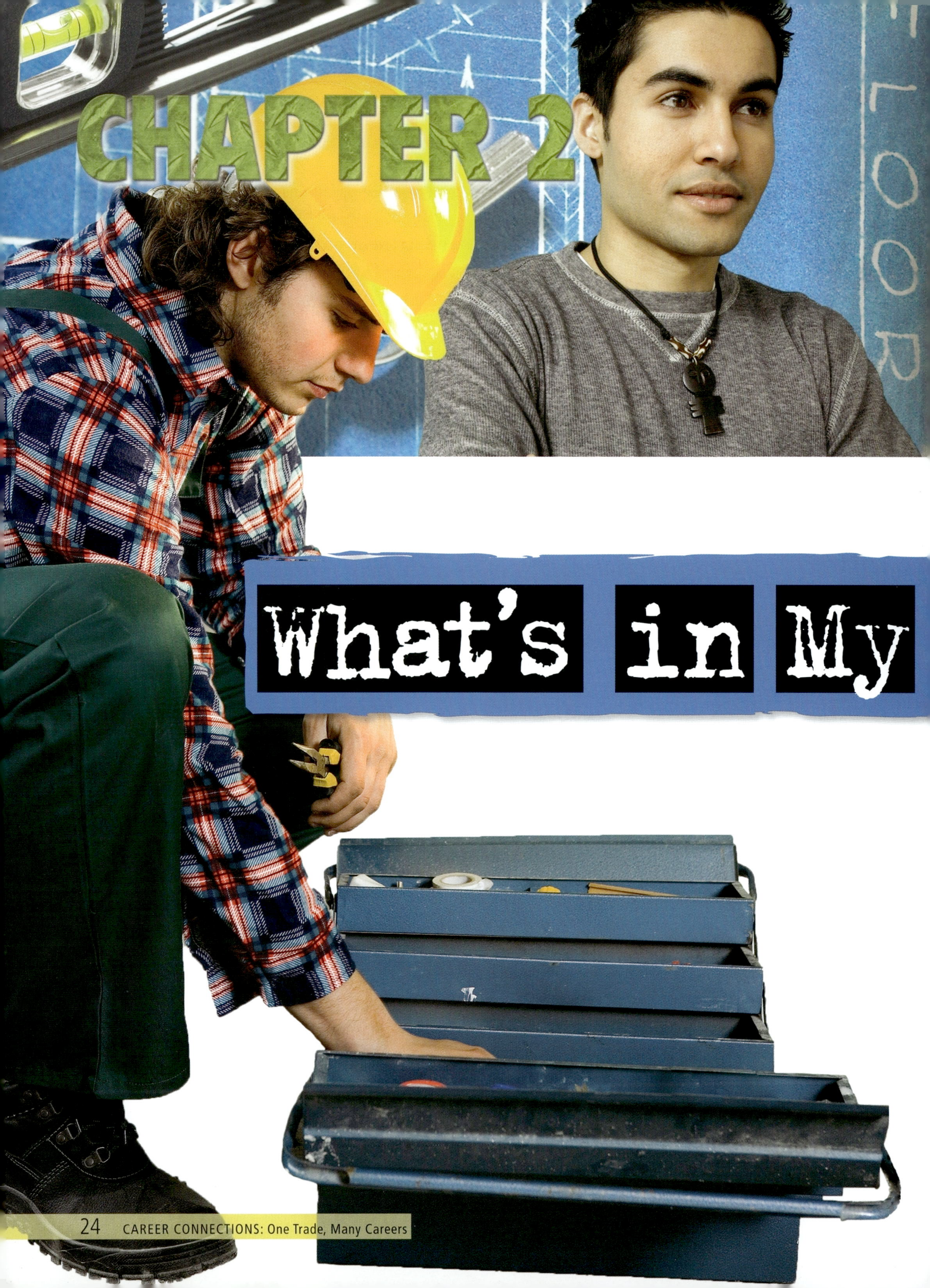

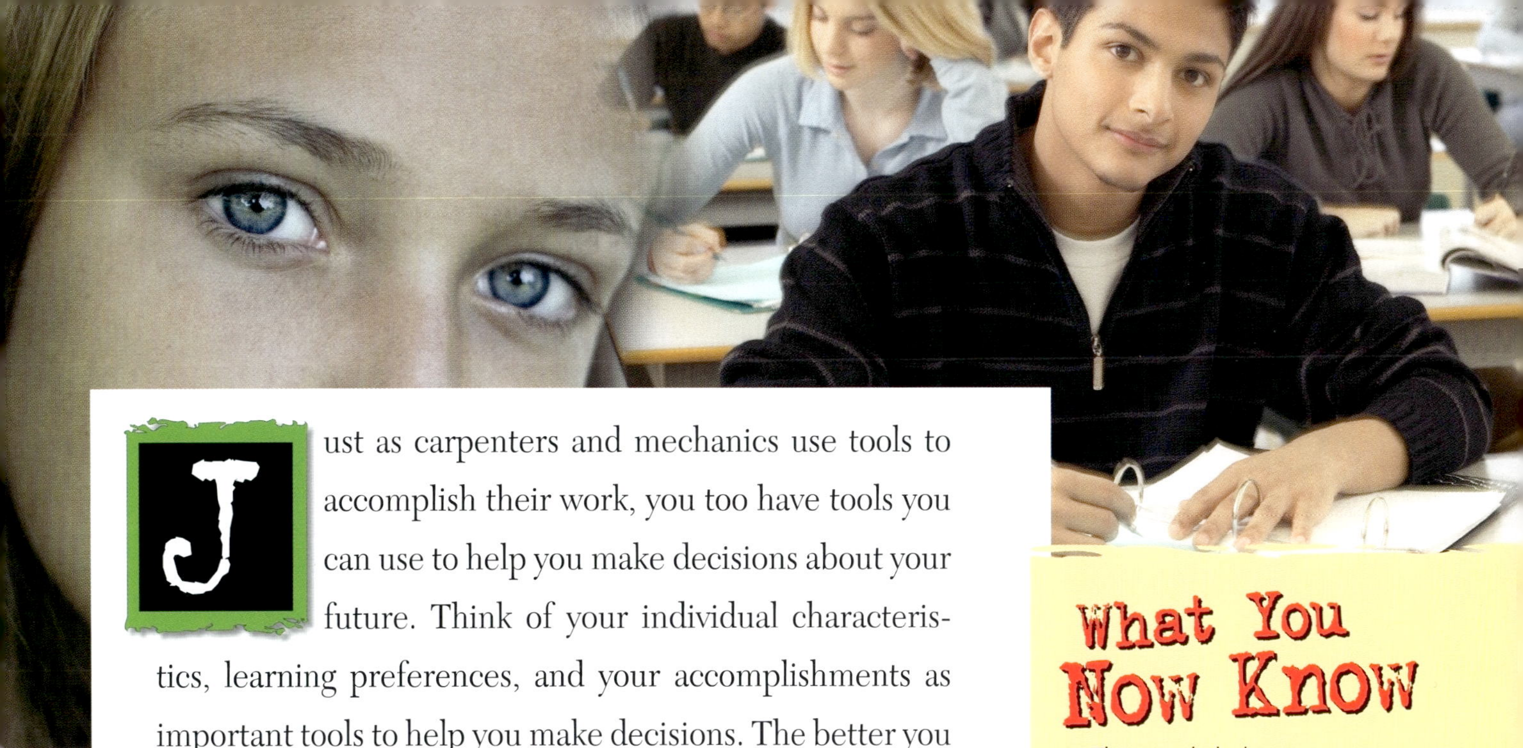

Just as carpenters and mechanics use tools to accomplish their work, you too have tools you can use to help you make decisions about your future. Think of your individual characteristics, learning preferences, and your accomplishments as important tools to help you make decisions. The better you understand these tools, the better you will be able to plan your future career.

Toolbox?

A plan for your future should be laid out in a similar way to a construction project. Before the building is constructed, you need a solid foundation. The finished building can only be as strong as the foundation on which it stands. Think of the foundation of your plan as what you have learned and achieved in your life. You may be surprised at how much you have learned and accomplished to get to this point in your life. Now it is time to make good use of all that hard work.

What You Now Know

- That goals help you achieve success
- How values influence your attitudes
- How to build on your achievements
- That every day is filled with some type of decision

What You Will Know

- How you prefer to learn
- How to make good decisions

. . . you too have tools you can use to help you make decisions . . .

1 What You Have Achieved So Far

You may think that you haven't done very much with your life so far. And it's probably true that your most important achievements are yet to come. Even so, you have probably accomplished far more than you may realize. Consider the skills you have now compared to the skills you had when you were born. You have learned to walk, talk, read, write, and make sense of complex numbers and equations. You have acquired a great amount of knowledge regarding literature, history, government, science, and the way the world works. You may have been in a choir, a band, or on a sports team where you learned about teamwork and the value of hard work. You may not think of any of these things as great accomplishments, but behavioral scientists will tell you they are really quite extraordinary. And just think, you have already accomplished all of this and much more.

framing your future

How many people do you think you'll meet in your lifetime? If you meet an average of 2 new people a day from the time you're 10 through 80, that would be 70 years X 365 days + 17 leap years X 2 people = 51,134 people. Of all the people you're going to meet in your life, how many do you think will be central to your life story?

CRITICAL THINKING What do you think you've achieved with your life so far? What are the accomplishments that make you the most proud? What life lessons have you learned from some of your accomplishments? Which of your accomplishments can you build on in the future?

Your Life Story A person's life is much like a novel. It is a series of significant and seemingly insignificant experiences that add up to a meaningful story. Even a relatively quiet life will feature plenty of thrills and action and will involve all sorts of fascinating people. There will probably be a few heroes and even a few villains. But since this is your story, you will always be the central character. And no matter what direction your life takes, you are the one who must decide which paths to follow.

Some people say life is an adventure.

Some people say life is an adventure. But unlike an action movie that may last two or three hours at the most, your adventure is likely to last 80 years or more. So, it is well worth giving some careful thought to how all those years are to be spent. After all, you are the author of your own life story and you can make it the way you want it.

What Your Story Says About You How you spend your life and the decisions you make reveal what's most important to you. If you value your home and family, your decisions should support these important aspects

of your life. Your life may also show a spiritual commitment. For some, this commitment may be outwardly expressed in the form of a church membership or similar religious affiliation. For others, it may take the form of a simple faith in the goodness and meaningfulness of life. Still another important part of your life will be your sense of allegiance to your school, community, state, or country. An allegiance to your country is called patriotism, and you may have the opportunity to demonstrate this by participating in government, serving in the military, or in some other important way such as registering voters.

An especially important part in your life story will be the career you choose to pursue. Your career will determine how you will spend much of your time and how you will provide support for yourself and your family. The work you do has a powerful influence on how you see yourself as a person and how others might identify you. How often have you heard someone described as a teacher, a baker, a salesman, or a carpenter? The career decisions you reach now will make a big difference not just in how you live your life but in how you see yourself and how others see you as well.

...the way you live says a lot about who you are

Choosing a career forces you to give very careful thought to the future. In order to make a good choice, however, it's often helpful to think about the past. Your choice of careers should be based at least in part on what you have learned and the experiences you have had up to this point in your life. You've grown up, gone to school, taken on part-time jobs, made close friends, and perhaps even fallen in love. The point is, you have already done a lot of living, and the way you live says a lot about who you are.

CRITICAL THINKING What are the things that give meaning to your life? What does the way you spend your time, energy, and money say about what is important to you?

Was It Fun or Was It Boring? By doing some careful thinking about the experiences you've had over the years, you'll learn a lot about yourself. Have you enjoyed school or would you rather have spent your time in the classroom in some other way? Did you accomplish any personal goals? How did you feel when you reached those goals? What personal losses have you suffered? How did you react to them? Your experiences and your responses to those experiences will reveal much about your personal interests, values, attitudes, people skills, and goals.

Obviously some activities are more enjoyable than others. Some are lots of fun. Others are downright boring. So when thinking about the activities you have engaged in over these last few years, ask yourself this question: was it fun or was it boring?

how i see myself

Often, the key to your career path goes back to what you loved doing as a child. What activities totally absorbed you? If you were fascinated by taking apart your toys, working with machinery might be a fun career for you. Do you recall a particular activity or interest from childhood that has left a lasting impression? How might this experience point to a career path?

Any activity that seems overly difficult may not be fully engaging your mind and emotions. That may mean you're not interested in it. People tend to devote far less time and effort to activities that don't interest them. If an activity is fun, you'll almost certainly invest more time, thought, and energy in it. And, no doubt, you'll also become better at it. Most people don't spend much time playing games or sports they don't enjoy.

Think about the kinds of things you enjoy doing. Do you like being outdoors, or do you prefer staying inside? Do you enjoy activities that involve books or computers, or do you prefer things you can do with your hands? Would you rather build things or talk about them? Asking questions like these about your experiences will help you learn more about yourself and your personal preferences. Answering these types of questions can also help you select a career that's right for you.

CRITICAL THINKING Think about some of the activities you have engaged in over the years. Which of these were fun and which were boring? Are any of these activities things you would enjoy doing as a career?

2 Your Learning Preferences

Experts in learning tell us there may be as many as eight different kinds of intelligence, or **learning preferences**. These preferences are determined by the ways individuals interact with the world around them. You have probably noticed that some people are more interested in how something feels to the touch than in how it looks. Some people are fascinated by colors while others pay closer attention to sounds. Naturally, these differences have a powerful influence on how people learn. The following list describes some learning preferences:

- **Verbal** preference for reading, writing, and storytelling; prefer receiving information in the form of words; often very successful in school and in careers that emphasize reading and verbal communication
- **Hands-on** preference for working with one's hands; enjoy finding out about things by touching solid materials and moving them around; often very good in athletics and at building or fixing things
- **Logical** preference for working things out in one's head; good with numbers and problem solving; may enjoy doing experiments
- **Visual** preference for picturing things in one's mind; can imagine how these things would look if they were changed in certain ways; like working with drawings, photographs, and maps
- **Musical** preference for music; sometimes said to "have an ear for music"; may often remember every note of an entire piece of music or follow rhythms without reading the music off a sheet; may prefer listening to music to reading a book
- **People Oriented** preference for being with people; feel comfortable and learn best in social settings; make friends easily and like being part of a group; usually communicate well with others and may enjoy helping people solve their problems

nailing it!

Do you feel you learn best by doing? And not just by using your hands, but by having your entire body in motion? You might be a "whole body learner." As kids, whole body learners need to move to learn. They learn geography by walking on a giant map, or they memorize a poem while tossing a ball back and forth. As adults, whole body learners need to think through a problem by working out at the gym, or they learn about construction by building a house. Careers for whole body learners include actor, dancer, carpenter, and tour guide.

Some people are fascinated by colors while others pay closer attention to sounds.

Are you people oriented?

- **Personally Oriented** preference for working and learning on one's own; less likely than others to have doubts about their thoughts and feelings; often confident enough to work with little input or support from others
- **Nature Oriented** preference for outdoor environments; may hear and see things in a forest, on a beach, or even in the sky that others would never notice; enjoy the outdoors and are good at working with plants, animals, and other aspects of the natural world

Learning preferences also explain why some people handle certain tasks much better than others. Your own learning preferences are closely linked to the rich store of talent you will bring with you into your career. The important thing is to choose a career that is well matched to your learning preferences and talents.

CRITICAL THINKING Which learning preferences do you think you have? Which do you know you do not have? What do you think your learning preferences say about you and your possible career choice?

preference for outdoor environments

3 How You Make Decisions

Whether you realize it or not, you make many decisions every day. You decide what clothes to put on in the morning and what to eat for breakfast. You may decide who to sit with at lunch, whether to buy gas for your car or wait until tomorrow, or whether or not to call that friend you haven't heard from in a while. These day-to-day decisions may seem important in the moment, but they probably won't make much difference to your future.

Other decisions, such as what career path to follow, may change the course of your entire life. In making decisions about your career, there is much to consider. Listed here are some of the important considerations that may relate to your choice in a career.

- **Location** – Do you want to work in the city or in the country? Do you like living in your hometown or do you want to move to another location? You might even prefer a career that keeps you on the road, or one that requires moving frequently.
- **Stability** – Do you want an opportunity in a growing industry such as alternative fuels or would you like a more stable opportunity as a carpenter?
- **Income** – How important is money to your career satisfaction? Most people want to make as much money as they can, but for some this is more important than for others. Where one person may be happy doing good work for an acceptable wage, another person may be dissatisfied and want to make more money. This leads to questions about working for a small company, working for a corporation, and even starting your own business.
- **Desirable work** – Do you want to work inside or do you prefer the outdoors? Do you prefer working at a desk or do you like more physical work? Do you prefer technical work or do you like less technically demanding work? Do like to work alone or do you prefer working with customers, co-workers, and supervisors?

shout out!

Derek Stump of South Bend, Indiana, has made three important decisions in his life. The first one was in high school, when he got his Dodge Ram pick-up truck. The second decision was to customize the truck and race it competitively. With 360 horsepower at the wheels and 866 foot pounds of torque, Stump became the defending national champion in Street Class with the Diesel Hot Rod Association. To earn enough money to support his love of racing, Stump made a career decision when he got out of high school: to become a union carpenter. "I'm a hands-on person, and I was always building stuff when I was growing up. In carpentry, you really feel like you've accomplished something once it's all done. It makes you feel good." Today, Stump is content with his career and lifestyle decisions. "I'm single. I own my own house. I have a truck I love. What more can I ask for?"

framing your future

First Lady Eleanor Roosevelt wrote in a letter to a friend, "Somewhere along the line of development we discover what we really are, and then we make our real decision for which we are responsible. Make that decision primarily for yourself because you can never really live anyone else's life, not even your own child's."

These and other decisions can be hard to make. The most difficult thing about making decisions is that you can't be absolutely certain you are making the right ones. Making a decision requires what is sometimes referred to as a "judgment call," and our judgment can mislead us. Maybe you were the one who picked the movie that turned out to be terribly boring. That may have been disappointing and perhaps even a little embarrassing, but it's hardly a disaster. It's just a decision you made that didn't work out as well as you had hoped. Everyone makes the wrong decision sometimes, and the results can be far worse than having to sit through a bad movie. That's why people occasionally get anxious when faced with a key decision.

The best way to ensure that you reach your own goals is to be in charge of your own decision making.

Decision-Making Styles

Interestingly, whether the choices you face are life changing or relatively insignificant, you tend to make most of your decisions in the same way. In other words, just as you have individual learning preferences, you also have your own decision-making styles, or methods. Read the following decision-making styles, and as you read, compare them to how you make your own decisions. You may relate to one or a combination of these styles depending on the situation or the decision to be made. The important thing here is for you to get a better idea of how you make decisions.

* **Dependent** Some people believe they are not good at making decisions and want others to make the decisions for them. When faced with an important choice or conflict, they invariably turn to their parents, siblings, teachers, bosses, or friends for help. Making a **dependent decision** of this sort often starts in childhood, when our parents make most of our important choices for us. However, this dependent approach is not very helpful later in life. The best way to ensure that you reach your own goals is to be in charge of your own decision making.

* **Intuitive** Often people rely on intuition or what we sometimes call a "gut feeling" to make decisions. An **intuitive decision** relies more on the "feeling" of a decision than on the facts. Although intuition may be an important component of a decision, most good decisions also include thoughtful deliberation about the facts.

* **Impulsive** An **impulsive decision** is made very quickly and without careful analysis. Think of the person who buys a used car simply based on its looks. This person may quickly find out that a car can look good without necessarily providing dependable transportation. Buying a used car, like most other important decisions, requires some thoughtful analysis. People who make impulsive decisions don't take the time to consider all aspects of the decision. This may be appropriate when selecting a flavor of ice cream, but it can be a problem when making an important decision. By not considering all the aspects of an important decision, you may have to live with some consequences you didn't expect or want.

★ Fatalistic If a person believes that his or her choices have no effect on the outcome of an event, then this person is engaged in making a **fatalistic decision**. This type of decision making can be described with the question: "What difference does it make anyway?" People with this attitude generally don't put much effort into making a good decision.

★ Thoughtful A **thoughtful decision** is one that is made after weighing both the facts and the feelings that surround potential choices. A thoughtful decision also takes into account the consequences of the available options. Thoughtful decision making takes time, effort, and discipline. By taking the time and making the effort to analyze the outcomes of each of your possible choices, you will greatly increase your chances of realizing a bad choice before you actually make it. This is hard work, but it is the best way to start on your career path.

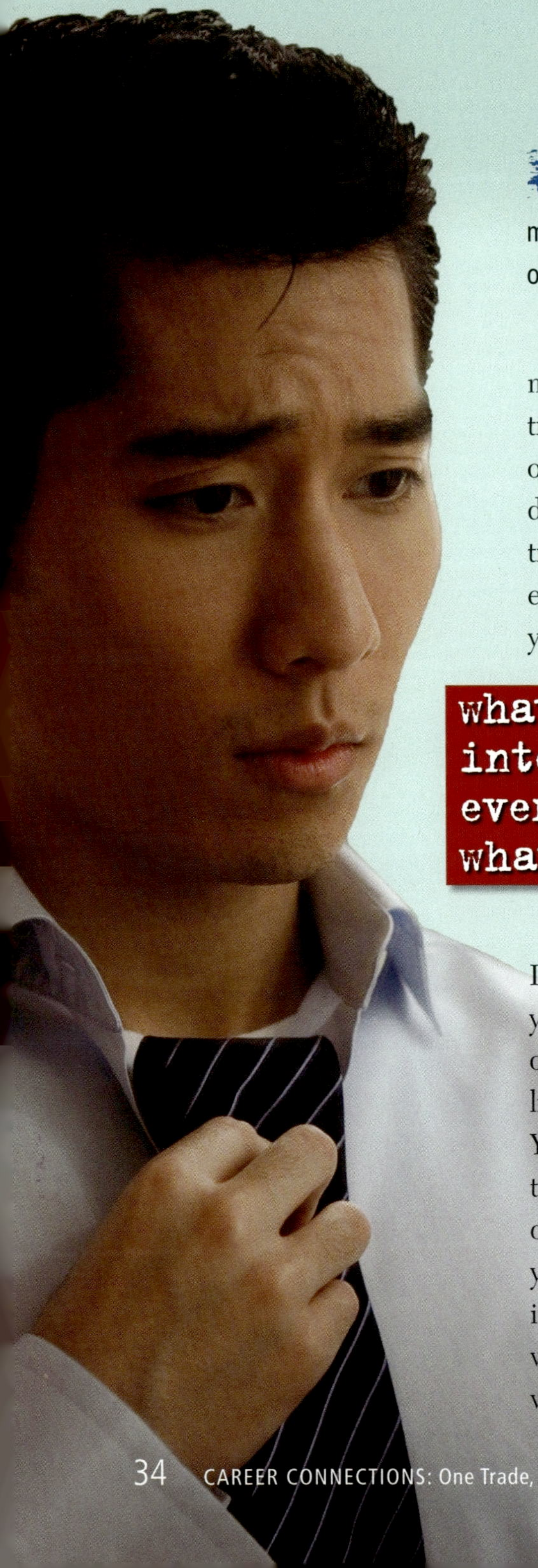

CRITICAL THINKING What decision-making style do you most closely relate to? Why wouldn't you want to use the impulsive style to make a career choice? Why do you think you are in the best position to make your own career decisions?

A thoughtful decision will usually produce better results than decisions made in a dependent, intuitive, impulsive, or fatalistic manner. By taking the time and effort to consider both facts and feelings, and the consequences of various choices, you will be able to reach a reasonable decision. This decision may not lead to the results you wanted—nobody gets it right all the time—but if things don't work out as you had hoped, you can learn from the experience. Since your decision was based on thoughtful decision making, you can identify the flaw in the process and then avoid this same mistake the next time you are faced with a similar decision. Even better, if things work out well, you will learn from that too and you will be able to repeat the success.

what to wear for a job interview might require even more thought than what you wear on a date

Making a truly thoughtful decision is a methodical, step-by-step process. It takes too much time and energy to apply this approach to every decision you make each day. For example, if you used this type of decision making to order lunch, your lunch hour might be over before you even ordered. Your life is filled with choices and minor problems that must be solved quickly. You can't afford to take a lot of time making such decisions. Deciding where to sit on a bus or which movie to see at the theater is more suited to intuitive or even impulsive decision making. Deciding on a magazine to buy or what you are going to wear on a date may still be thoughtful, but the thought we invest should match the importance of the decision. Deciding on what to wear for a job interview might require even more thought than deciding what you wear on a date.

Steps in Making Good Decisions

When making really important decisions, such as what career path you will follow, you should always apply a thoughtful decision-making process and invest plenty of time in that process. After all, you could be living with the consequences of this decision for a long time. The thoughtful decision-making process consists of the following seven steps.

1. **Accept Responsibility for the Decision** Sometimes making decisions can make us uncomfortable. Decisions often close the door on one opportunity even as they open the door on another, and this can be painful. You may wish to avoid making a painful decision or to put it off as long as possible, but you shouldn't. Once you recognize that a decision should be made, take responsibility for making the decision. In this way, you are taking responsibility for your own life. Also realize that by taking this responsibility, you are also accepting responsibility for the consequences of that decision.

2. **Identify the Problem** Think of a decision as a problem to solve. You can even think of an upcoming career choice as a problem that needs a solution. The problem is picking an appropriate career that you will be happy with. A good decision will provide an acceptable solution to the problem. A poor decision may delay the solution to the problem or even make it a more difficult problem. To solve any problem well, it is important to understand as much about the problem or situation as possible. It may be helpful to write out the problem and then list as many possible solutions you can think of.

your future might look very different after entering a union apprenticeship program as opposed to getting a part-time job

3. **Consider Alternative Solutions** Obviously some solutions to a problem will be better than others. After you have gathered as much information as possible on the problem and listed possible solutions, it is time to consider the likely consequences of each solution. Ask yourself what might happen if you actually made each of the choices you listed as possible solutions. This will give you insight about your future once each decision is made. For example, your future might look very different after entering a union apprenticeship program as opposed to getting a part-time job.

4. **Choose a Likely Solution** Once you have carefully considered all the reasonable solutions, one or more of them will seem more attractive than the others. Soon you should be able to narrow your list of solutions down to a single likely option. Make sure that this option fits in well with your goals and personal values and attitudes. If you don't find any conflicts, you have probably identified an acceptable solution. Be careful not to rush this step, and take the time to honestly evaluate your possible solutions.

5. **Make the Decision** If you are comfortable with the solution you have selected, you are now ready to actually make the decision. You may want to discuss your decision with friends, family, or others whose judgments you respect. This process should give you confidence about your choice. If it doesn't, you may want to reevaluate your decision. It is not too late to change your mind if you discover a good reason to do so.

6. **Implement the Decision** Decisions have little value until they are put into action. If you are not going to act on your decision, why would you bother to make the decision at all? Although implementing a decision may take a lot of hard work, determination, and more than a little patience, it is usually worth the effort. In fact, the harder you work in implementing a decision, the more likely the decision will be successful. However, if the results of your decision are not the ones you had in mind, further action may be necessary. You may even need a new decision.

7. **Evaluate Your Decision** It is not uncommon for people to omit the last and most valuable step in the thoughtful decision-making process. That is, they don't take the time to evaluate their decision. In fact, they may get so caught up in the consequences of a decision and the action it required that they forget why they made the decision in the first place. Although it is seldom useful to second guess your decision, it can be very helpful to evaluate the process you used to arrive at the decision. Did you correctly identify the problem? Did you list all the likely solutions? Did you gather enough information and correctly weigh the alternatives? Was the decision you made in keeping with your goals and personal values and attitudes? Were you satisfied with the result?

CRITICAL THINKING Why would you want to use the thoughtful decision-making approach when making a career decision? What possible solutions could you come up with in trying to decide on your own career? In evaluating these solutions, which solution seems to be the best option? What do you want to learn more about before actually deciding on a future career?

You can see that your tool box has some very useful tools to help you make smart decisions about your future career. Your tool box is full of individual characteristics, learning preferences, and your accomplishments. Your tool box now also contains more knowledge about how to make thoughtful decisions. You can use these tools to build the future you want.

Chapter Check

On a separate piece of paper, write your answers to the following questions:

Multiple Choice

1. A person who is good with numbers and problem solving has which type of learning preference?
   a) hands-on
   b) verbal
   c) logical
   d) visual

2. Which type of decision-making style is best for choosing a career?
   a) thoughtful
   b) impulsive
   c) dependent
   d) intuitive

3. What is the first step in a thoughtful decision-making process?
   a) identify the problem
   b) identify the reason for the problem
   c) make the decision
   d) accept responsibility for the decision

Fill in the Blank

4. Serving in the military or registering voters are ways to demonstrate ______________.

5. A person who enjoys outdoor environments has a(n) ______________-oriented learning preference.

6. People who make ______________ decisions don't take time to consider all aspects of the decision.

True or False

7. A person with a learning preference that is personally oriented learns best in social settings. *T or F*

8. Making an intuitive decision means relying on a "gut feeling." *T or F*

9. People who make fatalistic decisions put too much effort into their decision making. *T or F*

10. The last and most important step in the thoughtful decision-making process is to act on the decision. *T or F*

Important Words

Dependent decision A decision made for someone by someone else, such as a parent, teacher, or friend.

Fatalistic decision A decision made by someone who believes his or her choices have no effect on the outcome.

Impulsive decision A decision made very quickly and without careful analysis.

Intuitive decision A decision made based on feeling rather than facts.

Learning preferences Ways in which people acquire intelligence.

Thoughtful decision A decision made after weighing both facts and feelings about potential choices.

On the Trail of . . .

Think of someone you know who is good at decision making. It could be a parent, relative, neighbor, or local businessperson. Interview this person to determine his or her decision-making style. Find out why this style works for them, and ask for an example of a good decision they have made using this style. Write a short report on your findings.

.com

People with specific learning preferences are often tailor-made for certain careers. On a piece of paper or on a computer, create three columns. In the first column, list the learning preferences described in this chapter. In the second column, write a suitable career for each learning preference. For example, someone with a verbal learning preference would make a good public speaker or disk jockey. In the third column, name a well-known person for each of the careers listed. Use the internet to include some identifying information about each person, such as how long he or she has been in this career and notable accomplishments.

Being the First Choice

Thinking skills, such as decision making, problem solving, and visualizing, are basic skills you'll need to get a job and be successful in the workplace. To practice these skills, act out the decision-making process by making a decision about something right now. Using the thoughtful decision-making process, determine the seven steps you need to follow to carry out this decision. Draw a diagram that details each step.

PART 2

The World of

...entering the working world you realize that it is a serious place

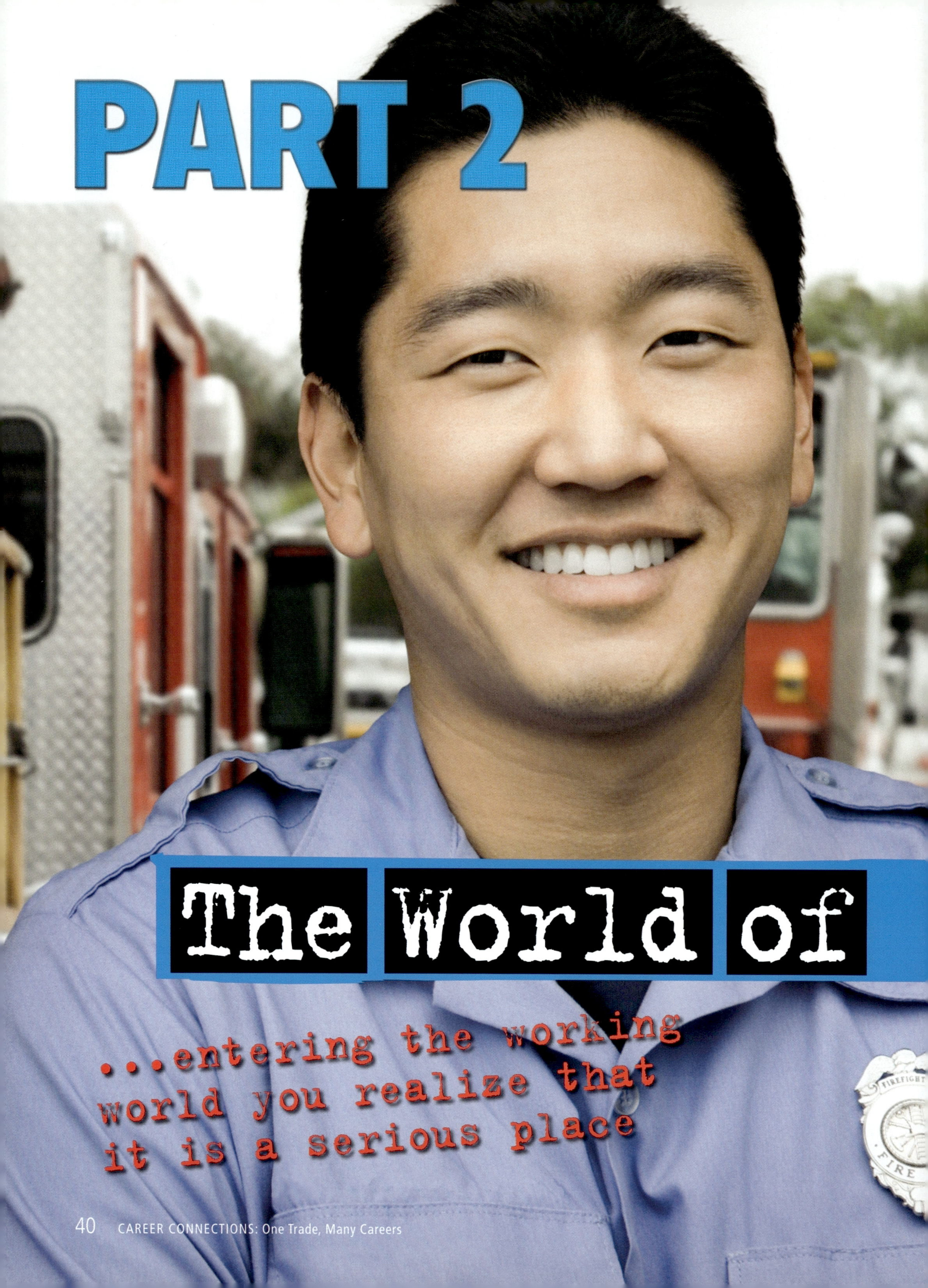

Work

Work is nothing new to you. You've been working and learning about work nearly all of your life. At school you've had assignments, and at home you've had chores to do. You may have had a part-time job to help pay for summer trips, to buy clothes, or to provide spending money for evenings out with your friends. Perhaps you have also done community service work such as helping to clean up the environment.

After you finish school, however, you'll be stepping into the world of work. If you are like most people you'll be spending a substantial portion of your life—perhaps as much as 100,000 hours of it—at work. When you make this enormous investment of time and effort, you'll want to be sure you enjoy the work you do. Fortunately, the working world is an exciting place, and it can offer you the opportunity to meet fascinating people and learn new things. You may also have the opportunity to develop fresh interests and achieve personal goals that were once only dreams.

Just as life itself is not always easy, neither is work. Once you have entered the working world you will quickly realize that it is a serious place. The world of work is competitive. It is also filled with challenges that must be faced and hurdles that must be overcome. But, the world of work is also a place where you can reach your highest potential. People often achieve some of their most important and memorable accomplishments at work and you may discover this is also the case for you.

To reach your full potential as a worker and to get the most out of your life-long investment in work, you should learn as much as you can about the working world before you enter it. The next several chapters will answer some of the questions you may have about work. For instance, what is it like at work? What skills will I need in a fast-paced, quickly changing workplace? What will my employers expect of me? And perhaps most important of all, what is the best way to choose a career that's right for me?

framing your future

The wise words spoken 2500 years ago by Chinese philosopher Confucius are still meaningful today: "Choose a job you love and you will never have to work a day in your life."

CHAPTER 3

The Modern

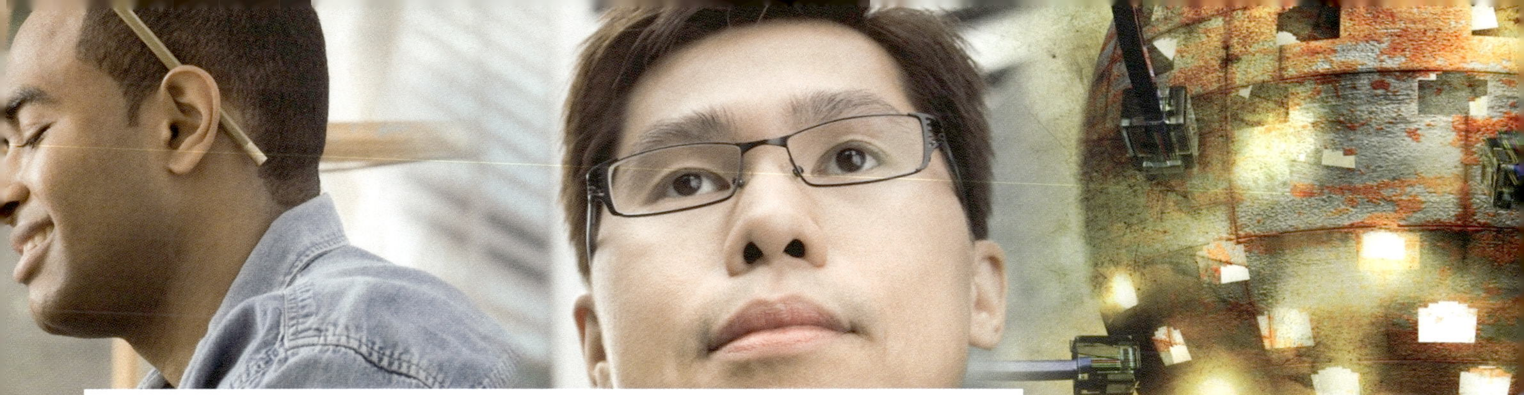

In recent years you may have heard about big changes in where people work, how they work, and even why they work. The global economy, the importance of technology and skilled labor, and the diversity of the workforce are common topics on the internet, on television, and in newspapers and magazines. You may be paying closer attention now that you are about to enter the workplace.

In order to be successful in the changing workplace, you'll need to constantly upgrade your skills. Adapting to changes in the workplace means that a critical skill for you is learning to learn. You'll need to adapt and to learn "the next big thing" in the field you have chosen as a career.

Workplace

Some characteristics of our changing work and workplace are that the workplace is:

- Increasingly focused on working in teams rather than having workers repeat one process in assembly-line fashion
- Providing more and equal opportunities for people of all races and ethnic backgrounds
- Committed to fair hiring practices, including more and better opportunities for women as well as providing accommodations for those challenged physically and in other ways
- More responsive to legislated safety rules and regulations

What You Now Know

- That knowing how you learn helps in achieving goals
- The importance of making good decisions
- That work is a part of everyday life

What You Will Know

- How the modern workplace functions
- What employers expect
- How to communicate effectively
- The importance of understanding and using information
- How to effectively manage time and resources

1 What Is Work and Why Do We Do It?

So, what is work, anyway? You might consider cleaning the house, mowing the lawn, and even studying for an exam as work. You would be right. Work can also describe packing for a trip, making a model airplane, or helping the kid next door repair his bicycle. In fact, any sort of useful activity can be defined as work. However, when people talk about work they do at their jobs, they are talking about the activities they do in order to make money.

CRITICAL THINKING If you didn't have to work for a living, would you choose to do some sort of work anyway, even if you didn't need the money? If you decided to work purely as a matter of choice, then what sort of work might it be?

People often say they work to "put food on the table," by which they mean they work to buy food and clothes, pay bills, and pay for rent or mortgages. But people work for many other reasons as well. Interestingly, many hard workers may not even be aware of all their reasons for working. If asked, they may say they work "to get paid," but their motives are likely far more complex. Some of the more important reasons people work are listed here.

building your future

- **To Build a Secure Future** Not all of the money that people earn is spent right away. Many people put a portion of their earnings into savings or retirement accounts. Some invest in stocks, bonds, or similar securities. Others may buy real estate, gold, or other things that may hold or increase their value over time. This type of spending is intended as an investment toward a future that will be financially secure. Preparing for such a future is one important reason for working.
- **To Get Out and Be Around People** Hanging around the house or apartment may be relaxing at first, but after a while it's likely to get boring. Television and video games can be fun, but most of us want interactions with real people. That's probably one reason you like to be around your friends. The workplace offers similar benefits to workers. It gives you a chance to be around and to interact with others. Often the people you meet at work are engaged in the activity of promoting the interests of the business. This shared experience frequently leads to long-lasting friendships.
- **To Enhance Personal Identity** Your choice of career is likely to make a big difference in how others see you and in how you see yourself. Once you've become involved in a career, you will likely find that you include your occupation when you talk about yourself.
- **To Have a Purpose in Life** Having a job or a career often gives you a sense of purpose. It also helps you to organize your life and feel as though you have something of value to offer.

CRITICAL THINKING Which of these reasons for working apply to you? Which one is most important to you? Are there other reasons you might want employment?

Once you've become involved in a career, you will likely find that you include your occupation when you talk about yourself.

2 What Do Employers Expect?

Do I have what it takes to get a good job and keep it? You may have already asked yourself this question. Another way to ask the same question is: what do employers expect? Obviously employers want to hire employees who will do a good job. You may not realize it, but doing a good job in the workplace takes more than good technical skills and the willingness to work hard. Among other things, employers want workers who can work well with others, be part of a team, communicate well, listen attentively, and speak clearly. Employers want workers who can understand information and use it effectively.

> . . . employers want workers who can work well with others. . .

They want people who can make reasonable decisions and can solve problems as they occur, often without supervision. They want workers who are organized, who can get to work on time, and who can meet deadlines. Increasingly, employers are also seeking workers who are able to understand and adapt to new technology.

> . . . workers who are organized, who can get to work on time. . .

Ability to Work with Others

You may know someone you think is difficult and hard to get along with. This person may be argumentative, overly sensitive, nosey, or unfriendly. This person may be self centered and egotistical, or overbearing and controlling. This list could go on, but the point is that you don't want to be viewed in any of these ways at work. Employers want workers who know how to get along with coworkers, customers, suppliers, and managers. Many a good worker has been let go from a job because of issues related to getting along with others. Workers who are able to get along with others are more effective, and help make the workplace more enjoyable. This is as much an attitude as a skill. If you maintain a friendly and helpful attitude at work, you are most likely to be viewed as friendly and helpful.

Cooperation

Many thousands of years ago people learned that they could achieve much more by working together than by working alone. For instance, in certain dry areas of the world, farmers worked cooperatively to build irrigation systems. As a result, these farmers were able to grow much more food than they could have if each farmer irrigated his own land. This same sort of cooperation has become especially important in the modern workplace. Employers today expect and need employees to work together cooperatively.

Cooperation is also the key to good teamwork. Regardless of whether or not the "team" concept is part of a particular workplace, cooperation with managers and with coworkers is essential. For example, understanding the company's goals and being prepared to work in accordance with these goals is a big step toward being cooperative. By acting cooperatively, you will be helping your coworkers, team members, and managers reach their goals.

Teamwork

In the world of sports, teams are groups of individuals who work together to score points or goals, or to prevent other teams from scoring them. In the music world, teams are groups of individuals who combine their instruments or voices to create a smooth harmonic sound. In the world of work, teams are made up of individuals with varying responsibilities, skills, and levels of experience. These people work together to help their company achieve its goals. Companies may have many different goals, but the most important of these is likely to be earning profits. These profits, in turn, are shared with the workers in the form of wages, salaries, and bonuses. In some cases, employees who work well together as a team make more money for their companies and also for themselves.

Teams may consist of many members or just a few. Usually, each team member plays a different role on the team based on experience or what that person does best. For instance, on a crew that is framing walls, someone does the layout, another cuts the studs and support members, someone else nails all the pieces together, and then the whole crew lifts the assembled wall into place. Another person on the team installs the backing while an apprentice does the clean up. The team is then ready for the next phase of the building process.

Teams play a large role in many carpentry careers. In fact, many employers place an emphasis on teamwork, and they are more likely to hire workers whom they think will make good team members.

nailing it!

In the early Middle Ages in Europe, there was a strong cooperative relationship, and interdependence, between the builder and the carver. The art of stone carving played a key role in building the great French Gothic cathedrals. So when the stone masons built their structures, they kept in mind the artistic creations of the carvers that would follow-- the figures of saints, the heads of gargoyles, or the wings of angels. The carvers and builders worked as a team to create magnificent structures that have inspired people for centuries.

Pulling Your Own Weight

It is said that no chain is stronger than its weakest link. No matter what your job, you are an important link. Each worker must handle a particular part of the overall task and complete it properly and on time. If one worker falls behind, a project may be delayed, and the overall goals of the business may not be achieved. Since no one wants to be the cause of harming the business or letting down their coworkers and teammates, most workers try to do their very best work.

Sharing Ideas

Good ideas are often as necessary as hard work in achieving a company's goals. For example, a good idea may help a whole team do better work and get it done faster and easier. Most work-related ideas don't belong to anyone in particular. They belong to the business and should be shared freely with team members and coworkers. Sharing the idea with others will open it up to improvement. Another team member may think of a way to improve on it. Someone else may think of a way to improve it even more or adapt it to the work of a different team. This process of improving and refining ideas by passing them back and forth among coworkers and team members is called **brainstorming**. Brainstorming may lead to a really great idea and an improved product or service that will bring credit to the workers and profits to the company.

CRITICAL THINKING What aspects of being part of a team do you like? What aspects don't you like? Have you ever experienced team spirit? How did it make you feel?

Helping New Coworkers

Think about a time when you went into a new and strange situation all alone. As you well know, this can be unsettling. This is not much different from starting a new job. On most jobs it is important that the new worker be brought up to speed fast, otherwise everyone might get behind. It is important that new coworkers be encouraged to fit in by being made to feel that they can contribute to the success of the project. If you are an existing member of a team, be sure that any new team members:

- are made to feel comfortable with other members of the team
- become familiar with the way the team works
- are given specific roles to fill and tasks to do that moves the project forward to completion

Resolving Conflicts

Obviously, people don't agree with one another all the time, and in the workplace some conflicts are inevitable. Conflicts may occur between supervisors and workers, between coworkers, and even between members of the same team. It is essential to prevent these conflicts from spiraling out of control. Most conflicts can be resolved in ways that avoid any lasting bad feelings.

One way to resolve a conflict is to talk about it in a reasonable and unemotional way. It may be that the conflict has to do with differing opinions. People can hold differing opinions on the same subject and still remain good friends, coworkers, and team members. However, if the disagreement is serious enough that some action must be taken, someone will have to decide how to resolve the conflict. Usually, the necessary decision will be made by the manager or supervisor who has been put in charge of the team or project. Decisions such as these can be very difficult to make. More often than not, the supervisor's decision will turn out to be the right one.

Following the Organizational Structure

One of the first lessons that new army recruits are taught is how to follow the chain of command. This means that soldiers must obey their immediate superior who obeys his or her immediate superior and so on until the chain reaches the commander-in-chief. In the military, following the chain of command can mean the difference between life and death. Therefore, failing to follow the chain of command is a very serious matter.

The organization of the working world is not as rigid as that of the military. Even so, most organizations have a structure that is a type of "chain of command" and employees are expected to follow it. In the world of work, nearly all businesses, divisions, departments, teams, or projects have a supervisor. Those supervisors are in charge. They pass along instructions to workers and provide help when it is needed. Most supervisors are given their jobs because they have a great deal of experience, are skilled at working with people, and are good at resolving conflicts in a productive way.

Supervisors are not always right, but it is their responsibility to make important decisions. They are also responsible for the success or failure of the projects placed under their supervision. This in itself can make decisions difficult. Add to this the fact that nearly all supervisors have bosses of their own to whom they must answer.

As you enter the world of work you may believe you are leaving a world where you were closely supervised by parents and teachers and are entering a world of independent action. Unless you work for yourself, you likely report to a supervisor or boss. The ability to respond well to supervision is, therefore, a critical skill. Interacting with supervisors in a positive manner is a key expectation that employers have of their workers.

CRITICAL THINKING How well do you respond to supervision? Do you have friends or acquaintances that dislike being supervised? What problems does this dislike cause them?

how i see myself

In his book *Leadership Gold*, John Maxwell lists 26 lessons for being a good leader. One of them is: "Leadership is the ability to submerge your ego for the sake of what is best." This is as important for a leader as it is for a team member – understanding that it's not about you, it's about the team, and what is best for everyone. Can you submerge your ego for the good of your team?

Leadership and Initiative

Even though supervisors are usually given the responsibility for leading and inspiring others, leadership abilities are also valued among workers and team members. While the coach may be in charge of the team, he or she may rely heavily on individual members of the team to assume leadership roles. This same thing happens in the world of work. For example, if you have the ability to motivate and inspire your coworkers, you may assume a leadership role on your team. Your leadership abilities might even lead to an even greater leadership role and even a promotion to supervisor one day.

You may also have the ability to motivate and energize yourself. A person with this ability is sometimes called a **self-starter**. Self-starters are committed to their work, anxious to see their projects successfully completed, and often take the steps to ensure a project's completion with very little or no supervision. In other words, self-starters show **initiative** in the way they do their work. A worker shows initiative by not waiting to be told what to do, but instead does whatever needs to be done to accomplish the job or finish the project.

CRITICAL THINKING In what situations have you shown leadership abilities? In what particular instances have you been a self-starter?

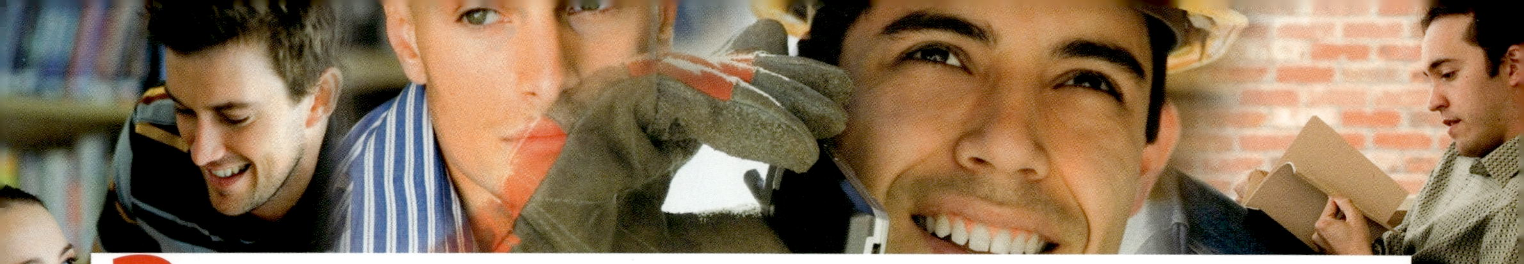

3 Effective Communication Skills

It would be very difficult to be a good worker or team member without effective communication skills. Your success in the world of work depends, in part, on your ability to listen attentively, speak clearly, and say exactly what you mean.

Listening Carefully Few skills are as important as the ability to listen attentively. For obvious reasons, people who listen carefully learn more than those who don't listen well. People with good listening skills tend to get things right more often in school and at work. That's because they are more likely to understand exactly what to expect and exactly what is expected of them.

Careful listening provides many benefits. For one thing, if you listen carefully when other people are speaking, they will be more likely to appreciate you as a coworker and a person. No doubt, you have heard people say to you or to others "You are just not listening to me!" When people say that, they are frustrated about not being heard. Most people consider careful listening to be a sign of respect. If you don't listen to what they have to say, they may think you don't respect them even though this may not be true.

Careful listening can also help resolve conflicts—sometimes even before they get started. It is a mistake to believe that you know what someone else is thinking. Even though you may be correct sometimes, you will be wrong just as often. The only way to know what someone is thinking is to listen carefully to what he or she is saying. If you listen carefully to another person's point of view, you are more likely to avoid misunderstandings and you may find that you agree after all. Even if you don't agree, you will at least have a better idea of what the other person is thinking and can take that into consideration.

. . . ability to listen carefully, to show concern for others

Active Listening People are not necessarily born good listeners. Listening is a skill not unlike the ability to throw and catch a ball. Some experts in social behavior teach what they call "active listening." They believe that people who practice active listening will be more successful at school or at work and get along better with friends and associates.

The process of **active listening** consists of two key parts. The first part is to pay close attention when another person is speaking. To do this you must stay focused and remain engaged in the conversation. You may want to check your understanding along the way by asking questions during the conversation. If you let your mind wander and start thinking about something else, you will lose track of what the other person is saying. In conversations, it is very common for people to be thinking about what they are going to say next while the other person is still talking. This is not a very helpful habit and one that is best avoided. The natural pauses in conversations usually provide plenty of time to consider your next remark. Furthermore, your responses will make more sense and have a greater effect if you have actually heard and understood what the other person has to say.

. . . stay focused and remain engaged in the conversation

...clarify what you thought you heard

The second part of active listening is to clarify what you thought you heard. You may want to paraphrase important parts of what you heard to make sure you understand. You may also want to ask questions for clarification. By responding in these ways, you are not only improving your understanding, you are also showing the other person that you were listening and care about what they have to say. This will make both of you feel more comfortable about the conversation. It will also improve your understanding of what was said.

Active listening is especially important and useful when receiving instructions or directions. For example, if your supervisor asks you to attend an important meeting that will be held in the department conference room on Thursday at 3:00 pm, you might repeat back the date, time, and location to confirm that you understood. Repeating the instruction ensures that you are both on the same page. While this may be a simple example, this step in the active listening process becomes more important as the instructions become more complicated.

communicate clearly

CRITICAL THINKING How do you feel when you're talking to someone and they're not listening? Does your mind wander during conversations or are you an active listener? In what ways do you think active listening would help you at work and in your relationships with others?

Speaking Clearly Have you ever said to a friend: "I can't read your mind!" This was probably because your friend was not communicating clearly. In matters where thoughts and feeling are important, it is important to speak clearly. This means that it is necessary to clearly tell people what you want them to know, rather than making people struggle to figure it out for themselves.

When talking about something important, it is usually best to keep your remarks as brief as possible and to use words that make your point entirely clear. Idle chatter is okay when you are relaxing with friends but not when you are communicating information at work and not when something important is at stake. Try to stay focused on the information you are conveying or the point you are making. Don't get off track or distract others with stories or ideas that are only distantly related to the topic. Sometimes an interesting story may help you illustrate a point, but it is usually best to make direct statements.

building a better u

Saying what you mean is particularly important in electronic communication. When you write an e-mail or instant message, make sure you're very clear in your message. You don't want your words to be taken the wrong way. Once you send a message, it becomes a written record that you can't take back.

speak clearly

Make sure that everyone involved in the conversation can hear what you are saying. Some people are shy and, as a result, speak so softly that others have difficulty hearing them. There is rarely, if ever, any need to shout, but if you have something important to say, talk loudly enough so everyone can hear you clearly.

Saying What You Mean Some thoughts can be hard to put into words. You may have had some conversations where you fell short of making the point you intended. The problem is that you may be judged by what you said, rather than what you meant to say. Also, there is a chance that someone could have taken a wrong action based on a misunderstanding because you didn't say what you meant to say. Here are some tips that may help you say what you mean.

- **Be Prepared** – Try to gather as much information as time permits before beginning an important conversation. Then, organize your thoughts before you speak.
- **Use Written Notes** – If the conversation involves a series of ideas or a complex process, it may be useful to make notes or even make a brief outline beforehand. That way, you can glance at the notes or outline to see if you are leaving out key information. Preparing in this way will also help you organize your remarks and avoid getting off track when speaking
- **Be Brief** – Nobody has time to waste, especially at work. So say what is necessary in as few words as possible.
- **Keep to the Topic** – Avoid the temptation of talking about things that are not related to the topic. If you stray off your topic, you may lose your audience or leave out important information.
- **Avoid Getting Emotional** – Emotional statements have their place, but they are seldom appropriate in work-related conversations. No matter how strongly you may feel about a topic, most topics at work are best discussed rationally rather than emotionally.

CRITICAL THINKING Have you ever had trouble communicating clearly? What tips listed here do you think would be most helpful for you? Why do you think clear communication is so important in work situations?

4 Ability to Understand and Use Information

framing your future

Studies show that the more you learn the more you earn. This means that the more highly skilled you are, the more value you bring to the workplace. The more value you bring, the better the opportunities you'll have. All of this translates into bigger paychecks.

In our global economy a high value is placed on information. Today, success is likely to depend not only on what you can do but also on what you know. Employers will expect you to acquire knowledge and put it to use in your job. To do this, you will need good listening skills as well as the ability to use what you already know to make decisions and solve problems.

Good Learning Skills If you are new to the world of work, it is unlikely that you will know how to do the job the moment you are hired. There is much you will have to learn. Even experienced workers who have been on the job for a long time must constantly refresh and update their knowledge and skills to keep up with new processes and advancing technology. For these and other reasons, employers are anxious to hire workers who know how to learn.

If you have performed reasonably well in school, then your learning skills are likely to be well developed. You know how to listen, observe, read a set of instructions, and study a process or a body of information until you have mastered it.

The following learning techniques may prove useful to you as you enter the world of work.

Concentrate To learn something, you must pay attention to it and observe it closely. To an extent, this is another way of suggesting that you take an interest in what you want to learn. If you can't find a way to be interested in the subject matter or process, you will find it much more difficult to learn.

Organize Some material must be learned in the proper order. For instance, when learning to play an instrument, you must learn how to hold it properly before you can learn how to play it properly. This type of learning is very common in carpentry. When learning how to do an ordered or stepped process, don't get ahead of yourself. Concentrate on the first part or step until you have mastered it. Then go on to the next part or step.

study a process

Repeat Most learning is accomplished by going over an idea or repeating a process until you remember it. Sometimes only a few repetitions are necessary, but it may take many repetitions to master complex ideas or processes. When the information is complex, you may want to take a break periodically and put it out of your thoughts. When you return to it later the information will seem much easier to learn and you may even remember it longer.

Associate When learning something new, it is often helpful to associate it with something that you already know. For example, if you are learning how to build a table, it might help to associate this new process with the process you may have learned while building something similar such as a desk or chair.

Refresh Time has a way of making people forget. Over time even things you learned well may become hard to remember. The best way to remember something you learned is to refresh your memory periodically. Keeping and reviewing notes can come in very handy in helping you retain valuable knowledge and skills. Remember, skills and knowledge learned but never used will be soon forgotten.

Test From your experience in school, you may have the idea that tests are about grades. But in the workplace testing is not about grades. Tests are an important and necessary part of the learning process. There are at least two very good reasons to test your knowledge. The first reason is to make sure you understand the information so you can use it on the job. When you are to be tested, you are more likely to put the time and energy into learning the material. The second reason is to help make what you have learned a more permanent part of your memory. When our knowledge is put to the test, we recognize that it is important. And people tend to remember things that they think are important.

Keep at It An important thing to know about learning is that it takes time. Some people learn faster than others, but everyone can learn if they keep trying. If you don't do well the first or second time your knowledge is tested, then continue with the learning process. Eventually, you will pass the test and prove to yourself and others that you can learn what you set out to learn.

CRITICAL THINKING How would you rate your learning skills? Why do you think it is harder to learn things you are not interested in? How might this relate to the grades you got in school? How might your grades in certain subjects relate to the career you choose?

Ability to Solve Problems

When it comes to working with tools, materials, processes, and people, it is important to be able to solve problems. When something gets broken, or something doesn't fit, or a mistake is made, or some other unforeseen obstacle gets in the way, the entire project could be delayed. Employers place high value on workers who can find ways of overcoming problems when they occur. With the right attitude and by learning a few skills, this is the kind of worker you can become.

Problem solving is basically a matter of clearly identifying the problem, suggesting solutions, analyzing the solutions, and then selecting a solution or aspects of several solutions that best solve the problem.

The next time you are faced with a problem you want to solve, try asking the following questions.

- what is the problem?
- what are possible solutions?
- what are the benefits of each of the possible solutions?
- which possible solution or combination of possible solutions is best?

Once you arrive at a satisfactory answer to the final question, you have a solution you can implement. The best solution is not necessarily the easiest one to implement. Other important factors such as cost, time, effort, and resources must also be taken into consideration.

problem solving

Here's how you might use this method of problem solving. Let's say you are assembling a bicycle and you discover that one of the parts doesn't fit properly. Here are some questions you might ask to clearly identify the problem.

* Is this the right part?
* Am I using the right technique for fitting the part?
* Is the part damaged?
* Is the bicycle damaged in some way that prevents the part from fitting?

Having considered each of these possibilities, you come to the conclusion that the part is damaged. Now you must consider likely solutions to the problem. After some careful thought, you come up with the following possible solutions.

* Assemble the bicycle without using the part.
* Repair the part.
* Replace the broken part with a new part.

In analyzing each of these possible solutions, you draw the following conclusions.

* The part is critical to the operation of the bike. The bike would work temporarily without the part. But riding the bike without the part would cause even more damage.
* You don't have the materials on hand to repair the part and even if you had the materials, the repair would take a lot of effort.
* A nearby bike shop has a replacement part in stock and it is not too expensive.

In analyzing each of these possible solutions, the final solution becomes clear: You will buy and install a new replacement part. This solution avoids the issues of making a new part as well as the damage the bike would receive if assembled without the part. The final solution is convenient, inexpensive, and will allow the bike to work properly.

CRITICAL THINKING Why do you think employers want to avoid hiring workers who feel helpless when faced with problems? Why do you think it is so important to accurately identify the problem before you start thinking about solutions? Why is it important to carefully analyze a solution before you start implementing it?

Ability to Make Decisions

Work-related decisions usually carry important consequences, so they should be made in a thoughtful manner. As you have learned in Chapter 2, decisions can be made in a variety of ways. You learned that people can make the mistake of making important decisions using other methods: dependent, intuitive, impulsive, or fatalistic. These methods rarely produce good results at work and should be avoided. The best method to use is called the thoughtful decision-making method. In this method, both facts and feelings are weighed and consequences are carefully considered before a decision is made.

When making any decision, it is important to take responsibility for both the decision and the result. This means that the decision maker accepts the possibility that the decision may or may not turn out as expected. Even if the decision turns out poorly, the decision maker can learn from the experience. Regardless of the consequences, if the decision was thoughtfully made, the outcome can provide valuable information and a learning experience for everyone involved.

CRITICAL THINKING What does accepting the consequences of a bad decision say about the decision maker? Why would this behavior be of value to an employer? Can you think of a situation where any decision is better than no decision?

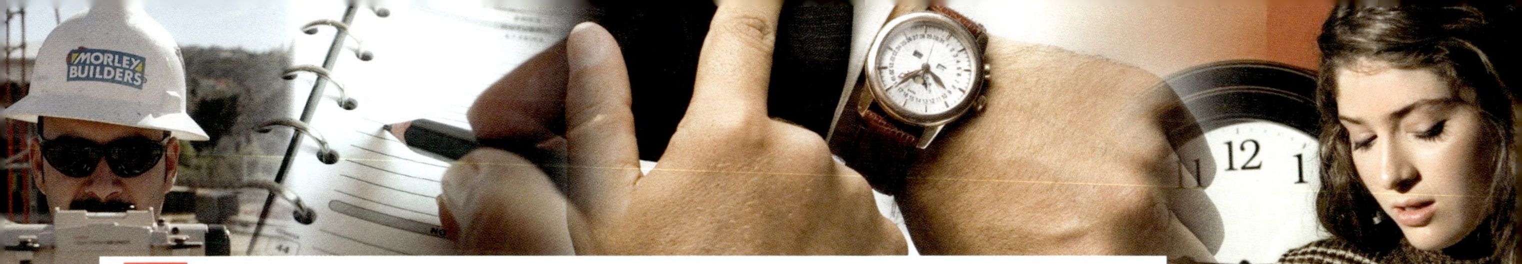

5 Ability to Manage Time and Resources

You have probably heard that time is money. In the world of work, this is usually true. For example, if you are late to work and don't finish a project on time, both you and your employer are likely to lose money. Getting to work on time and getting things done on time are sure signs that you are responsible and organized. By being organized and responsible, you are more likely to handle resources and materials carefully and efficiently. Wasted materials are like wasted time—they both cost the employer money. It is no wonder that employers look for people who can handle their work in a responsible and organized fashion.

Getting to work on time and getting things done on time are sure signs that you are responsible and organized.

Wasted materials are like wasted time— they both cost the employer money

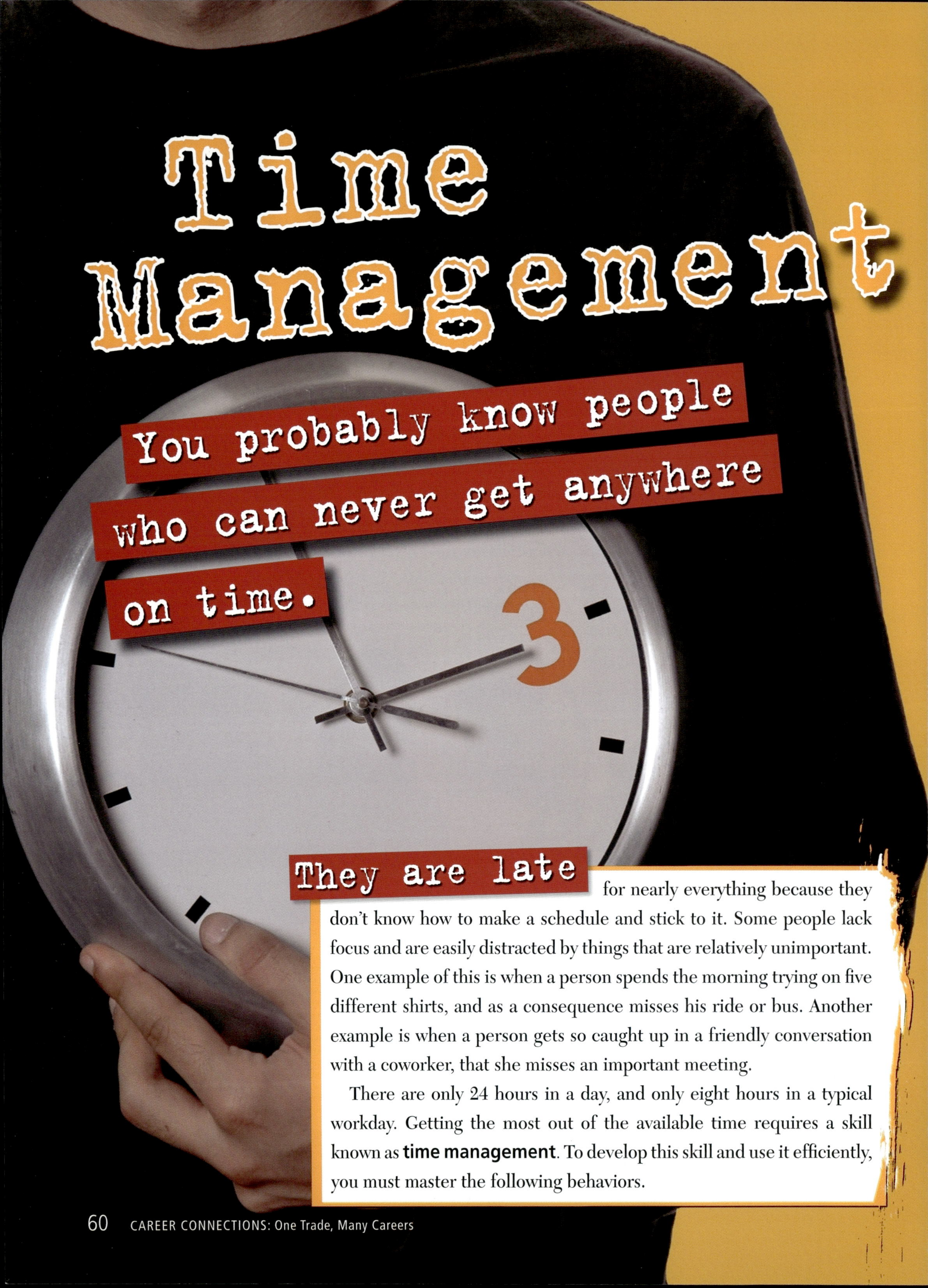

Time Management

You probably know people who can never get anywhere on time.

They are late for nearly everything because they don't know how to make a schedule and stick to it. Some people lack focus and are easily distracted by things that are relatively unimportant. One example of this is when a person spends the morning trying on five different shirts, and as a consequence misses his ride or bus. Another example is when a person gets so caught up in a friendly conversation with a coworker, that she misses an important meeting.

There are only 24 hours in a day, and only eight hours in a typical workday. Getting the most out of the available time requires a skill known as **time management**. To develop this skill and use it efficiently, you must master the following behaviors.

Recognize the Importance of Deadlines Successful workers understand that deadlines keep the project on track and profitable. When deadlines are given, successful workers work efficiently to meet them. Even without official deadlines, successful workers tend to create their own deadlines to help them stay productive and efficient. Workers who have a track record of meeting deadlines are very highly regarded by most employers. On the other hand, most employers don't tolerate missed deadlines for very long.

Establish Priorities Which is more important: getting to work on time or looking exactly right once you get there? While it may be important to look your best, getting to work on time is probably more important. So it wouldn't make much sense to be late for work simply because you couldn't decide what to wear in the morning. In this example, getting to work on time is an established priority. A **priority** is something we recognize as more important than other things we might choose to do instead. The ability to establish priorities is essential for good time management.

Set and Stick to Schedules A schedule is a list of places we need to be at a certain time, or a list of things we intend to get done by a certain time. Sometimes, the places or activities listed on the schedule are linked to one another in some way. The places must be reached or the activities completed in a certain order. A class schedule is a good example of this type of schedule. You may have math class at 9:00, English at 10:00, history at 11:00, and so on. Essentially, a schedule is a series of deadlines. If you are good at meeting deadlines, then you should have no trouble sticking to an established schedule.

Keep Track of Schedules There are many ways to keep track of an important schedule. You could write out a schedule on a sheet of paper and post it on a wall. You could use a desk or wall calendar to help you keep track of certain long-term schedules. You could create a schedule on a computer and either print it out or use it electronically. You could even create and track a simple schedule on a cell phone.

Use Reminders Even with the most organized schedule, it is possible to forget to do an important task. You will be less likely to miss a scheduled appointment or deadline if you prompt yourself with reminders. Some computer software will provide reminders. Most cell phones can be set to provide reminders. You could even attach reminders to the refrigerator or on some other object you are likely to see. The reminders don't have to be complex. They just need to jog your memory of important tasks. For example, a reminder may simply say: "Don't forget your meeting today at 10:30 am."

CRITICAL THINKING What would be the most effective way for you to create a schedule? What would be the best way for you to remind yourself of an important deadline?

building a better u

A written to-do list is one way to help you remember tasks. But what if you lose the list? One trick for remembering the tasks on your list is to imagine associations between each task. Suppose your list says you need to go to the library, call your friend Jim, and buy milk. Think of an association between "library" and "Jim," and between "Jim" and "milk." For example, imagine that when you walk into the library, Jim is the librarian, and he pours you a glass of milk. The more ridiculous the associations, the more likely you'll remember the tasks.

Resource Management

other important resources include tools, materials, and even the workplace itself

People who are good at working toward deadlines and sticking to schedules are often good at **resource management** as well. Every company has resources that are used to accomplish its business. The skilled workers are the most important resource. But other important resources include tools, materials, and even the workplace itself. Like time, these resources are limited and they cost money, so employers expect them to be used with care and efficiency.

Managing Tools

If you borrow a tool from a friend you will likely take extra care when using it. That's because you wouldn't want to damage something that belongs to a friend. You should treat any company-owned tool in the same way. Treat them with respect. Use them properly and only for the tasks for which they were designed. When not in use, store them properly and safely. Damaged tools can be dangerous, and are more likely to fail, creating costly delays and wasting materials. If you encounter a damaged tool, tell your supervisor so it can be removed from service and repaired or replaced.

Managing Materials

For any assigned task it is important to use the proper materials. Using substitute materials may lead to costly failures or delays, and they may prove unacceptable to the client. Materials are also costly, and employers will expect you to do your job properly using the least amount of materials possible. Using materials efficiently is a huge money-saving concern. Even when materials are not being used, they still need to be managed carefully. Not storing materials properly, can result in costly damage and work delays.

Managing Workspaces

Have you ever tried to work in a cluttered environment? You probably found that it was hard to get anything accomplished. Most people prefer a clean and organized environment, whether at home or in the workplace. In fact, cleanliness and tidiness are even more important at work than they are in the home. A cluttered workspace is inefficient, and it can be dangerous. For these reasons and others, employers expect the workspaces they provide to be kept clean and orderly.

CRITICAL THINKING What do you think are some safety hazards related to a messy workspace? If a tool is abused and breaks on the job, how might this affect the project?

Chapter Check

On a separate piece of paper, write your answers to the following questions:

Multiple Choice

1. Successful workers understand that which of the following keep the project on track and profitable:
   a) deadlines
   b) reminders
   c) ambition
   d) concentration

2. What is the recommended way to speak clearly about an important matter?
   a) keep your remarks brief
   b) use repetition to get your point across
   c) speak with emotion
   d) rely on a related story

3. Which of the following is a learning technique you would use to help acquire knowledge on the job?
   a) control
   b) concentrate
   c) connect
   d) contact

Fill in the Blank

4. The best way to remember something you learned is to ________________ your memory periodically.

5. A(n) ________________ is a list of places you need to be at a certain time.

6. ________________ management means managing skilled workers as well as materials.

True or False

7. In the learning process, the technique "associate" means learning how to do something in an ordered or stepped process. *T or F*

8. While practicing active listening, you can ask questions to check your understanding. *T or F*

9. Few skills are as important as the ability to listen attentively. *T or F*

10. In the world of work, teams are made up of people with the same general level of experience and skill. *T or F*

Important Words

Active listening The process of paying close attention when another person is speaking and then clarifying what you heard to improve your understanding.

Brainstorming Improving and refining ideas by passing them back and forth among coworkers and team members.

Initiative The ability to do what needs to be done in a job without waiting for prompting or direction from others.

Priority Something that is more important than other activities and must be dealt with first.

Resource management Practices that show you respect and value people, materials, and your workspace.

Self-starter A person who can motivate and energize himself or herself and can work with little or no supervision.

Time management Practices that allow you to make the best use of your time.

On the Trail of ...

In your experience, why do people work? Interview 5 people you know who have jobs. These people could include young adults (over 18 years of age), family members, teachers, neighbors, or other adult acquaintances. Try to get a cross-section of ages. Ask each person for the top 3 reasons why they work. Summarize your results and write a brief statement with your conclusions.

.com

You may be familiar with team building activities from school or camp. Team building is also important in the workplace to motivate team members, improve communication and performance, and build working relationships. Imagine you're in a job where the teamwork is lacking. You need to work together to accomplish a particular goal, but your fellow team members are not feeling connected or motivated. Suggest to your boss a team building activity that you would enjoy and that you believe would help the team work together to achieve its goal. Use the internet for team building activity ideas. Write a short report that describes your imagined (or real) work situation and your team building idea.

Being the First Choice

Knowing how to learn is an important thinking skill that is required for being successful in the workplace. To practice this skill, get a piece of thick string or twine about 3 feet long and teach yourself how to make a square knot. This is a basic knot – if you already know how to make it, teach yourself a figure-eight knot, or a butterfly loop. The point is to demonstrate your ability to acquire and apply new knowledge. Use a book or an online source to acquire the knowledge.

CHAPTER 4

What and Personal

At least some of the training necessary for a job is done after you are hired for the job. Even so, employers still expect the people they hire to bring a set of skills and positive personal traits to the workplace. These include basic skills, such as reading, writing, and arithmetic, and personal qualities, such as honesty and reliability. Most of these skills and qualities are the same ones that helped you in school. You will continue to need these skills and qualities in the world of work. Without them it will be very difficult to get a good job and keep it.

Basic Skills Qualities Do I Need?

What You Now Know

- How to communicate effectively
- How to make decisions and solve problems
- Your basic skills and personality

What You Will Know

- The basic skills necessary to be successful in the workplace
- The important role that thinking skills play in the workplace
- How your personal qualities affect your success

1 Basic Skills

Everyone has a different experience at school. Some love school, others don't like it as much, and there are others that are bored and can't wait to get out. No matter how you feel about school, it has provided you with an opportunity to prepare yourself for your life ahead. If you have worked hard and have been successful in school, then you already possess many of the skills you need to hold a job. At a minimum you will need the basic skills of reading, writing, and math. But you'll also need to know how to think clearly and logically about important matters.

reading

There are few skills that will be as important to you on the job and in life as the ability to read. Depending on the type of work you do, you may be asked to read forms, reports, written instructions, manuals, memos, and many other written materials. If you have difficulty reading and understanding these materials, it will be very hard for you to do your job effectively. This is why employers want workers who can read well.

How do you know if you are a good reader? If you enjoy reading, then you are almost certainly a good reader. If you can read this book without much difficulty, then you are probably a good reader. If you often read newspapers and magazine articles or read novels for fun, then you are very likely a good reader. On the other hand, if you feel you're getting lost or off track when reading something that is more than one or two paragraphs in length, then you may need a little help with your reading skills.

Fortunately, one of the best things about reading is that it is something everyone can learn to do well. Once people have learned to read at a basic level in school, all they need to do to be really good at it is to read and keep reading. And another good thing about reading is there is plenty of reading material available just about everywhere. Newspapers, magazines, the Internet, the library, bookstores, and even the checkout counter of the grocery store, all provide good sources for reading. Be sure you select materials that interest you. This will make reading practice much more enjoyable.

how i see myself

"My mother and my father were illiterate immigrants from Russia. When I was a child they were constantly amazed that I could go to a building and take a book on any subject. They couldn't believe this access to knowledge we have here in America. They couldn't believe that it was free." The actor Kirk Douglas's childhood memory of reading raises the question: In what ways do you value your right to read?

If, after practicing your reading every day for a period of time, you are still not satisfied with your reading skills, you should not be shy about asking for help. You can ask for extra help from teachers or advisers at school, or your parents. Also, most communities have programs to help adults or recent high school graduates improve their reading skills.

CRITICAL THINKING Are you a good reader? Do you have difficulty reading newspapers or long magazine articles? How do you think your reading skills will help you succeed in the world of work?

reading comprehension

Most of the reading you do on the job will be very different than the reading you do for pleasure. Most work-related reading involves information that will be important to you, your coworkers, and your project or company. For this reason, you must be sure that you correctly and completely understand, or comprehend, what you are reading. You can use the following steps to make sure you comprehend a set of instructions, a memo, or any other written communication:

1 scan

Your first step should be to scan the document to get the basic idea of what it is about. Scan the document quickly to ask questions such as: Is the document meant only for you or for a group of people? Does the document call for a treply? Does it require you to take some action or is it intended only for general information? Do any parts of the document seem more important than others?

2 read

Once you have scanned the document, it is now time to read it carefully. Be observant as you read, paying close attention to the main points as well as the details. Sometimes the most important information contained in a document is found in the details.

3 analyze

Carefully sort through the main points of the document and see how they relate to one another. If you have any questions concerning one or more of these points, check to see if they are answered somewhere else in the document. Perhaps the answers to your questions are in details that you overlooked.

4 check

Does everything in the document make sense to you? If there was anything you didn't understand, read the relevant parts of the document again. If you still don't understand, it may be necessary to ask your supervisor or a coworker. Be sure the document is not confidential before sharing information with a coworker.

5 summarize

One way to be sure you understand what the document says is to ask yourself if you can summarize its contents. What are its main points? What are the most important details? One way to identify the main points and important details is to underline or highlight them right on the document. If for some reason you can't mark on the document, write your summary on a separate sheet of paper. Not only will your summary help you remember the contents of the document, it will provide you with a quick reference if you need to answer a coworker's question or to draft a reply.

writing

Not all jobs require good writing skills. However, many jobs do. And some jobs require excellent writing skills. Depending on your job, you may have to produce emails, letters, memos, reports, and many other types of written material. If you are required to do much writing on the job, you will need to have good writing skills. The better your skills, the more successful you will be.

Just like reading, writing is an important skill not just in the world of work but also for day-to-day living. That is why writing, or composition as it is often called, is taught in every school. However, the writing you will do at work may have different goals than the writing you did at school. Writing at work may be done to bid for a job, to sell a concept or product, to promote safety, or for a variety of other reasons.

every written document should be

Clear

To avoid confusion, all documents should be written in a style that is both clear and direct. The reader should have no trouble understanding all of the information in the document.

Concise

To avoid wasting time, the document should be brief and to the point. It should be no longer than is necessary to clearly cover the required information.

Complete

The document should thoroughly address all of the relevant information. The reader should be able to easily comprehend the purpose and the contents of the document.

Convincing

The document should be persuasive. The reader should think that the person who wrote the document knows the subject thoroughly and is confident in what is written.

Free of Errors

A document should have properly constructed sentences, appropriate punctuation, and correct spelling. Documents that contain a lot of errors may not be taken seriously and may even cause the reader to question the writer's competence. Before a document is passed along to others, it should always be carefully proofread at least twice to make sure it doesn't have any errors.

Fortunately, most word-processing programs can help check spelling and grammar. However, these programs are not perfect, and they don't catch all errors. For example, they won't catch the problem of using the word "there" when you should have used "their." So don't think that just because you used a grammar and spell check on your computer that the document is error free. If the document is long, complex, or concerns critical information, you may want to have a coworker with good writing skills also proofread it before you send it.

building a better u

A dictionary can be your best friend when you need help with words. But how do you look up a word if you can't even spell it? You can sound out the word and then scan the dictionary in hopes of finding the word you want. Or, you can look up a synonym—another word that means the same thing. You'll very likely find the word you're looking for under the definition of the synonym. Another option is to use an online dictionary. You can type in just the letters you know and then choose from a list of possibilities.

Proofreading TIPS

Read for meaning

Read the document to check for meaning, clarity, and logic. As you read, imagine you are one of the people receiving the document. Sometimes, statements that seemed logical to the writer are not to the reader. Reading the document out loud will help in this process.

Read for grammar, spelling, sentence structure, and punctuation

Once you have proofread for sense, proofread a second time to check the mechanics of the writing. Some sentences may need to be reworded to make sure they are both clear and correct.

Compare drafts

When finding errors or making changes, mark them on a draft of the document. Then transfer the changes to the final draft. To make sure the final draft contains everything essential, place the final draft beside your first draft and compare them line by line.

Test read

If the document is particularly important or will be widely distributed, you may want to try it out on a test reader. The test reader should be someone who has not seen an earlier draft of the document. The test reader can give you honest feedback about whether the document makes sense and has the desired impact.

Rewrite

Don't be discouraged if your document doesn't read as well as you had hoped. Just try again. Some important documents may need to be rewritten one or more times before they are clear and ready for distribution.

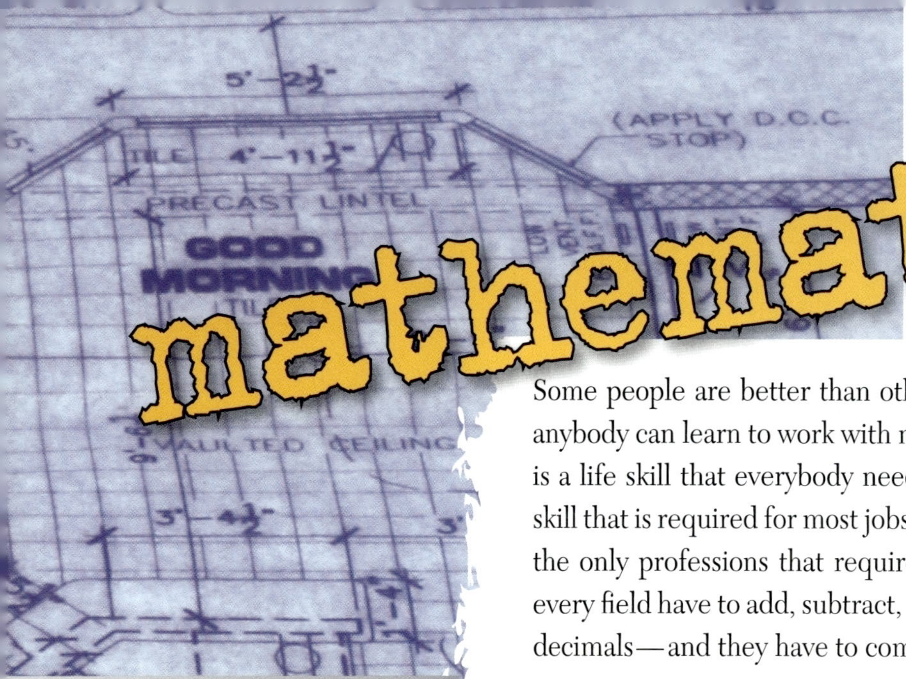

mathematics

Some people are better than others at handling complex calculations, but anybody can learn to work with numbers. The ability to work with numbers is a life skill that everybody needs and that anyone can master. It is also a skill that is required for most jobs. Accountants and financial analysts are not the only professions that require "number crunching." Workers in nearly every field have to add, subtract, multiply, divide, or work with fractions and decimals—and they have to come up with the correct answers.

you will need an excellent grasp of math if you want a career in any of the construction trades

You will need an excellent grasp of math if you want a career in any of the construction trades. Principles of math and the use of math formulas are involved in all aspects of properly laying out and building structures, including commercial buildings, homes, and bridges. Having trouble solving basic math problems could prevent you from getting the job you want or succeeding in the career you have chosen.

Fortunately, it is not too late to improve your math skills if that is what you want to do. All you need to do is ask for help. You can ask for extra help from teachers or advisers at school or from your parents. Also, most communities have programs to help adults or recent high school graduates improve their math skills.

framing your future

Math skills are critical—not only for just about every job you'll ever have but for functioning in the everyday world. Math is everywhere. In the kitchen when you're cooking, at the car dealership when you're deciding to buy or lease, in the office when you're balancing a checkbook. You need to do mental math to make quick calculations in stores, restaurants, or gas stations. Every time you pull out a tape measure or pull out your wallet, you're doing math. Strong math skills will help you plan your future.

ability to work with numbers is a life skill that everybody needs

6068 SGD
13'–6"
2050 SH
4050 SH
CONC
2'x3' SLAB
WP/GFIP
TILE
PRECAST LINTEL
GOOD MORNING
TILE
15'-10"
VAULTED CEILING
5 1/2" WALL
40 1/2" AFF
TOP TO BE 1x6
GFIP
D/W OUTLET
D/W
CERAN
RANGE
GFIP
SINK SPRAYER
TILE
ON/C
OFF
LN
LOG
TAN
COS
9
=

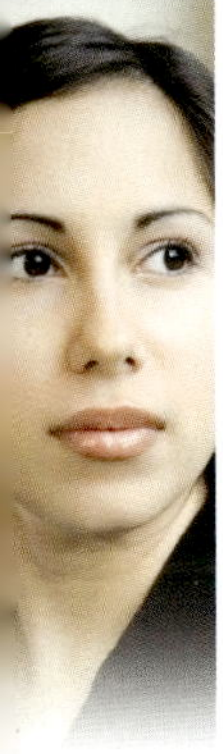

2 Thinking Skills

Every day we acquire more and more information in our heads. People who have acquired a lot of information are often regarded as being smart. But being smart is less about knowing a lot of information and more about applying that information. People who are truly smart know how to apply knowledge to new situations, think creatively about what they have experienced, and are able to solve problems. In other words, smart people have developed strong thinking skills. And like other skills, thinking skills can be learned and improved with practice. Thinking skills involve a variety of other skills, but the cornerstones are focused attention, logical reasoning, creative thinking, and critical analysis.

Focused Attention Strangely enough, the most common mistake people make when thinking about something is that they don't think about it long enough. When considering a problem, they may be satisfied with the very first solution that pops into their heads without considering any other possibilities. For example, let's say your supervisor at work passes you in the hallway and doesn't say hello. In considering what happened, you may quickly conclude that your supervisor doesn't like you. However, by giving this matter more thought, other possibilities might occur to you. Your supervisor simply might not have noticed you, or he or she may have been in deep thought about some important issue.

Random thoughts are the enemies of focused attention. Random thoughts such as what you are going to do tonight, the price of a video game, or the cool car you saw that morning are constantly competing for attention in your brain. It's perfectly natural to have such thoughts, but they must be controlled if you are to focus attention on solving a problem or answering a question. When random thoughts start invading your thinking, simply pause for a moment and refocus. By keeping your thoughts on track, you will be practicing mental discipline.

random thoughts are the enemies of focused attention

CRITICAL THINKING Why is it important to consider all the likely possibilities when trying to answer a question or solve a problem? What do you do when you are easily distracted by unrelated ideas or memories when trying to think clearly about something important?

Logical Reasoning Logical reasoning is the ability to come to a rational conclusion based on facts, rather than emotions. We all use logical reasoning every day to make all kinds of decisions. For example, in choosing a cell phone to buy, you would want to base your decision on the facts about each phone.

here is a career related example

Suppose you already know that you don't want a career that would require you to work at a desk in an office. Your friend hands you a pamphlet or points you to a website that describes careers in carpentry. Part of the information has photos showing carpenters working outdoors. Since it is clear that a career in carpentry fits at least one of your major career criteria, you decide to gather more information and consider carpentry as a career. Your action was a response to logical reasoning.

innovative original

creative thinking

requires an open and flexible mind

Creative Thinking is the ability to think of original and innovative ideas. Although there is no one way to be a creative thinker, creative thinking usually requires an open and flexible mind. For example, when a chemist working at the 3M Company accidentally created a new adhesive that was not very strong, he did not just assume it was a failure. Instead, his thinking was open and flexible enough to find a new application for this weak adhesive. This is how he invented the very popular Post-It® Notes.

Creative thinking involves brainstorming, which is a technique of allowing yourself and others the freedom to generate ideas without any judgments about their worth. Brainstorming encourages a great many ideas that may broaden your thinking. Later, when you analyze the ideas, you may discover a great idea, or you may need to combine several ideas to form a great idea.

Another good tool when thinking creatively is to practice what is called **associative thinking**. This is the skill of associating one thing with another. For example, the inventor of Velcro® thought of this unique fastening method when he was brushing his dog and saw how tightly burrs stuck to the dog's coat.

As you can see, there are many skills that can help you become a good creative thinker. In the world of work you will probably have opportunities to use and practice many of these skills. They go hand-in-hand with problem solving. And, as you learned in the last chapter, employers place high value on workers who know what steps to take in order to solve problems. Whether you are defining the problem to be solved, coming up with possible solutions, or determining which solution is best, you will need good creative thinking skills.

Critical Thinking is basically a matter of asking and answering probing questions when you are considering something or trying to solve a problem. For example, when you consider a possible career, many questions may come to mind.

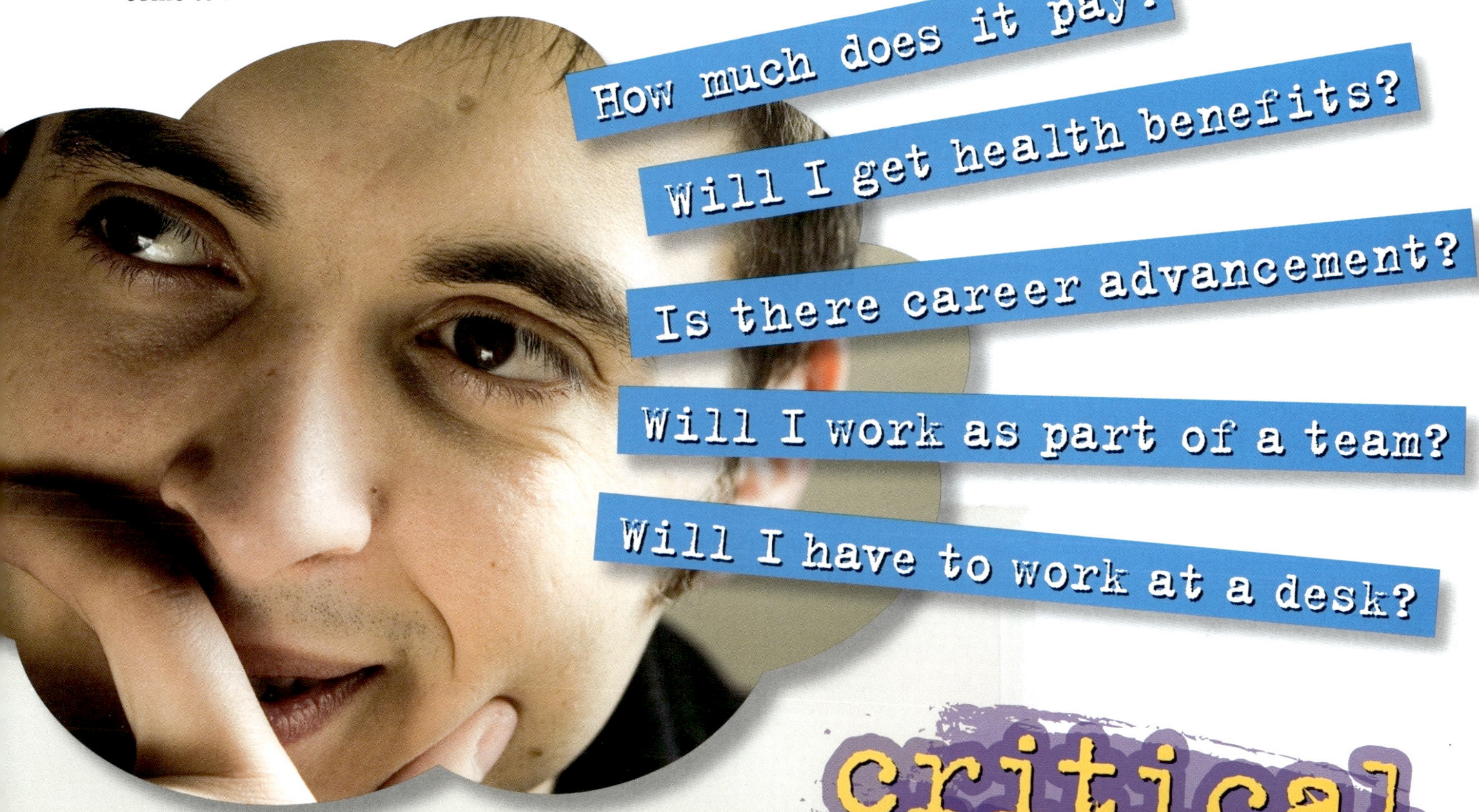

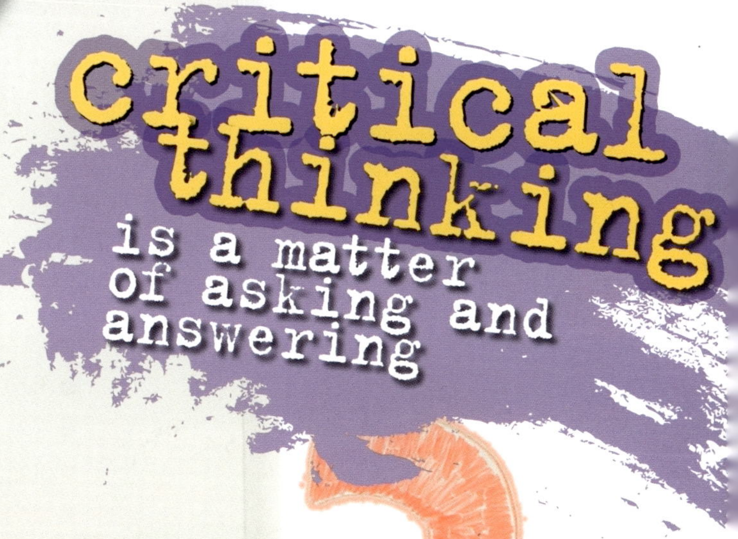

Just by asking these questions, you have engaged in the type of critical thinking that will help you in making your important decision about a career.

Critical thinking can be a big help in the workplace. For example, you may be part of a work team that uses a particular process to reach its goal. The process works, but asking the following questions about it may prove worthwhile:

- Is it the quickest process to get the job done?
- Is it the least expensive process to get the job done?
- Does the process produce the highest quality results?

Asking and answering questions like these represent critical thinking in action. You may even have situations in your personal life that could be improved as a result of asking and answering some probing questions.

CRITICAL THINKING How have you applied logical reasoning to make a recent decision? Can you think of a time when you used creative thinking to come up with a new idea? In what situation in your life might you use critical thinking to solve a problem?

3 Personal Qualities

No matter how many important job skills you have mastered, they will not make up for negative qualities like being dishonest or being undependable. It is no exaggeration to say that employers have very little tolerance for workers who do not have the qualities of honesty and reliability. Employers also want workers who do quality work and who take pride in a job well done.

Honesty Honesty means being truthful in what you say and what you do. Honest people do not lie, cheat, or steal. For obvious reasons, employers expect workers to be honest in their words and their actions. Employers value honesty in workers because honesty contributes to a trusting work environment and to the company's overall success. Examples of honest behavior in the workplace include the following:

- Working diligently during the entire work day
- Taking breaks only during designated break times
- Admitting responsibility for mistakes and accidents
- Avoiding practical jokes or pranks that may endanger yourself, others, equipment, or materials

Employers do not hire workers they believe to be dishonest. And when an employer discovers that they have hired a dishonest person by mistake, they are likely to end the employment. Most employers would consider the following behaviors to be dishonest:

- Lying about qualifications on a resumé or during a job interview
- Reporting more hours on a timecard than actually worked
- Lying about reasons for taking time off from work
- Removing items from the workplace without permission
- Covering up or shifting the blame for errors or mistakes
- Lying to clients or customers
- Personally accepting a reward or praise for the work of others
- Covering up safety violations

...reliable means word can be and you can be

Reliability is the quality of being dependable or trustworthy. Being reliable means that your word can be trusted and you can be counted on to meet expectations. Without reliable employees, a company can't possibly operate smoothly and efficiently. Reliable employees also make more significant contributions to a company while requiring less oversight. A reliable employee can be recognized by the following behaviors:

- Shows up to work on time prepared to begin the work day
- Operates in a manner that is consistent with the mission of the company and the requirements of the job
- Completes work assignments on time and with high quality
- Performs tasks with little or no supervision
- Arrives at meetings on time and prepared

It is reasonable for companies to put such a high value on reliability. Imagine trying to run a business where the employees showed up whenever they wanted, were late to important meetings, missed deadlines, and produced poor-quality work. Such a company would certainly not be in business very long. Can you imagine any customer who would be willing to put up with this type of service?

CRITICAL THINKING Do you consider yourself to be an honest and reliable person? What makes you think so? What kind of feedback have you gotten from others about these qualities in you?

that your trusted counted on...

Having an eye for quality is something you must learn.

Quality Conscious All companies try to balance cost with quality. In other words, they try to produce the highest-quality products or services for the cost. If you were having a house built and you had a lot of money, you might be able to use the most expensive materials and include the latest in technology. On the other hand, if you were building a house on a budget, you would probably opt for less expensive materials and fewer bells and whistles. In either case, however, you would want your house built well. You would want the workmanship of your house to be of the highest quality possible.

Employers also want to be sure that their products are of the highest quality within the limits of the cost. They want workers who will strive to do the best job possible whether working with expensive materials or more economical materials. Employers want to maintain a standard of quality that will satisfy their customers and make their business successful. They do not want to turn out products that may or may not be of high quality depending on who worked on it. This would be very bad for business.

Like all skills, an eye for quality is something you must learn. No one is born with the ability to do quality work. You have probably already developed a sense of relative quality when you evaluated various products before you purchased them. Quality was probably a prime consideration in your evaluation. Employers will want you to recognize quality and to consistently produce quality work.

CRITICAL THINKING What are some characteristics of a high-quality product that you may want to buy in the near future? Why would you decide to spend more money in order to get the higher-quality product? Why would you decide to get a lower-quality product?

Pride in a Job Well Done There is an old saying: anything worth doing is worth doing well. Those who succeed in the world of work generally agree with this statement. They want to do an excellent job because they see their work as a reflection of their character. Employers prefer to hire people who take pride in their work because they usually work hard, require less supervision, and produce excellent results.

Taking pride in your work is really the same as taking pride in yourself. You can probably think of times when you have been filled with pride from doing some excellent work. This excellent work probably even boosted your self esteem. It's a great feeling to be able to take pride in a job well done. Your future customers, supervisors, and coworkers will recognize and appreciate your ability to take pride in your work. They will know it as a sure sign that you are doing the best work you can offer.

...anything worth doing is worth doing well.

nailing it!

Imagine a home that can produce as much energy as it consumes. Building "zero-energy homes" is a long-term goal for the U.S. Department of Energy's Building America program. The program currently builds homes that use less energy, are faster to build, cost less, and provide a healthy environment. Building America creates teams of architects, planners, engineers, manufacturers, builders, and materials suppliers, who all work together to boost a home's performance and cut costs. Over the past 10 years, these teams have built more than 20,000 houses that use 30-90% less energy. Architect Betsy Pettit, one of the project managers for the program, describes these homes as "affordable the day you buy them and every day afterward."

Chapter Check

On a separate piece of paper, write your answers to the following questions:

Multiple Choice

1. Which one of the following words describe a persuasive work document?
   a) complete
   b) complex
   c) convincing
   d) quality conscious

2. Reading for meaning is something you do to a document when you are doing which of the following?
   a) proofreading
   b) scanning
   c) summarizing
   d) associative thinking

3. What type of thinking are you engaging in when you ask about the pay and benefits of a job you are considering?
   a) constructive
   b) associative
   c) critical
   d) creative

Fill in the Blank

4. To make sure you understand a written document, the first step is to ______________ the document by looking it over quickly to get an idea of what it's about.

5. When proofreading an important document, you can ask a ______________ reader, someone who has not seen the document before, to read it and provide honest feedback.

6. Showing up on time for work every day and doing your job with little or no supervision demonstrates that ______________ is one of your personal qualities.

True or False

7. Emotions play an important role in logical thinking. *T or F*

8. By definition, being quality conscious means using expensive materials. *T or F*

9. Every written business document should be persuasive. *T or F*

10. Innovators use associative thinking to come up with new ideas. *T or F*

Important Words

Associative thinking The ability to relate one thing to another while thinking creatively.

Creative thinking The ability to think of original and innovative ideas.

Critical thinking The ability to ask and answer probing questions when considering something or trying to solve a problem.

Logical reasoning The ability to come to a rational conclusion based on facts.

Reliability The quality of being dependable or trustworthy.

On the Trail of ...

Inventors use creative thinking to come up with original ideas and new products. Research an invention and its inventor. Write a short report on the inventor's thought process. How did he or she get the idea for the invention? Was associative thinking involved? How did the inventor's attitude and open-mindedness influence the process? What has been the impact of this invention on individual users or on society?

.com

Team up with another student. One of you is in the market to buy a certain product or material. The other one is the seller. Decide together what that product or material is. The buyer writes an email to the seller asking some questions, perhaps about product availability, price, delivery, color, and so on. The seller writes back with detailed answers. Both buyer and seller can use the internet for product ideas and information. Buyer and seller should print each other's email and correct it for spelling and grammar.

Being the First Choice

Knowing how to write and being able to display positive personal qualities will make you a valuable asset in the workplace. Imagine that you have an opportunity to be a team member for an exciting building project. The building project could be the set for a school play, a jungle gym for a local park, a deck for a friend's house, an 8-foot sailboat – anything that you'd be thrilled to help build. All the training would be provided on the job. With this dream project in mind, write a letter to your teacher, who will be the project manager. In the letter, list all the personal qualities you would bring to the project. Describe the ways in which you would demonstrate honesty, reliability, quality consciousness, and pride in your work.

CHAPTER 5

Choosing That Is Right

A whole world of career options awaits you. Selecting a career that is right for you will not be easy, but you have already made a good start. You have learned more about yourself—your values, preferences, qualities, and strengths. You have learned about some of the important elements of the modern workplace, and about the many skills that are required. You have also gained a better understanding of how to solve problems and make good decisions. Now your task is to match your personal characteristics to an occupation that will help you reach your long-term goals.

a Career for You

What You Now Know

- What employers expect from employees
- That you will have to eventually choose a career
- That the career you choose will affect your lifestyle

What You Will Know

- The difference between a career and a job
- How to narrow your career choices
- How to use information gathered to decide on a career
- The education required for a successful career

A whole world of career options awaits you.

1 Job vs. Career

By this point in your life, you probably have a good idea about the meanings of the words "job" and "career." So far in this book, these words have been used many times. But, how are the meanings of these two words different? Generally speaking, a career is an occupation that you expect to have for an extended period of time, perhaps even for your entire working life. A job, on the other hand, is usually considered to be more short term. A job can also be thought of as the work you do in order to draw a paycheck. You may not intend to have the job very long or for it to lead to a career. However, it is also true that jobs can lead to careers and careers can include many related jobs. But when you are preparing for your future, you will want to focus on the career you want.

Not everyone decides on the career they are in. Some people take a job when they are young because it is available. Years later they are still at that job, or a similar job. By default, they end up making that particular line of work their career. They may keep the job for the rest of their working life without really giving much thought as to whether it is the right career for them. Sometimes jobs can turn into rewarding careers. Often, however, they don't. Those who plan their careers generally find more satisfying and better paying work than those who jump from job to job without a plan.

framing your future

"I found every single successful person I've ever spoken to had a turning point. The turning point was when they made a clear, specific unequivocal decision that they were going to achieve success. Some people make that decision at 15 and some people make it at 50, and most people never make it at all." What do these comments by author and motivational speaker Brian Tracy suggest to you about the importance of making timely choices about your career?

Sometimes jobs can turn into rewarding careers.

Which career is right for you?

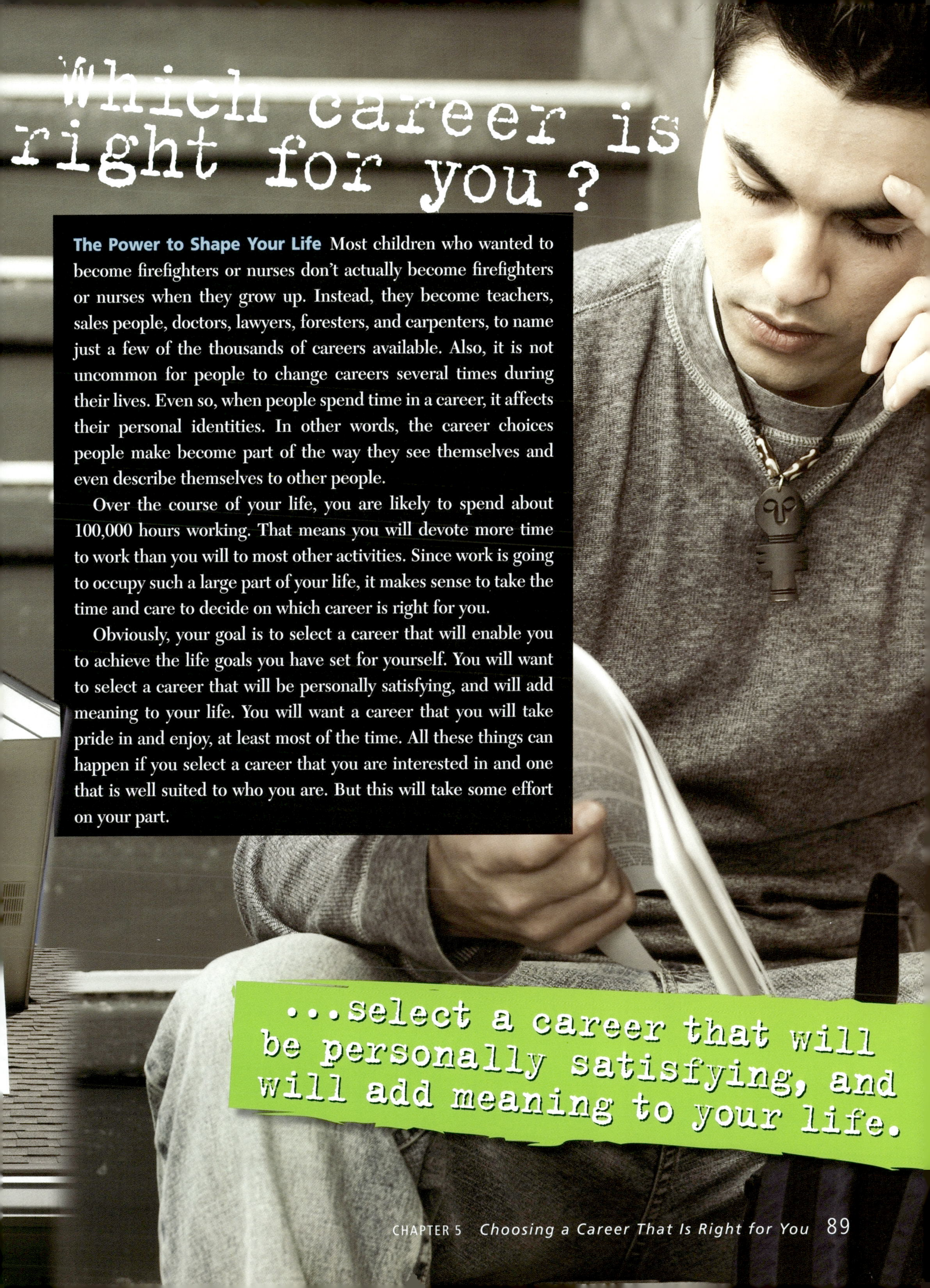

The Power to Shape Your Life Most children who wanted to become firefighters or nurses don't actually become firefighters or nurses when they grow up. Instead, they become teachers, sales people, doctors, lawyers, foresters, and carpenters, to name just a few of the thousands of careers available. Also, it is not uncommon for people to change careers several times during their lives. Even so, when people spend time in a career, it affects their personal identities. In other words, the career choices people make become part of the way they see themselves and even describe themselves to other people.

Over the course of your life, you are likely to spend about 100,000 hours working. That means you will devote more time to work than you will to most other activities. Since work is going to occupy such a large part of your life, it makes sense to take the time and care to decide on which career is right for you.

Obviously, your goal is to select a career that will enable you to achieve the life goals you have set for yourself. You will want to select a career that will be personally satisfying, and will add meaning to your life. You will want a career that you will take pride in and enjoy, at least most of the time. All these things can happen if you select a career that you are interested in and one that is well suited to who you are. But this will take some effort on your part.

...select a career that will be personally satisfying, and will add meaning to your life.

There are thousands of potential careers to choose from, and some will interest you more than others.

Some careers will fit well with your unique set of preferences, talents, and experiences, while others will not. To make career exploration easier, the Department of Labor has defined sixteen career categories, or clusters. These career clusters and the occupations within them are all listed in the *Dictionary of Occupational Titles* (DOT). The list includes the following career clusters:

1. Professional, Technical, and Managerial Occupations
2. Clerical and Sales Occupations
3. Service Occupations
4. Agricultural, Fishery, Forestry, and Related Occupations
5. Processing Occupations
6. Machine Trades Occupations
7. Benchwork Occupations
8. Structural Work Occupations
9. Miscellaneous Occupations

This list and the DOT will come in handy as you consider what careers you might be interested in. The more time you spend thinking and learning about possible careers, the better your chances will be of finding a career that's just right for you. Once you find a career and then make the decision to pursue it, you will have the power to shape your own life.

2 Narrowing Your Career Choices

Considering all the possible career choices can be overwhelming. But don't let it worry you. Approaching this situation methodically will help you cover a lot of ground quickly. First, carefully consider each of the career clusters from the DOT listed above. Pick out one or two of the clusters that most interests you. Keep in mind that each cluster contains many different types of careers. Make a list of any careers that appeal to you. In addition, you may want to add to your career list by researching possible careers on the internet, or in books and other publications you may find at the library or even at the local employment office. Also, you may want to talk to your parents, teachers, and school advisor or counselor about possible career ideas, and then consider adding these ideas to your career list.

Once you have a list of potential career ideas, you can then start your evaluation. When you read the list, you will probably notice that some of the occupations on your list appeal to you more than others. Underline or make a separate list of the occupations that sound the most attractive to you. You may want to do some additional research on these careers.

> Once you have a list of potential career ideas, you can then start your evaluation.

Questions to Consider When you evaluate each of the careers on your list, you will want to answer the same questions about each one. That way you will have enough information to compare these careers thoroughly. You might like the working conditions of one career, but prefer the amount of pay for another career. Learning these kinds of facts about possible careers will help you narrow the field.

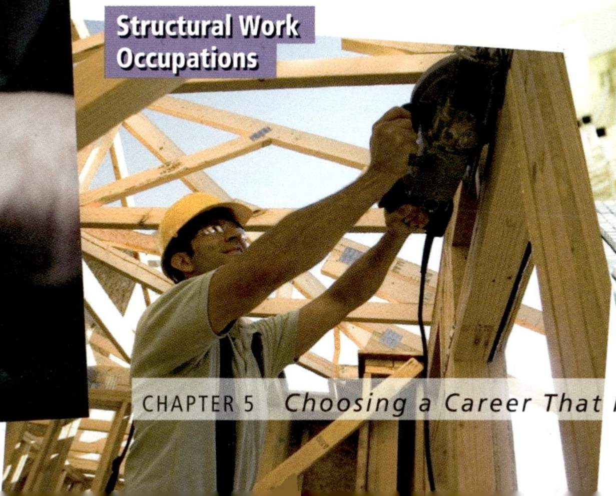

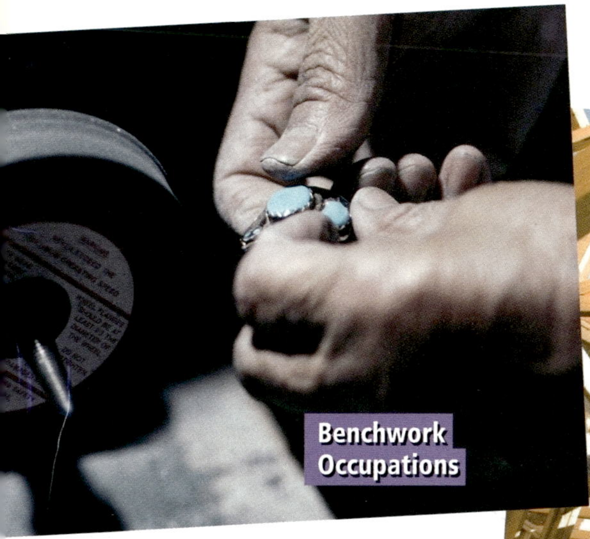

...questions you might want to answer about each career on your list

What does it pay? Some careers pay more than others. Some also have more potential for pay increases. But the amount of pay is only one factor out of many that may point to a good career fit. Also, you should think about how much money you need at first to support yourself, and then perhaps later to support a family. Take the time to understand the cost of housing in your area, whether rental or house purchase. You also need to take into account the cost of food, entertainment, transportation, and utilities. Only by knowing these approximate costs can you judge whether the paycheck will be too little, adequate, or generous.

How will you spend your time at work? If you don't like working with people, you may not want to consider careers in social work or health care. If you like working with your hands and enjoy building things, you may want to consider careers in carpentry and other building trades. The point is to make sure you pick potential careers that fit how you like to work.

What are the hours? Some occupations have regular hours while others may require you to work on weekends or at night. Some careers may require frequent travel assignments that would extend your work week. These may be important considerations, especially if you want to spend time with friends and family.

What are the working conditions? If you don't want to work at a desk, you would probably be unhappy with a career that requires you to work in an office at a desk. On the other hand, if you don't like the idea of working outside, you may want to consider careers that will keep you indoors most of the day.

Is the work physically demanding? If you work out and enjoy lots of different kinds of physical activity, you might enjoy a career that requires hard, physical work. If you don't like strenuous physical activity, you should consider careers that don't require much muscle power. If you want a physical career, you may want to consider how challenging the work would be in 20 years. For example, many construction careers are strenuous. However, carpentry career paths also include less strenuous positions such as foreman, superintendent, and even teaching positions.

What skills and talents are required? Most careers require a specialized set of skills. In many cases these skills can be learned if you don't already have them. Keep in mind, however, that some occupations, such as those in the art, music, and acting fields, require both skills and special talents. You must have the required talents to be successful in these careers.

How much education or training is required? Nearly all occupations require some training beyond high school. You will want to find out what training is necessary and how long it would take. For some occupations, on-the-job training is provided to those who are hired into entry-level positions. Keep in mind that to advance within many careers often requires additional formal training.

nailing it!

Did you know that only 4 out of 100 college graduates earn more than a skilled worker in the building trades? And that 7 out of every 10 jobs in the United States require trade skills, not college?

Does the career have a future?

Is this career in demand? You will want to determine how many people are presently employed in the careers that interest you. You should also look for data that describes the outlook for those entering the field in the next few years. You will probably want to look for careers that will have lots of positions available for qualified workers. You are much more likely to get a job in a career that has a high demand.

Does the career have a future? When you analyze your potential career choices, do you think any of them might become obsolete in the future? Do you think they might become more automated as technology improves and new machines are developed? Such advances sometimes replace people, reducing the demand for workers. Automation has affected many manufacturing careers. Also, the demand for certain workers has decreased when jobs are moved to other countries where the labor is cheaper. If any of these things were to happen to your job, you might be forced to change your job and possibly even your career.

Are the skills you need transferable? Skills that can be applied to more than one career are **transferable skills.** Certainly most of the basic skills, thinking skills, and people skills that you have acquired so far are transferable skills. But when evaluating your career list, look for required skills that could be applied to other careers. These are the transferable skills that would make it easier to switch careers later on. So, if during your career you find that there is no demand for your services or you want to try something else, you will know what other careers you would be qualified for. Remember, just because you pick a certain career now, does not mean you will necessarily have this career the rest of your working life.

What are the opportunities for advancement? Many occupations provide the opportunity for promotion and better pay while others do not. Right now, you may not be interested in advancement. But, it is important to understand that better pay is usually tied to promotions, which almost always require increased responsibilities. Of course, another advancement option is to learn everything you need in order to become an independent consultant or start your own business. Not all careers offer the same opportunity for these options, but many do.

CRITICAL THINKING

What instances do you know of where someone has changed careers because their former job is no longer in demand? What careers do you think are most in demand today? What careers do you think will increase in demand?

research

Researching Your Choices In addition to all of the questions listed here, you probably have other questions you would like to answer about the occupations you are considering. In addition to your school advisors and local employment office, the following resources are available to answer most of the questions you might have:

»Internet

The Internet is a very powerful tool in researching careers. Many websites are available that contain information on careers. Online search engines can help you reach them. Enter the name of the occupation along with the words "occupational information," and then hit Enter. For instance, type "carpenter occupational information" and then hit Enter. All kinds of web sites will pop up, which, in turn, may have even more links to other web sites of interest.

»Companies and Businesses

Most large companies and businesses publish information about the career opportunities they have available and the skills and education required. The Internet is the best place to find company materials. In addition to information about career opportunities, company web sites may also contain information about company history and the products or services they offer.

»Library

Local libraries offer a wealth of useful information on occupations. By visiting a library you might discover how helpful librarians are in finding reference books, magazines, and web sites that contain the information you are looking for. You may also discover **trade journals**, which are work-related magazines. These journals might give you an inside look at the occupations you are interested in.

»Government Agencies

The U.S. Department of Labor (USDL) and the Bureau of Labor Statistics (BLS) provide many worthwhile resources for researching career options. For instance, the BLS publishes the *Occupational Outlook Handbook* which is updated every two years and provides information on hundreds of occupations. You can find the handbook in your school or local library, or in the guidance counselor's office. You can also find it on the Internet at www.bls.gov, or you may even be able to have a copy sent to you through the mail. Most states have their own Department of Labor that provides useful information on the types of work people do in specific areas.

Talking with Workers One of the best ways to get information about an occupation is to talk to people who actually work in that occupation. Most people like to talk about themselves and what they do for a living, and most would be more than willing to speak with you. Be sure to prepare your questions before you meet with anyone. Also, be sure to ask each person what they like and what they don't like about their career.

» talk to people who actually work in that occupation «

Finding people to talk to is a matter of asking around. Someone in your own family might know of someone to talk to. You could even make some calls to local companies to ask if there is someone there who would be willing to talk with you about his or her career. You might be surprised at how receptive people are when it comes to helping you get the information you need to select a career.

Try the Job Yourself The best way to learn about a career is to actually try the work yourself. This may not be possible, especially if you lack the necessary training and qualifications. However, there are plenty of opportunities to learn about occupations while working on the job.

research

...best way to learn about a career is to actually try the work yourself.

Here are possibilities you may want to consider:

Apprenticeships Some unions, companies, and trade schools offer apprenticeships to qualified applicants. Basically, an **apprenticeship** allows you to work as a paid assistant alongside a more experienced and well-qualified worker, called a **journey worker**. As an apprentice, you could learn about your chosen occupation directly from experienced workers who have mastered the skills it requires. Apprenticeships can last for several years, so you will not want to get one until you are fairly certain of your career choice.

Internship An **internship** is similar to an apprenticeship except it typically lasts for a shorter period of time (usually 6 to 12 weeks) and it is not as skill intensive. However, internships are a good way to learn about a career by working alongside experienced career professionals. Also, some internships even pay.

Part-Time Jobs You may be able to get an entry level job doing work similar to that of the occupation you are considering. Most entry level jobs are part time and require less training than you would need as a fulltime career worker.

Job Shadowing Frequently as part of a career exploration class, students may spend a day or two working with and observing at a particular company or job site. This is called **job shadowing**, and it allows you to see first-hand what the work is like. Companies and businesses sometimes have a shadowing program that may last from one to several days for interested high school students.

Volunteer Work If you are willing to work for free as a volunteer, you may be able to get experience in certain careers such as those in civic, nonprofit, or charitable agencies. Although you won't get paid for this work, you may receive a wealth of experience and information about the occupation.

Cooperative Education Many schools offer **cooperative education** programs that allow you to work for a company for a specified number of hours per week while you are still attending high school. Cooperative education programs allow you to put your skills into action on the job. At the same time, the work experience adds to your knowledge about the world of work as well as a particular occupation. It is not unusual for a cooperative-education student who liked the work and who did a good job to be offered a permanent job with the company after graduation.

CRITICAL THINKING What methods do you intend to use to research your potential career options? What people or companies might you call to ask for some first-hand insights about the careers you are considering?

3 Deciding on a Career

Now that you have narrowed your list of potential careers to just a few and you have researched them well, you are getting very close to making a decision about your initial career path. But, there is still some work to do to ensure that you make the best possible choice. First you will want to do a good job of evaluating your potential careers, and then you will want to use good decision-making skills.

Evaluating Career Options Complex tasks, such as choosing a career, can be aided by writing important information down in an organized way. Doing this will make it easier to remember and compare important pieces of information. To help you evaluate your career options, you may want to create a career evaluation table for each of the occupations that interest you. A sample portion of a career evaluation table is shown below. By using a table like this one, you can compare your career choice with your goals, values, personality traits, and education and training. Remember, the better the career matches who you are and what you want, the better fit it will be for you.

Name: ____________ Career: *Carpentry*

Personal Characteristics	Career Characteristics	Match Yes or No
Long-term Goals		
Own a home	Pays well but pay varies from region to region	Yes
Be in a management position	Has a career path: journey worker to supervisor/foreman to superintendent	Yes
Want to work for myself one day	Can become independent contractor—own business	Yes
Values		
Contribute to the good of society	Build needed structures—homes, bridges, offices, etc.	Yes
Stay close to family geographically	May work on jobsites that are away from home sometimes	No
Need free time to pursue interests	Work is pretty constant and sometimes involves long hours	Unsure about work hours

continued on next page

continued from previous page

Personal Characteristics	Career Characteristics	Match Yes or No
Personality/Personal Traits		
Good with people	Must be able to work well with people in a team	Yes
Honest	Must be honest	Yes
High energy	Requires physical strength and endurance	Unsure about strength
Like working with my hands	Must have good hand-eye coordination	Yes
Like to do a good job	Requires attention to detail	Yes
Like to figure out how to fix things that are broken	Requires ability to solve problems	Yes
Education/Training		
Will graduate from high school	High School education preferred but not required	Yes
Not keen on four more years of school without pay	Offers 4-year apprenticeship, can earn while learning	Yes
Need to earn pay while training	Offers continuing education to upgrade skills	Yes
Not any good at math	Requires good math skills	No

before you decide... consider

Although this table may look complicated, it really isn't. First fill in your name and career and then fill in the first column with information about yourself. You can add anything about yourself that you think is important in selecting a career, but before you decide, consider using the categories listed below in your table.

- **Goals** Include at least your long-term goals, but you may also want to include short-term goals as well.
- **Values** Include any of your personal values that you think may affect your career choice.
- **Interests** Include any interests, activities, and hobbies you particularly enjoy like being outdoors, working on cars, painting pictures or working out.
- **Personality** Include important personality traits such as being shy, being quick to anger, having high energy, or being good with people.
- **Skills** Include your existing skills such as being good at working with your hands or being able to install and maintain software.
- **Training** Include any sort of career-related training you have had.
- **Education** Include the level of education you have had and how much time and energy you are you willing to devote to continuing your education.

Once you have completed the first column of the table, it is time to complete the second column. However, before you do so, it would be a good idea to make several copies of the table with only the first column filled in. By doing this, you will not have to go to the trouble of filling in the first column for each career that you decide to evaluate.

Now, using one of the copies, fill in the name of the potential career that you have researched and list its characteristics in the second column. It will be very helpful if you can line up the career characteristics with the personal characteristics you put in the first column. Then, in the third column, identify the match between your personal characteristics and the career characteristics by writing either "Yes" or "No." If you are not sure, write "Unsure" followed by a brief note.

Once you have created tables for as many careers as interest you, you are ready to look at the matches. Obviously, if it happens that the third column in any one of the tables is filled with "No's," then that career is not for you. However, most of your tables will probably have both yes and no answers in the third column. By simply comparing the number of "No" answers in the third column of each table, you will get a quick assessment of which career may be the best fit for you. However, be sure it is a fair comparison by carefully comparing the tables of close careers side by side.

At this time, you will also want to further explore any comparisons marked "Unsure." You may even want to consider things you are willing to change about your personal characteristics. For example, you might want to take steps to improve your math skills. Also, if no careers provided a good match, this would be a perfect time to rethink your potential choices in careers.

CRITICAL THINKING How do you think making career tables will help you to evaluate possible careers? How do you think your personal characteristics will match up with the characteristics required for the careers that interest you most?

...perfect time to rethink your potential choices in careers.

Making Your Career Decision The final step in your career selection process will be to make your decision. Even with all your preparation, this may not be an easy decision to make. Rarely is any career a perfect match. In the end, you should select the one career that continues to interest you, that seems suited to you, and that you are willing to work to achieve. It should also be a decision that you make carefully using a thoughtful decision-making style. But, even with every precaution, you may still make the wrong choice. Don't worry, if the career you select doesn't work out as well as you had hoped, you can always make a new career decision.

4 Preparing for a Successful Career

You! No matter what career you select, preparation will be the key to success. Today's global economy certainly requires skilled workers and anyone lacking the necessary training, education, and skills will be at a severe disadvantage when looking for a job. Fortunately, there are a number of ways you can get the education and the training you need.

High School By giving serious effort to your studies in high school, you will be building a solid foundation for your career. Employers often reason that students who do well in school also perform well at work. This is why many employers prefer to hire workers with good high school records.

Some high schools offer occupational training courses as part of what may be called technical preparation or **tech-prep** programs. Tech-prep courses vary widely and may include carpentry, agriculture, applied science, business, and health science. Usually, these courses are taken during the last two years of high school and include a blend of classroom study and hands-on vocational training. High school tech-prep programs may also be linked to similar programs at local community colleges. This allows students to continue their tech-prep training even after they graduate from high school.

CRITICAL THINKING In what ways have you made an effort to match your high school classes to your career interests? In what ways are your classes pointing you in the career direction you intend to follow? Does your school offer specific courses to prepare you for a career? If so, have you considered taking advantage of them?

Give serious effort to your studies in high school.

Postsecondary Education There are many careers that require **postsecondary education**, which is simply education or training beyond high school. While some companies may offer entry-level jobs that require as little as a high school diploma or GED, advancing further along a career path might well require a two-year or four-year degree. If your career choice requires postsecondary education, you will want to consider the options listed below:

- **College or University** High school students are often asked, "Are you going to go to college?" Those who answer "yes" will probably enroll in a four-year degree program at a university or college that offers the education they want at a price that they can afford. A college degree provides an excellent platform for a successful career. However, there are a great many rewarding careers that do not require a four-year college degree. Your high school teachers or advisors can help you decide whether a four-year degree program is right for you.
- **Community College** As an alternative to a four-year college program, many people attend community colleges. Community colleges offer one- and two-year certificates in certain career fields as well as two-year associate degrees. One of the advantages of community colleges it that they are relatively inexpensive and are often close by. Another advantage is that they often hold classes at night or other convenient times so that students can hold part-time or full-time jobs and still attend classes. You may want to check with the admissions office of your local community college to see if there are any programs that would meet your needs.
- **Career Colleges** Career colleges go by a wide variety of names including business colleges, trade or technical colleges, and technical institutes. What all of these postsecondary schools have in common is that they are dedicated to specific career fields such as business, computer programming, electronics, criminal justice, and health science. These schools offer one- or two-year certificate programs, two-year associate degrees, and even four-year degrees in some cases. Like community colleges, career colleges generally hold classes at convenient times so that students can learn while holding either part-time or full-time jobs. Depending on your interests and career goals, a career college or technical school might meet your needs.

CRITICAL THINKING Are you interested in a career that requires postsecondary education? What type of postsecondary education do you think will best suit your career needs?

building a better u

If the career you're interested in requires education or training beyond high school, you might qualify for financial aid and scholarships to lower the cost. The U.S. Department of Education offers financial aid for all types of education, including technical and trade education. Check out the possibilities online at www.studentaid.ed.gov. To find out if you're eligible, or to apply online, go to Free Application for Federal Student Aid at www.fafsa.gov. Visit a school or career guidance counselor for more information and application procedures.

On-the-Job Training

shout out!

Helmets to Hardhats is an apprenticeship program that transitions veterans into careers in the building trades. A group of Illinois apprentice carpenters in the program, who had already served their country well in the military, reported to duty to aid a fallen Marine's mother. Lori Fraher lost her only son when 19-year-old Ray was killed in Iraq. When asked by Lt. Governor Pat Quinn if there was anything he could do to help Fraher, a single mom, she said her house needed its roof repaired. She had put the repair off, waiting for Ray, who wanted to become a member of the building trades, to return home and do the work. As it turned out, the house needed more than roof work—it was falling down. Plans were made to tear down the house and build a new one. The Helmets to Hardhats apprentices arrived in the summer, ready to learn and help. By autumn, they worked with other area tradespeople to reconstruct the new house as a tribute to Ray.

On-The-Job Training No matter what career you choose, some of your training will probably occur after you have been hired and are already on the job. For some workers, on-the-job training is the only type of training they will ever receive. On-the-job training has several advantages. It is usually free, and you can often earn pay while you learn. More importantly, on-the-job training is very specific and is perfectly suited to the job that you will be doing. However, even though on-the-job training provides excellent training, many of the better paying jobs require education or training before you even get hired.

Internships Some businesses offer internships to high school and postsecondary students on summer break or who are taking time off from school to gain work experience. Usually, interns agree to work on a low-paying or volunteer basis for a few weeks or months while they learn about an occupation. Many interns use their internship as a form of career research. Unlike other forms of on-the-job training, internships are usually short term and may or may not lead to long-term employment.

Apprenticeship Programs Apprenticeships allow an inexperienced worker to work as a paid assistant alongside one or more experienced and well-qualified workers. This is one of the oldest forms of on-the-job training. Centuries ago, highly skilled artisans and craftsmen, such as goldsmiths, furniture makers, and carpenters hired apprentices to help them with their work. The apprentices agreed to work for low wages in exchange for the opportunity to learn the skills of the craft from a master. After several years, capable apprentices became master craftsmen and were then able to take on apprentices of their own. In this way, skills and expertise were passed on from one generation to the next.

earn pay

...hands-on experience at worksites under the supervision of qualified journey workers.

Apprenticeships in many skilled trades are still offered by certain schools, unions, trade associations, and employers. Today, however, most apprentices do not learn from just one master craftsman as in the past. Instead, they take part in specific programs that usually involves both classroom instruction and hands-on experience in the workplace.

In the classroom, apprentices are introduced to the tools, techniques, and procedures of the trade. They are also given hands-on experience at worksites under the supervision of qualified journey workers. From these journey workers, apprentices learn the art of the craft, respect for tools and materials, and pride in making a perfect product. But whether in a classroom or at the jobsite, there is always an emphasis on safety, including safety awareness, safety regulations, and safe practices.

A typical apprenticeship program in the carpenters union takes about four years to complete, although some may take longer and others are shorter. During this period, apprentices earn a percentage of the journey worker's wage for their work, and as their skills increase, they receive increases in their rate of pay. Of course, they will earn much more once they complete the program and become journey workers themselves. Their participation in the union ensures that they have representation with various employers, and that they also get health and medical benefits as well as a pension plan.

while you learn

framing your future

There are over 450,000 active apprentices in over 850 apprenticable occupations in the United States. To find out more about these occupations and apprenticeship programs, go to the Apprenticeship website of the U.S. Department of Labor, Employment & Training Administration at www.doleta.gov/oa.

Carpentry is just one of hundreds of technical careers that can begin with an apprenticeship. Most apprenticeship programs require applicants to have either a high school diploma or GED. Some apprenticeship programs may prefer applicants with junior college or college backgrounds. If you think you might be interested in an apprenticeship, it is not too early to find out about the requirements. If you are still going to school, you may want to take courses that will better prepare you for the apprenticeship program. For example, if you want a career and an apprenticeship in carpentry, you might want to take math courses, as well as courses such as computer aided design (CAD) and carpentry.

CRITICAL THINKING How do you think an apprenticeship program would fit into your career plans? Do you know if apprenticeship programs exist for your career choice? How might you find out?

Being able to learn new things is an essential element in advancing your career.

Learning Is a Lifelong Process You may think of your education as something you get in school or at college. Once you have earned a diploma or degree, your education is finished. Of course, this couldn't be further from the truth. You learned things long before you ever went to school and you will continue to learn things long after you are out of school. In other words, learning is a lifelong process.

Learning at work will be vitally important. You will have to learn tasks at work that you have probably never done before. You will have to learn about unfamiliar procedures and processes. You will have to learn about unfamiliar tools, equipment, and materials that you may be required to use. You will also have to learn about an unfamiliar worksite and about how to interact with your new coworkers and supervisors. No wonder people feel very stressed when they start a new job. There is so much to learn!

Even once you have become an old hand at work, learning will still be important. You will want to learn about new materials and techniques as they are introduced to improve efficiency. You will want to learn about any new equipment that is put into service and about any safety hazards that may arise. You may need to learn how to work with new team members, coworkers, and supervisors. You may even want to learn how to do your job so well that you would be considered for a promotion to a better job. Being able to learn new things is an essential element in advancing your career. The more knowledge and skills you acquire, the more responsibility you will be ready to handle.

CRITICAL THINKING Do you like to learn new things or do you do so reluctantly? How might your willingness to learn affect your chosen career path?

5 Planning Your Career

When you think about it, you probably do quite a bit of planning already. For example, you probably make plans for something as simple as getting together at a restaurant with your friends. Without a plan, your friends might not even show up at the right restaurant or at the right time to actually get together. As you can see, a plan is really important to the success of even simple activities. And since your career will be one of the most important activities of your life, it makes sense to plan it carefully.

...a decision about what career you would like to pursue is in itself a major milestone.

Making a decision about what career you would like to pursue is in itself a major milestone. This milestone is also a good starting point for a detailed career plan. Fortunately, a career plan can be fairly simple. It is really just a statement of your long-term career goal followed by the medium- and short-term goals that you must achieve to meet your career goal. Your career goals may include getting the kind of job you want and earning enough money to live a comfortable life. However, you are likely to have set for yourself many lesser but, nonetheless, important goals. For instance, your goals may include gaining the necessary certification to do certain types of highly skilled work or handle certain kinds of delicate or dangerous work-related materials. You may envision becoming a supervisor, manager, or independent business owner. You may want to build a solid reputation as being extremely skilled in your chosen craft, a goal that can only be achieved with years of training, practice, and hard work. Whatever your career goals may be, a career plan can help you work toward and achieve them.

TIPS how to set worthwhile career goals and make them work for you

Understand your career goals

Set clear career goals and make sure you understand what achieving them will mean for you and others. Achieving only some of your goals may not provide the benefits you expected.

Select realistic career goals

Your career goals should fall within your abilities as well as your available time and money. For example, if you have picked a career that requires extensive math skills, make sure you have the ability and the time to acquire these skills. And, if the courses you need are not free, make sure you can afford the cost.

Consider costs and rewards

Some career goals are well worth what they will cost you in time, money, and effort. Others are not.

Develop short-term career goals

Most long-term career goals cannot be reached in a single leap forward. To reach them you must set and achieve short-term or medium-term goals that will move you along toward your intended objective.

Establish reasonable timelines

Your career goals should be achievable within a set time period. Open-ended career goals, that is, goals without an established deadline, may be little more than dreams that will never become a reality.

Develop a written career plan

Your long-term goals, medium-term goals, short-term goals, and timelines should be written down. Keep your written goals and timelines in a place where you can refer to them frequently. That way you can check on your progress and make sure you aren't neglecting any important short-term goals.

One page is usually as long as your career plan needs to be. For example, if your career goal is to be a journey worker carpenter, your career plan might look something like the one shown here.

Name: ________________ Date:__________

Career Goal

Journey worker carpenter- Acquire the skills and experience necessary to get full time employment as a journey worker carpenter

Short-Term Goals

Take available carpentry classes in high school: 1-2 years
Completed: ________________

Gain experience working in a group or go out for a team sport: 1 year
Completed: ________________

Graduate from high school: 3-4 year
Completed: ________________

Medium-Term Goals

Take community college math courses: part-time over 2 years
Completed: ________________

Enter apprenticeship program: 4 years
Completed: ________________
Work during apprenticeship: 4 years
Completed: ________________

Long-Term Goals

Complete apprenticeship program successfully: 2-5 years
Completed: ________________

Work fulltime as a carpenter and continue to take upgrade classes: 5 years

Successfully apply for a supervisor's position at the end of 5 years
Achieved: ________________

Chapter Check

On a separate piece of paper, write your answers to the following questions:

Multiple Choice

1. Which of the following involves classroom instruction as well as hands-on experience?
   a) job shadowing
   b) internship
   c) apprenticeship
   d) volunteer work

2. Which of the following lasts for the shortest amount of time?
   a) internship
   b) apprenticeship
   c) cooperative education
   d) job shadowing

3. What is the minimum education requirement for most apprenticeship programs?
   a) some community college
   b) community college certificate
   c) high school diploma
   d) no minimum education but some work experience

Fill in the Blank

4. The type of on-the-job training that requires the greatest commitment is a(n) ______________________ program.

5. When creating a career evaluation table, it's important to include ____________________ as a category if you want to evaluate how much family time a career would allow.

6. Skills learned from life experience or from a part-time job, which you can use in a career, are called ____________________ skills.

True or False

7. By definition, a career is more short term than a job. *T or F*

8. You start a tech-prep program when you are in community college. *T or F*

9. An internship is usually done when taking time off from school. *T or F*

10. Apprentices who complete their program become journey workers. *T or F*

Important Words

Apprenticeship Program that provides a way to learn an occupation by working as a paid assistant alongside experienced professionals for a period of years.

Cooperative education Program that provides work at a particular company for a specified number of hours per week while still attending school.

Internship Program that provides a way to learn an occupation by working, usually without pay, alongside experienced professionals for a period of weeks or months.

Job shadowing Program that provides a way to learn about a particular company or jobsite by observing it for a period of days.

Journey worker Experienced and skilled worker who has completed a specified training program as an apprentice.

Postsecondary education Education or training beyond high school.

Tech-prep Occupational training program offered in high school.

Transferable skills Skills that can be applied to more than one career.

Trade journals Magazines related to specific areas of work.

On the Trail of . . .

Now that you know the difference between a job and a career, interview one person with a job, and another person with a career. What does each person get out of their work? Ask how they feel about their pay, hours, benefits, and working conditions. Find out their level of skill, education, and overall job satisfaction. Divide a sheet of paper in half. Use one side to profile the person with the job and the other side to profile the person with the career. What are the similarities and differences? How might their work choices influence your own?

.com

Use the internet to locate the Occupational Outlook Handbook online. Find a job that interests you. For example, you'll find Carpenter under the category Construction. For the job you select, find out the education, training, and other qualifications required; the job outlook over the next ten years; the earning potential; and at least one website where you can find more information. Write a summary of your research.

Being the First Choice

Being able to think creatively, visualize, use information, and communicate with others will help make you more valuable in the workplace. Team up with another student. Each of you will take turns "trying on" a career. With a desired career in mind, take on the identity of this worker. Describe yourself to your classmate: "I am a ________. Every day I do ________. I do this work because ________. This work suits my personality because ________. After five more years of this work, I'll look forward to ________." Doing this verbal role play might require some research, or you can use the job information you researched in the previous activity.

PART 3

The World of Construction

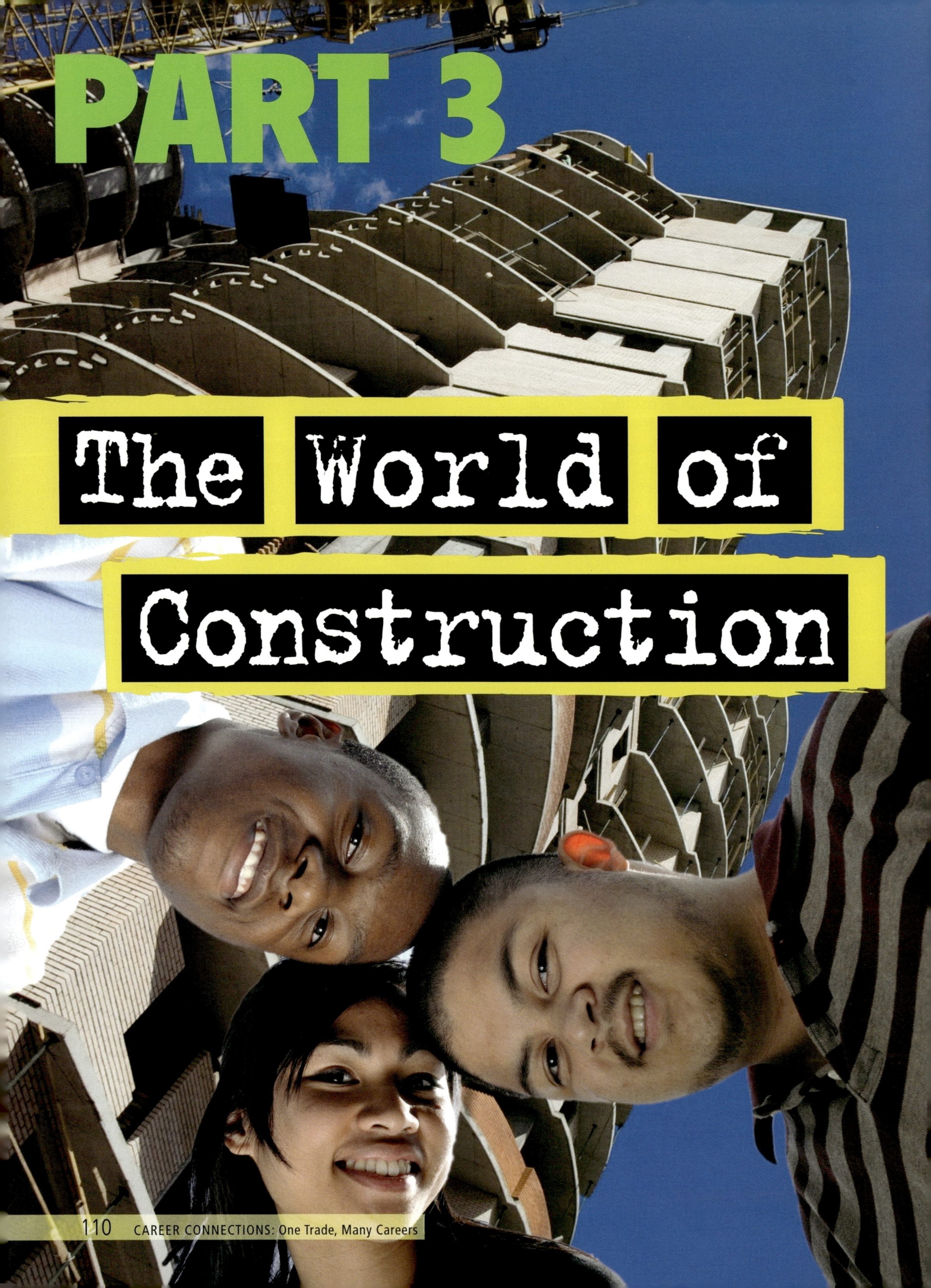

You are probably reading this in a classroom, the library, a bookstore, a coffee shop, or at home. Wherever you are, you're probably in some kind of building that was built by construction workers. Look around you. The walls, windows, flooring, furniture, and perhaps even the desk or table in front of you, have all been created by construction workers. These skilled workers include carpenters, pile drivers, millwrights, lathers, floor layers, cabinet makers, and a variety of other construction professionals.

Construction workers have been building places for people to live, work, store things, and worship for thousands of years. Some structures, such as the pyramids in Egypt, the Parthenon in Greece, and the Roman Coliseum in Italy, have even lasted for that long. These structures are truly magnificent, but so are many of the structures being built today. It is very possible that many of our modern structures will still be considered magnificent thousands of years from now.

The construction workers of today are not only building impressive structures, they are building a lot of them. Twenty-first century construction workers build houses, apartments, schools, museums, hospitals, government buildings, office buildings, and skyscrapers. They also build dams, roads, bridges, and airports. They build unusual structures like public aquariums, planetariums, art museums, sports arenas, theme parks, nuclear power plants, and even pads for launching space vehicles.

> **Construction workers have been building places for people to live, work, store things, and worship for thousands of years.**

Construction workers also enjoy a kind of job satisfaction unavailable to workers in many other occupations. When they drive through a city, suburb, or business park, they are surrounded by structures built by workers just like them. Occasionally, they may even be able to point to a house, a business, or a skyscraper and say, "I helped build that."

Recessions can produce tight job markets and unemployment, but people aren't going to stop building, maintaining, and changing structures, so construction work is a relatively secure occupation.

shout out!

When Margaret Kato, executive director of Habitat for Humanity in Michigan, heard that students in Flushing High School were taking a new home improvement class, she talked to officials about students constructing sheds for Habitat houses. "It's very important for us to be able to tap into our youth and make the projects they are doing in class functional," Kato said. "They can drive by the houses some day and say, 'I built that shed.'" Chad Selvig, a senior, said he and his 15 classmates did every step from start to finish when building the sheds. They calculated measurements and determined the sheds' costs. "We got to build something from the ground up," ninth-grader Ryan Roddie said. "I will remember what we learned. It will help later in life."

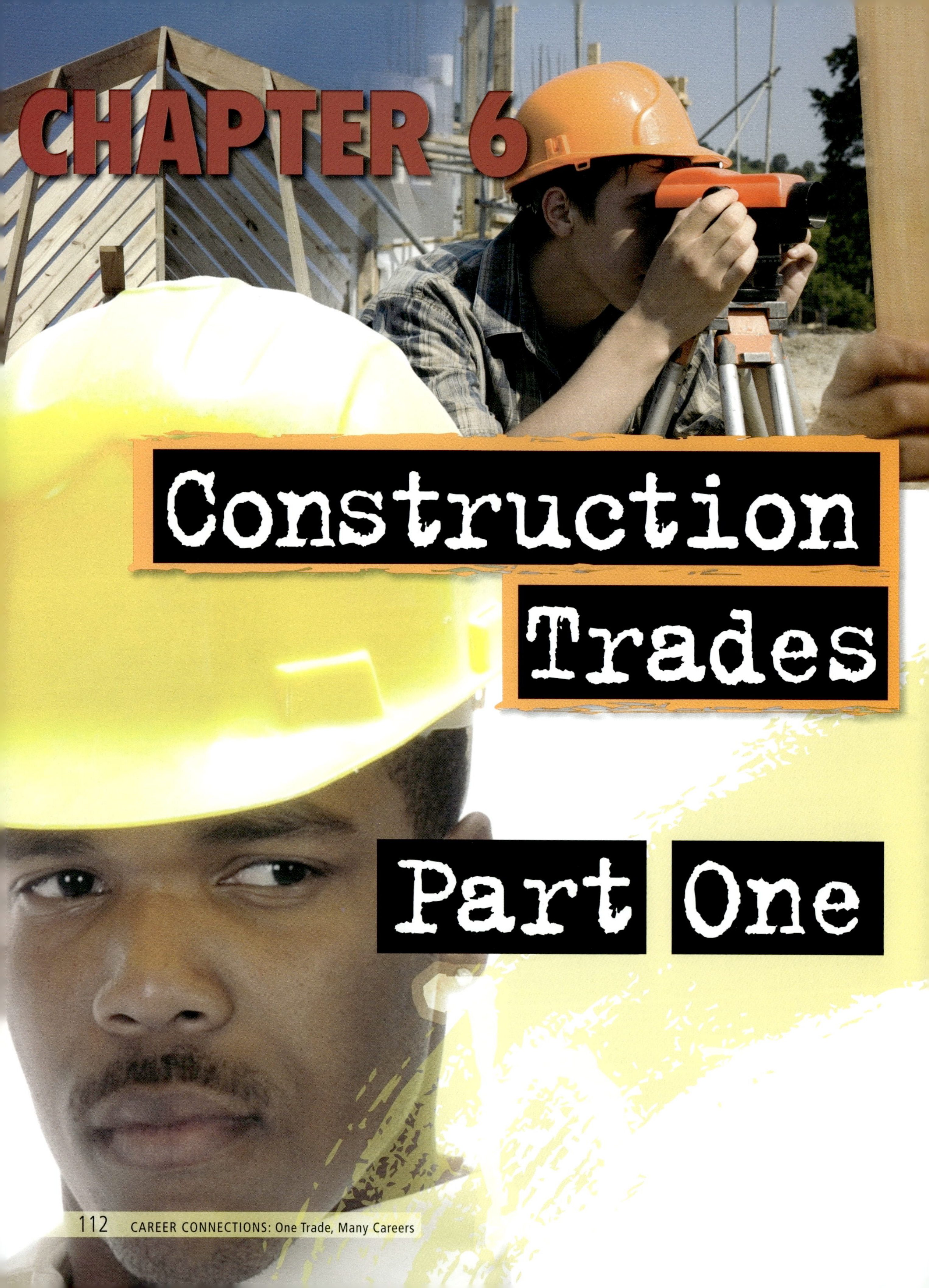

CHAPTER 6

Construction Trades

Part One

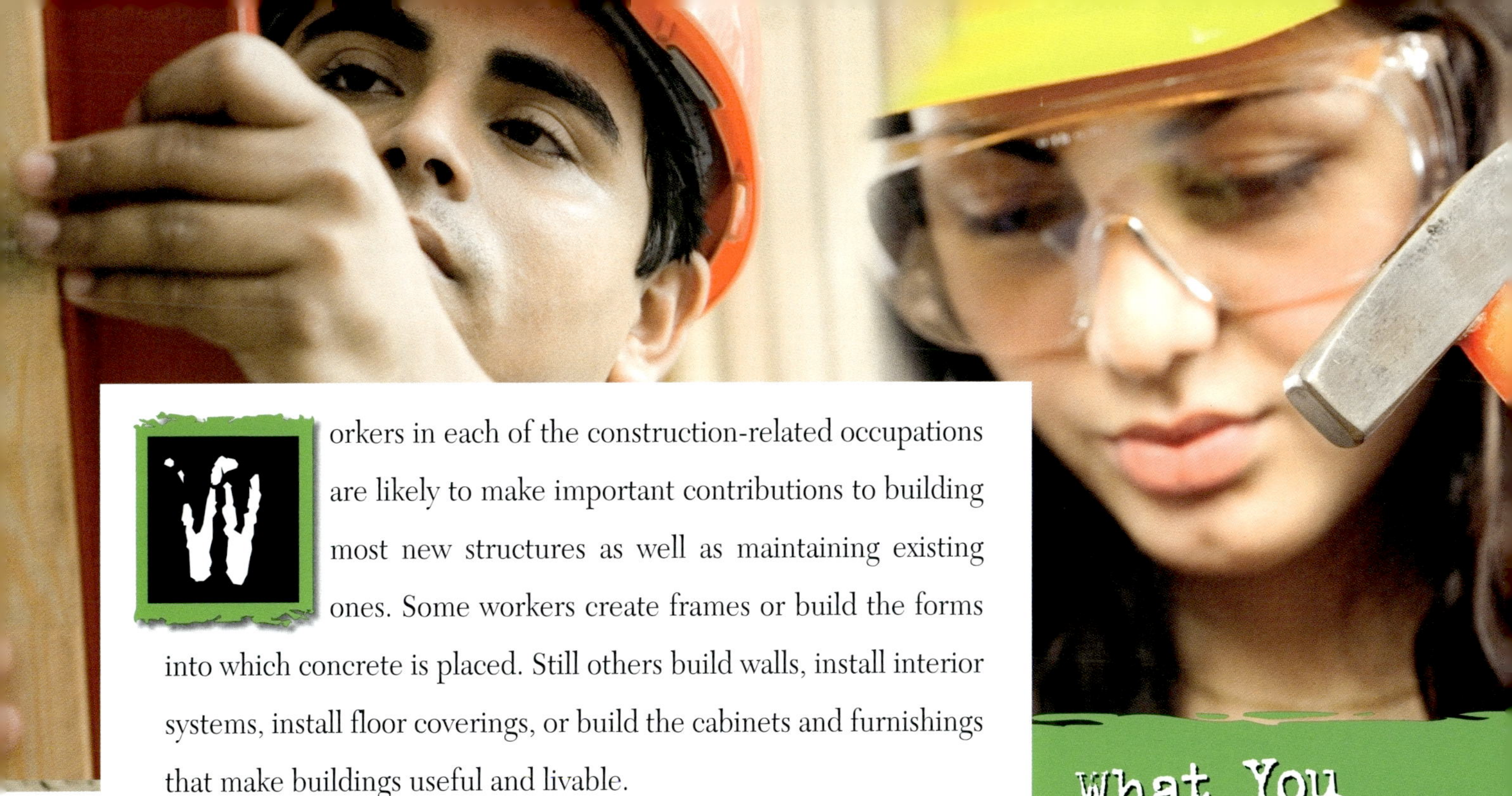

Workers in each of the construction-related occupations are likely to make important contributions to building most new structures as well as maintaining existing ones. Some workers create frames or build the forms into which concrete is placed. Still others build walls, install interior systems, install floor coverings, or build the cabinets and furnishings that make buildings useful and livable.

In this chapter you will explore what it takes to be a construction worker and what it is like to work in the following important construction occupations:

- residential carpenter
- commercial carpenter
- interior systems carpenter
- mill-cabinetmaker

Remember that each of these occupations makes an important contribution in building the structures that we rely on every day. Although each of these occupations requires different skills, they all require similar education and training.

What You Now Know

- Success in a career comes with planning
- That your likes and dislikes are important considerations when choosing a career

What You Will Know

- The educational requirements for a career in construction
- What a carpenter does
- How the job of a carpenter differs according to the type of carpenter
- What a cabinet maker does

1 Education and Training Requirements for the Construction Trades

consider
construction trades

Construction jobs are available for workers with a wide variety of backgrounds, interests, skills, and talents. Depending on how you decide to get your training, it could cost you the price of an associate degree, or it could cost you almost nothing or even be free through an apprenticeship program. In fact, apprenticeship programs offered by some trade schools and unions make it possible for workers to be trained free and to earn pay while they learn their craft. As you can see, there are many reasons why you may want to consider a career in the construction trades.

how to Get the Necessary Education and Training

High school is a good place to start the process of learning to be a carpenter. Classes in shop and Computer-Aided Design (CAD) are helpful. Classes in math, including geometry and algebra, are also helpful. And don't neglect English classes. Workers who cannot read and write well are less likely to succeed in any occupation. You will also want to be physically fit since most occupations in the construction trades are physically demanding. Taking physical education classes and participating in outdoor activities are good ways to get fit and to stay fit. Regardless of the classes you choose, you will want to be punctual and have good attendance to enhance your employability.

Beyond the preparation of high school, there are a number of paths that you might take to be trained for a career in construction. One path is to attend a community or technical college. Another path is to get a construction job where you can learn from more experienced workers. However, perhaps **the surest path to a successful construction career is to** complete a state or federally registered apprenticeship program. An apprenticeship in carpentry, for example, typically lasts approximately four years although some programs may be longer or shorter. During the apprenticeship, you would receive a minimum of 144 hours of classroom and hands-on instruction per year. You would spend the rest of the time working in the trade and being paid for your work.

building a better u

A study published in the Journal of Exercise Physiology shows that employees with higher levels of cardiovascular endurance tend to be less tired, more efficient, more productive, concentrate better, and feel more satisfied with the quality of their work. Physically fit employees also feel less stress, less anxiety, and increased self-esteem on the job. How might having a job that makes physical demands and builds strength have a positive effect on you?

> ... how the finished product should be made, what it will look like, and how it will function

Required Skills

Most construction workers must know how to read and understand construction plans, which are called **prints**. A carpenter, for example, should be able to determine how the finished product should be made, what it will look like, and how it will function—all from looking at the prints. Carpenters must also know how to use a variety of measuring and layout tools to accurately measure and lay out the project so that the materials end up in the right place, are the right size, and fit together properly. To do this, carpenters use tools such as tape measures, squares, levels, and a variety of other measuring tools.

Carpenters must also be familiar with many different kinds of materials and must know how to cut, shape, smooth, place, and fasten these materials. All workers in the construction trades must have a high level of skill in using a wide array of hand and power tools safely. The tools used by carpenters include saws, planes, chisels, hammers, staplers, nail guns, drills, and routers, just to name a few.

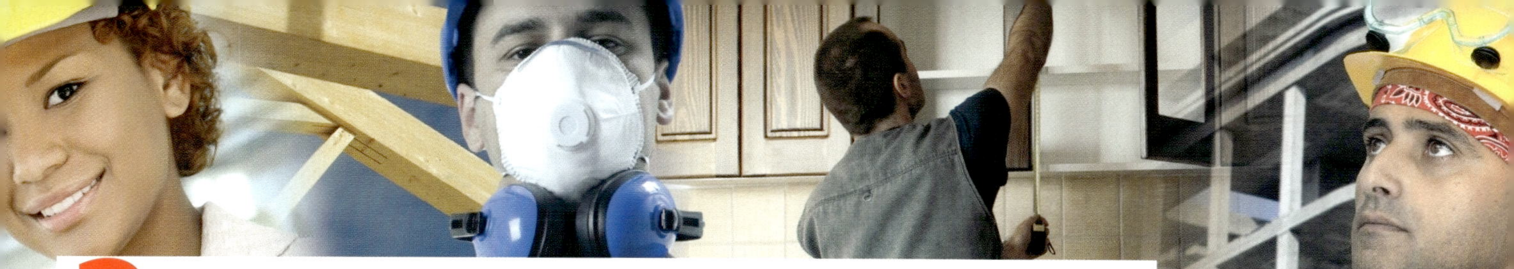

2 The Carpenter's Craft

All members of the United Brotherhood of Carpenters and Joiners of America (UBC) are professionals. The UBC carpenters have the designation of professional because they are well trained and highly skilled. The word carpenter is broadly interpreted by the UBC to include trained and skilled workers of a number of crafts, including carpentry, floor laying, lathing, millwrighting, pile driving, and mill cabinetry. The title of this book, *One Trade, Many Careers*, expresses the vision of the UBC.

Carpenters make up the largest group of skilled workers in either the United States or Canada. According to the U.S. Bureau of Labor Statistics, there are about 1.5 million working carpenters in the United States alone. The need for carpenters is expected to grow over the next decade, so carpentry is a promising field for those seeking a stable and rewarding occupation. Depending on the kind of work they do, carpenters may be called residential, commercial, or interior systems carpenters.

What Is a Carpenter? When you hear the word "carpenter," you probably think of the skilled worker who builds houses. But the trade of carpentry is much more involved than just that. Sure, carpenters build houses, but they also build amusement parks and zoos. They renovate museums and restore historic buildings. They make decorative furniture, cabinets, and build movie and theater sets. They are also responsible for creating most of the reception counters found at banks, hotels, and resorts. Carpenters also build restaurants, stores, dams, bridges, and even the tallest of skyscrapers. In fact, just about any building or structure that you can think of has either been built by or worked on by a carpenter.

The materials with which carpenters work are as varied as the structures they create. Traditionally, carpenters worked mainly with wood. Today, in addition to wood, they also work with fiberglass, drywall, metal, vinyl, plastic, and many other materials. Carpenters also use a wide variety of hand and power tools to shape these materials according to plan. Yes, carpenters still use hand tools such as hammers, chisels, saws, and planes for some jobs. But carpenters more often use the latest generation of power tools including nail guns, power saws, power drills, power sanders, and even measuring tools that incorporate lasers.

> UBC carpenters have the designation of professional because they are well trained and highly skilled.

How Carpenters Do Their Jobs

Every carpentry project is different, but most involve the same basic steps. First, an architect, designer, or supervisor provides a set of plans called prints. With these prints in hand, the carpenters do a layout. This means they measure, mark, and arrange the necessary materials so that they can be efficiently assembled in accordance with safety codes and quality standards. Next, they cut, shape, and may even smooth and finish the pieces that will be needed for the assembly. Then they assemble the prepared pieces using fasteners such as nails, screws, staples, brackets, or adhesives. This process also requires careful checking with levels, plumb bobs, squares, or surveying equipment to make sure it is all going together perfectly level and plumb and according to plan. The final step is to check the work to make sure it meets the quality expectations as well as the safety requirements of the project.

project is different, basic steps

...other carpenters choose to specialize in a particular type of work

In building a house, carpenters may perform most of the tasks needed to complete a project. However, in building a bank, carpenters may only perform certain tasks such as making the cabinets. In both of these examples, specialized carpenters may work on only part of the project. For example, specialized carpenters may build the frame for a house, and then other carpenters might do the siding or interior trim. On other projects, one carpenter may perform a much wider range of jobs. For example, a carpenter hired to remodel a home or small business might build walls, install windows and doors, install flooring, build countertops, and make cabinets. Carpenters who can handle these types of projects must have a broad range of carpentry skills.

Still other carpenters choose to specialize in a particular type of work. For instance, they may choose to only erect scaffolding, build forms for concrete, install prefabricated stairs or wall panels, or put up braces for underground passageways. And, since these carpenters handle the same sort of work most of the time, they can become highly skilled and highly paid specialists. However, it is also true that specialization can limit their employability.

how i see myself

For many people, working outdoors is essential to their well-being. Author and newspaper columnist Tom Stienstra has made the outdoors his life's work for the past 25 years. "People who have careers in the outdoors have their lives filled with adventure, and are not only happy in their work, but are paid well for it." Stienstra goes on to say, "The outdoors is good for the soul. An outdoor-related job can be rewarding on all levels . . . physically, mentally, spiritually and financially." How important is working outdoors to you?

...work can be strenuous and often requires physical effort...

What's It Like at Work? Not all carpentry work is outdoors, but carpenters are likely to spend more time than most workers out in the sun and weather. Carpentry work can be strenuous and often requires physical effort such as standing for long periods, climbing, or lifting. Since carpenters use a variety of tools, handle heavy materials, and often work in high places or cramped spaces, carpentry can be dangerous. For this reason, carpenters must take care to wear protective gear and job-appropriate clothing. A carpenter's protective gear usually includes a hard hat, work boots, eye protection, and gloves. Training for carpentry work must always emphasize safety.

Depending on the project or the job that needs to be done, carpenters may work alone, with a partner, or in a group. On large construction projects, carpenters may work alongside other carpenters or in cooperation with iron workers, plumbers, or electricians.

Carpenters often start work early in the morning so that they can take full advantage of available daylight. It is also necessary to start early when environmental conditions such as extreme afternoon heat can cause unsafe and less productive working conditions. Sometimes, because of deadlines, carpenters may be asked to work longer than the standard 40-hour week.

Wages and Benefits Construction work pays well. Many construction workers are paid relatively high hourly wages. The Bureau of Labor Statistics (May 2007) states that the average hourly wage of a carpenter is $19.84. Typically, carpenters receive overtime pay for working more than eight hours in one day or more than 40 hours in one week. Workers may get "time-and-a-half" or "double-time" for overtime work. Many carpenters receive health care and other benefits that are as good as or better than those offered by most other occupations. Today, good health benefits are worth 30% or more of a worker's salary.

CRITICAL THINKING Why do you think carpentry is North America's largest skilled occupation? In what ways is carpentry different from other trades? Do you think you would enjoy working as a carpenter? What appeals to you about the trade?

3 What Is a Residential Carpenter?

A **residential carpenter** is primarily engaged in the construction of new homes, apartments, condos, and residential complexes. In other words, residential carpenters provide places for us to live, and in many cases, help us achieve the American dream of owning our own homes. Residential carpenters also repair and remodel existing residences.

When building a new house, residential carpenters start by assembling and erecting the home's structural framework and exterior windows and doors. Then they install flooring, drywall, hang interior doors, install trim work, and do much of the finish work. Residential carpenters have experience in nearly every aspect of residential construction. Because they have a wide range of skills and can handle many different tasks associated with the construction of a home, they may stay on the project from start to finish.

How Residential Carpenters Do Their Jobs Residential carpenters work with a wide range of lumber, manufactured wood products such as plywood and fiberboard, and a variety of other materials. Carpenters also use many types of tools and fasteners to shape, assemble, and install the different materials they use. Residential carpenters use hand tools such as hammers, squares, and tape measures, and also power tools such as power saws, power drills, pneumatic nail guns and staplers, and a variety of other specialized tools. They also use fasteners such as nails, screws, brackets, staples, pegs, and various adhesives.

What's It Like at Work? Residential carpenters may face a wide variety of conditions on the work site. They may spend part of their time outside and part inside depending on the job. Weather conditions may influence a residential carpenter's hours along with the project schedule. Residential carpentry is as dangerous as other construction work, and safety must always be the first consideration. Residential carpenters must remain aware of their surroundings, which may include low overhangs, sharp corners, sharp tools and equipment, other workers, and materials. Hard hats and work boots are a necessity. Residential carpenters also wear eye protection, protective clothing, and other safety gear to protect them and help ensure safety while on the job.

safety must always be the first consideration

Like other carpenters, residential carpenters may work alone or in groups and for either large or small construction companies. Also, they often work in cooperation with the workers of other trades, such as painters, electricians, and plumbers.

CRITICAL THINKING Do you like the idea of building homes for people? Do you think you would enjoy working as a residential carpenter? How might this career be a good fit for you?

framing your future

"Measure twice, cut once" is perhaps the fundamental rule of carpentry. Traditionally, it means you should double-check your measurements for accuracy before cutting a piece of wood, or you might have to cut again and waste time and material. How can you translate this rule into practical advice for other areas of life?

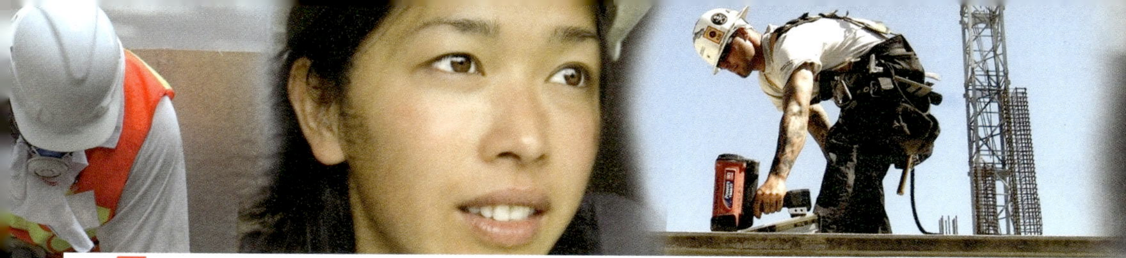

4 What Is a Commercial Carpenter?

A **commercial carpenter** is someone who works primarily on structures other than residences. Often, these structures are so advanced or well designed they are known around the world. The Empire State Building in New York City, the Golden Gate Bridge in San Francisco, and the Sydney Opera House in Sydney, Australia, are three good examples. Commercial buildings and structures include all of the office buildings, malls, schools, theaters, hospitals, bridges, and highways that we rely on every day.

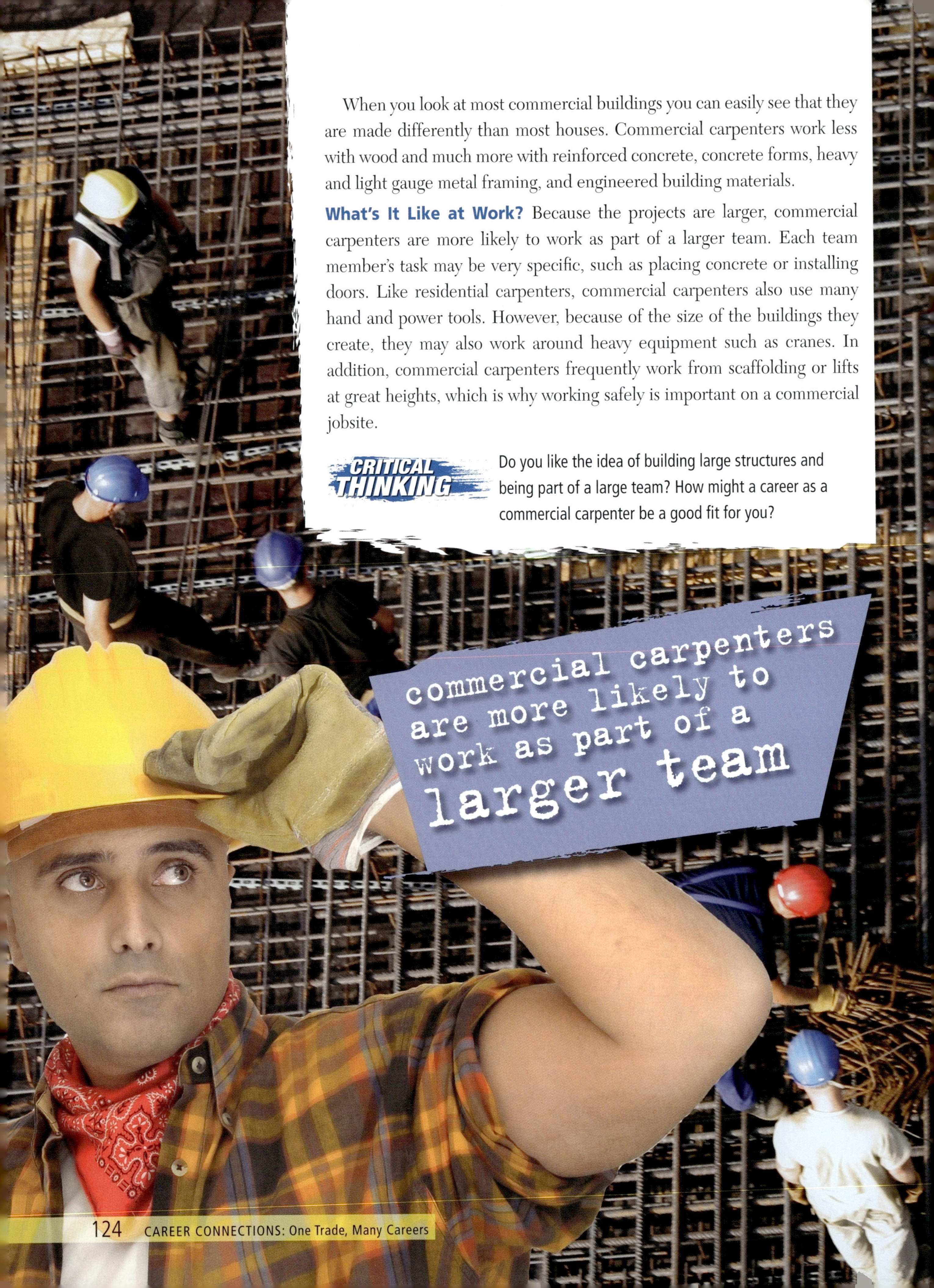

When you look at most commercial buildings you can easily see that they are made differently than most houses. Commercial carpenters work less with wood and much more with reinforced concrete, concrete forms, heavy and light gauge metal framing, and engineered building materials.

What's It Like at Work? Because the projects are larger, commercial carpenters are more likely to work as part of a larger team. Each team member's task may be very specific, such as placing concrete or installing doors. Like residential carpenters, commercial carpenters also use many hand and power tools. However, because of the size of the buildings they create, they may also work around heavy equipment such as cranes. In addition, commercial carpenters frequently work from scaffolding or lifts at great heights, which is why working safely is important on a commercial jobsite.

CRITICAL THINKING Do you like the idea of building large structures and being part of a large team? How might a career as a commercial carpenter be a good fit for you?

commercial carpenters are more likely to work as part of a larger team

5 What Is an Interior Systems Carpenter?

Just because a building is erected, that doesn't mean it is finished. In order to have their own unique character, many buildings are made with decorative elements on both the inside and out. What would the Notre Dame Cathedral be without its gargoyles or a palace without its ornate trim? Many of the decorative elements that transform a plain room into an appealing place to live, work, or visit are the work of an **interior systems carpenter**.

Of course not all of the work done by the interior system carpenter is decorative. Much of it is functional as well. Have you ever looked up at the ceiling in an office building and noticed the grid pattern of metal strips, tiles, and fluorescent lights? If so, you have seen the work of an interior systems carpenter. You may have even been in the main computer room of a building and stood on the raised floor that the electric, telecommunication, and fiber optic cables run below. This raised floor is also the work of an interior systems carpenter.

nailing it!

Steel framing, once the domain of commercial construction, is becoming more and more popular in home building. Not only is it stronger than wood, it's also lighter, more uniform, mold- and insect-resistant, fire-resistant, and recyclable. Because it's inorganic, it will not rot, warp, split, or crack. The strength of steel framing results in a safer structure that requires less maintenance and ages more slowly.

When you look at the exterior of a large commercial, government, or institutional building, what you see are the walls, windows, and doors. Of course, there is much more to these buildings than their outer shells. Inside they are likely to have acoustical ceilings or raised access floors. They may also have metal framing, wall partitions, built-in furnishings, and many other features that are designed for comfort, ease of use, and to give the building an attractive design. The materials and equipment that make these features possible are installed by interior systems carpenters.

How Interior Systems Carpenters Do Their Jobs The interior systems carpenter often works with prefabricated products that have been manufactured for specific purposes. These products are shipped in marked crates and boxes to the worksite where they are carefully unpacked and assembled. Interior systems carpenters use technical data supplied by the manufacturers to guide their assembly and installation work. Most of the work is done using metal-cutting saws, hammers, drills, wrenches, screw guns, and a variety of other hand and power tools. Some assembly work may also require welding. The finished systems and assemblies of interior systems carpenters may fill part of a single room, or an entire floor, or even the entire building.

interior systems carpenters often work with prefabricated products that have been manufactured for specific purposes

What's It Like at Work? Interior systems carpenters work on the same projects as both commercial and residential carpenters. Interior systems carpenters most often work on the inside of buildings but may also work outside. They may work at floor level or at heights where safety is always the first consideration. Because interior systems carpenters often work with light gauge metal, cuts or lacerations are possible from sharp edges. For protection, interior systems carpenters wear sturdy work clothes, gloves, and appropriate safety gear such as hard hats or eye protection.

The skills needed by interior systems carpenters are specialized and somewhat different from those of other carpenters. Interior systems carpenters may refer to prints occasionally, but they must also be able to read and follow the instructions and complex technical data provided by the manufacturers of the systems they will assemble.

CRITICAL THINKING Are you good at following detailed written instructions? How might a career as an interior systems carpenter fit your interests and abilities?

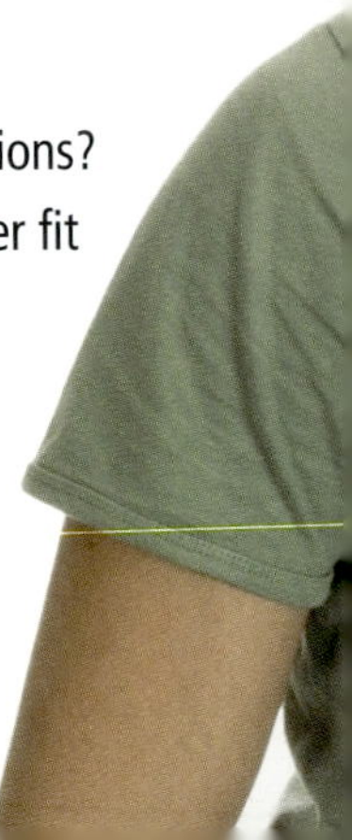

6 What Is a Mill-Cabinetmaker?

A **mill-cabinetmaker** is a type of skilled artisan that has been making cabinets and building furniture for thousands of years. Today, mill-cabinetmakers are still creating products that add beauty, comfort, and functionality to people's lives. Applying skills developed over the centuries, mill-cabinetmakers create their products using a wide variety of fine lumber, including exotic woods and veneers. They may also incorporate plastic, vinyl, metal, plywood, fiberboard, and many other manufactured materials into their finished products.

Mill-cabinetmakers cut, shape, assemble, finish, and install an endless variety of beautiful and highly functional products. Mill-cabinetmakers create commercial and residential cabinets and other furnishings such as desks, tables, and chairs. They may make display cases used to display items in retail stores and for exhibits. They may even make custom architectural millwork used to enhance the beauty of buildings.

How do you think mill-

How Mill-Cabinetmakers Do Their Jobs Mill-cabinetmakers may be expected to apply not one, but an entire range of skills as they juggle many different tasks. The mill-cabinetmaker's workday may include studying and making sense out of hand-drawn or computer-generated plans, selecting appropriate wood and other materials, and using various tools and stationary equipment to measure, cut, shape, and apply a finish. A mill-cabinetmaker's work may require the assembly of components into a finished chair, bookcase, store fixture, or set of cabinets. Often, mill-cabinetmakers go to construction sites where they install the products they build.

Some mill-cabinetmakers may work alone, while others may work in small shops or in large plants. Mill-cabinetmakers who work in large manufacturing facilities are likely to concentrate on a single stage of production such as rough cutting materials, assembly, or finishing surfaces. Many mill-cabinetmakers work in exhibit construction shops where they build the displays that are used at large conventions and trade shows. Mill-cabinetmakers who work alone or in smaller shops may personally handle many different cabinet-making tasks.

Mill-cabinetworkers, like many carpentry crafts, are on the cutting edge of technology. Possessing computer skills can be an advantage to someone interested in a career as a mill-cabinetmaker.

What's It Like at Work? Mill-cabinetmakers generally spend much of their time inside a shop or a large plant where they create their products. Since this trade involves the use of machinery, tools, materials, and chemicals, mill-cabinetmakers pay close attention to their safety and health. When at work, cabinet makers may wear work boots and other appropriate safety gear such as eye protection and ear protection.

Mill-cabinetmakers must be familiar with a wide range of woods and veneers, and also with a wide variety of hardware. While mill-cabinetmakers seldom select the type of wood they are to work with, they need to be able to recognize and adjust their techniques to the specific properties of each type of wood. For example, a soft wood like pine has very different properties from hardwood like oak. These properties must be considered in how the wood is handled, shaped, joined, and finished.

CRITICAL THINKING Do you like using fine wood to build things? How do you think a career as a mill-cabinetmaker would fit your level of creativity?

craft

a career as a
cabinetmaker
would fit your level of
creativity?

Chapter Check

On a separate piece of paper, write your answers to the following questions:

Multiple Choice

1. If you use exotic woods and veneers to builds objects, which occupation are you most likely to have?
   a) commercial carpenter
   b) mill-cabinetmaker
   c) interior systems carpenter
   d) residential carpenter

2. If your job is to install acoustical ceilings in an office building, which occupation are you most likely to have?
   a) commercial carpenter
   b) mill-cabinetmaker
   c) interior systems carpenter
   d) residential carpenter

3. Which type of tradesperson frequently works from scaffolding at great heights?
   a) commercial carpenter
   b) mill-cabinetmaker
   c) interior systems carpenter
   d) residential carpenter

4. Which type of tradesperson typically works with prefabricated products that have been manufactured for specific purposes?
   a) commercial carpenter
   b) mill-cabinetmaker
   c) interior systems carpenter
   d) residential carpenter

Fill in the Blank

5. Every carpenter must be able to read ________________, which are created by an architect or designer and show the look and function of a finished product.

6. All carpenters must wear ________________ gear, including a hardhat and work boots.

7. A(n) ________________ carpenter is more likely than other carpenters to work around heavy equipment such as cranes.

True or False

8. A residential carpentry team is more likely to be larger than a commercial carpentry team. *T or F*

9. Interior systems carpenters work on the same projects as both commercial and residential carpenters. *T or F*

10. Mill-cabinetmakers create products for residential, not commercial structures. *T or F*

Important Words

Commercial carpenter Carpenter engaged in the construction of structures other than residences, such as office buildings, malls, schools, hospitals, and bridges.

Interior systems carpenter Carpenter engaged in the decorative and functional finish work of residential and commercial structures.

Mill-cabinetmaker Skilled worker who makes cabinets and builds furniture for commercial and residential use.

Prints Set of plans used to prepare construction materials.

Residential carpenter Carpenter engaged in the construction, remodel, and repair of homes, apartments, condos, and other residential complexes.

On the Trail of . . .

Now that you know what different types of carpenters do, which one appeals to you most? On a piece of paper, draw a three-column table. At the top of the first column, write "Residential Carpenter," at the top of the second column, write "Commercial Carpenter," and at the top of the third column, write "Interior Systems Carpenter." Think of an ideal building project for each type of carpenter, and write the project below each carpenter title in the table. Below each project, list what you would enjoy about being part of the project team. Below that, list any reservations you would have about being part of such a project. On the other side of the paper, do the same thing for mill-cabinetmaker. See if this exercise points you in a particular direction.

.com

Carpentry has a language all of its own. Words that are second nature to carpenters sound like a foreign language to people outside the trade. Imagine that you are a carpenter and someone is asking you to explain the following common terms: plumb, pneumatic tool, aviation snips, and coping saw. Use online sources to look up these terms. Write a short, easy-to-understand explanation for each term.

Being the First Choice

Increasing your technology skills will make you more marketable in the workplace. Computer numerically controlled (CNC) equipment is used by many mill-cabinetmakers. Research how mill-cabinetmakers use this equipment—for what purpose and with what type of CNC machines. What computer skills are required and how could you get training? Write a short summary of your findings.

CHAPTER 7

Construction Trades Part Two

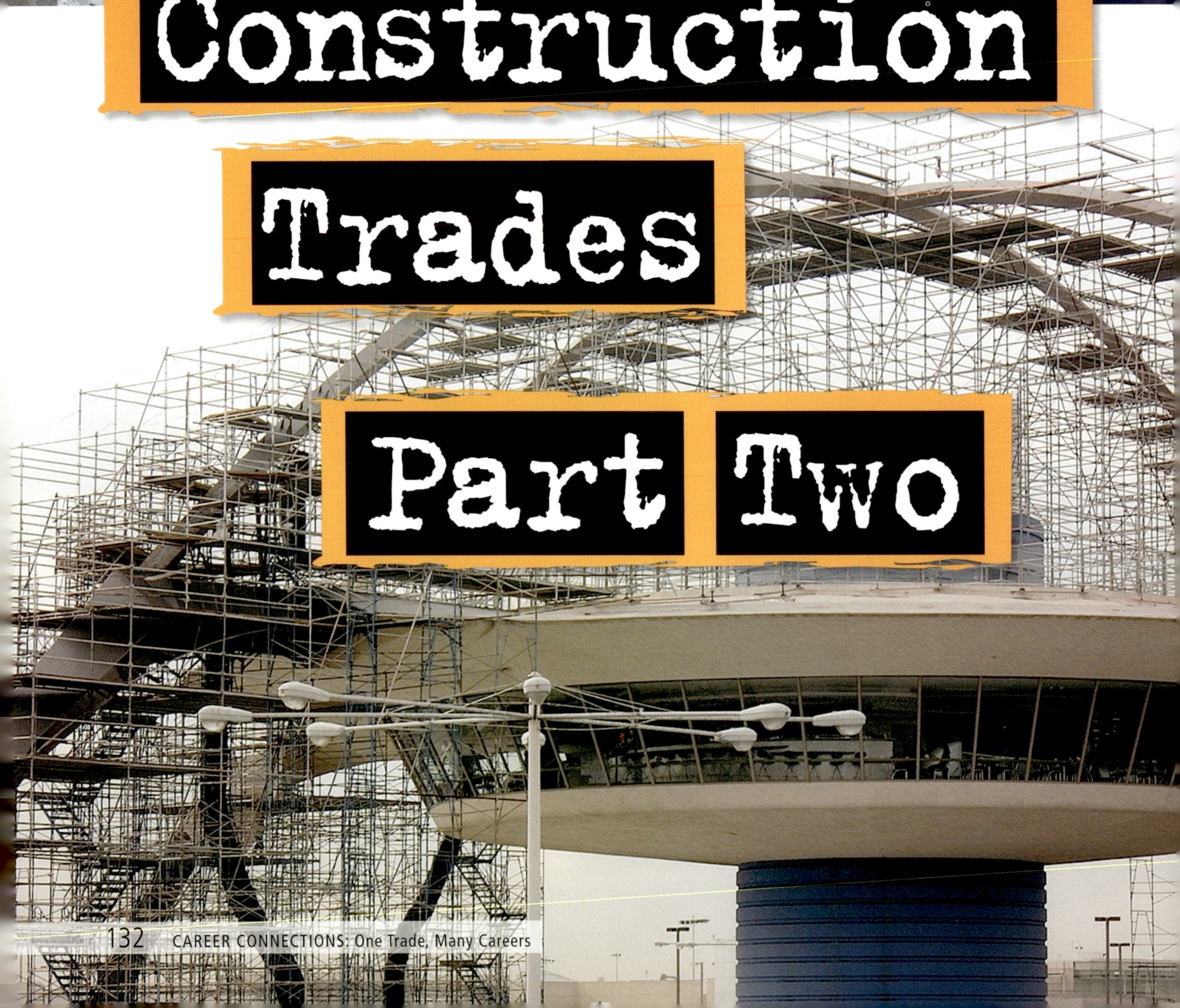

Skilled construction workers make vital contributions to creating and maintaining the buildings in which we all live and work. This chapter explores in detail four additional construction occupations: floor coverer, lather, millwright, and pile driver. Also, this chapter introduces 13 other construction occupations, from boilermaker to sheet metal worker.

What You Now Know

- That you are interested in a career in construction
- The educational requirements for that career
- What a carpenter is and does

floor coverer lather
pile driver
millwright

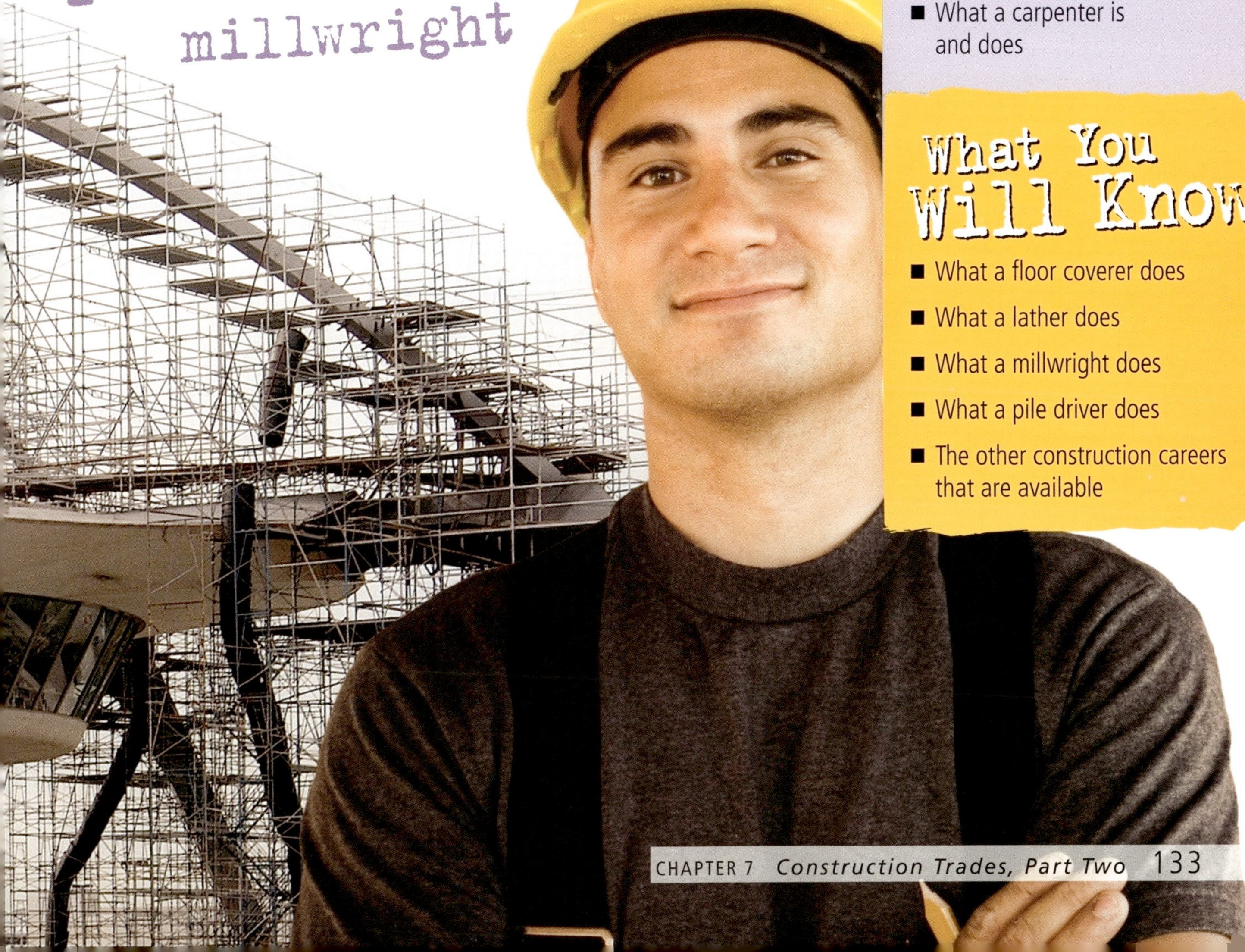

What You Will Know

- What a floor coverer does
- What a lather does
- What a millwright does
- What a pile driver does
- The other construction careers that are available

1 What Is a Floor Coverer?

how i see myself

How would you like to transform dull grey concrete into a spectacular high-gloss floor that looks like marble? Floor coverers are always up on the latest trends in new materials, and concrete flooring is one of them. Using special techniques, concrete can be colored, painted, stenciled, and stamped to look like expensive tile or natural stone. Decorative concrete flooring is durable and cost-effective. It is now thought of as a beautiful design element that only a skilled floor coverer could install.

A beautiful floor can set the tone for an entire room. Intricate tile patterns and beautiful marble are staples in the entryways of many high-priced hotels, restaurants, and resorts because they draw the guest's eye and create a luxurious ambiance. Floors can be very simple or very spectacular, and it is the floor coverer who makes those floors possible.

A **floor coverer** installs a wide variety of floor covering materials including carpet, wood, tile, sheet vinyl, and laminates. Floor coverers also maintain, repair, or replace existing flooring. They may work on new buildings or help renovate old ones. They work on both residential and commercial structures. They even install artificial turf in sports stadiums.

Some floor coverings are so beautiful and intricately designed that they can be considered fine works of art. Whether or not a floor is designed to draw attention, **floor coverings are a very important element of any interior design.** With this in mind, floor coverers creatively match complex patterns and carefully place or align seams. The end result of their efforts is often a breathtaking expanse of artfully designed floor covering that is as beautiful as it is useful.

How Floor Coverers Do Their Jobs Floor coverers execute their work to the specifications provided by architects, interior designers, facility managers, or homeowners. First, they must estimate the amount of carpet or other floor covering materials needed to complete the project. Materials must be cut so that they fit the space being covered. Careful consideration is given to matching tile patterns, the direction of carpet pile, or the direction and appearance of wood grain. By paying close attention to these details, **the floor coverer ensures that the finished floor will be both beautiful and durable.**

Before installing various floor covering materials, the surface on which they are placed must be prepared. The surface must be clean, dry, and level before any flooring is installed. The floor coverer must understand the requirements for preparing various surfaces, depending on the type of the flooring material that is to be placed. For example, vinyl tile and sheet vinyl are glued in place.

When carpet is being laid, the floor coverer may use adhesives or other fastening systems to attach carpeting to the floor. Some carpets may be stretched and held in place with tack strips instead of glue. Because floor coverers usually work inside finished buildings, they must take care to avoid damaging walls, doors, entryways, or furnishings. However, this is not usually a concern when they are installing flooring around pools, on sports fields, or in similar outdoor locations.

Some floor coverings are so beautiful they can be considered fine works of art.

installing flooring involves heavy lifting bending over, and kneeling

What's It Like at Work? The installation of many floor coverings requires teamwork, so floor coverers often work alongside a partner or as part of a larger team. Floor coverers often work in buildings where the floors consist of bare concrete, metal, or rough wood. They may also work on floors where previous flooring materials have been removed or are being removed. In most cases, the buildings are nearly complete when floor coverers begin their work. Even so, buildings where floor coverings are being installed may be active construction sites where appropriate safeguards must be taken to prevent injury. Several safety issues apply to floor laying. For example, some flooring materials and adhesives may give off dangerous fumes. When using these materials, adequate ventilation is an important consideration. Also, installing floor covering involves heavy lifting, bending over, and kneeling. All these actions should be performed in a safe manner to avoid any health risks.

CRITICAL THINKING Does the idea of working with carpet, wood, and other flooring materials appeal to you? How do you think a career in floor laying would fit you?

Does the idea of working with carpet, wood, and other flooring materials appeal to you?

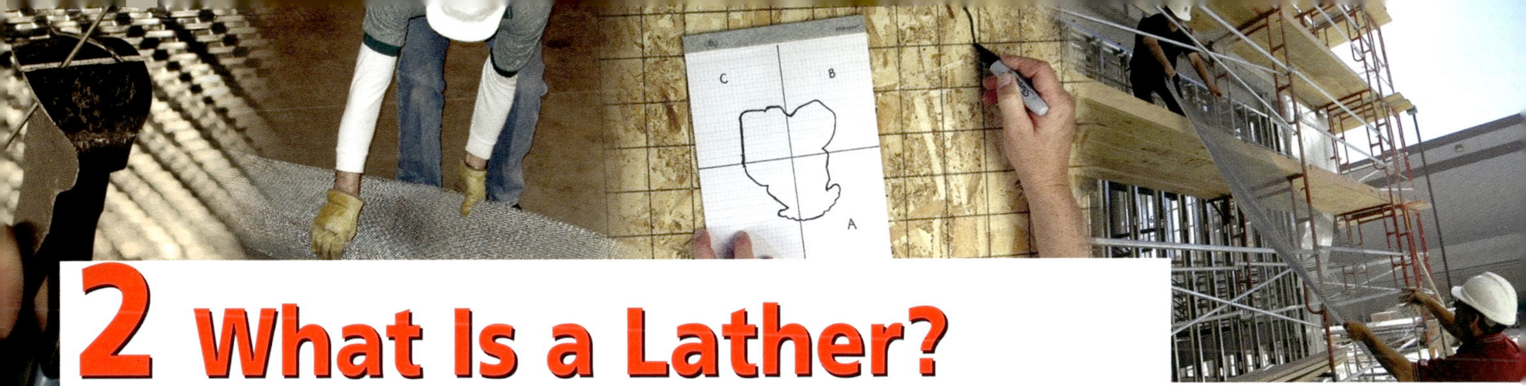

2 What Is a Lather?

Have you ever been to Disneyland? Did you know that many of the decorative elements on many of the rides in the park were created by lathers? Maybe you have been to a zoo and have been impressed with the creative habitats that have been built for the animals to more closely resemble their natural environment. False trees, rocks, and themed structures all have a framework inside them that was built by lathers.

Lathing is a small but important trade that employs thousands of workers in the United States. It's a very old occupation that dates back to the days when palaces and cathedrals were built with stone, wood, and plaster. At one time, a **lather** worked with thin wooden strips called laths, which was how this occupation got its name. Plaster was then used to cover the lathing, which held the plaster in place. Today wooden lathing has been replaced by metal studs and a framework of metal mesh. Modern lathing serves the same function of holding plaster in place. The plaster is what you see as the finished surface of the wall, ceiling, or object. Modern lathing makes it possible to create the ornate walls and ceilings seen in large buildings as well as fancifully shaped creations featured in resorts and theme parks.

building a better u

What does it take to build a 20-story mountain? About 1,800 tons of steel, which holds up Expedition Everest, the high-altitude, high-speed roller coaster attraction in Walt Disney World Resort. The mountain takes up about an acre of land and is the tallest artificial mountain at the resort. All of the outer rockwork is plaster, which took months of carving and shaping to make it look like a real mountain. The structure has to be strong enough to withstand the 60 mph speeds of the coaster, without cracking. What skills would you need to help build a massive steel and plaster structure like this one?

The work of lathers is complicated and the skills necessary for accomplishing it are highly specialized. The lathing put in place by lathers may become the foundation for extraordinary patterns and sculptures. Lathing and plaster can be used to create roaring lions and leaping dolphins. They can be used to create an endless number of geometric shapes and swirling patterns. And they can make the walls or ceilings of a building look like cake frosting or appear to be floating in air.

How Lathers Do Their Jobs Lathers work in a number of ways to erect metal structures that will later be covered with plaster or some other surfacing material. The process may involve anchoring a metal grid or framework to a wall or ceiling with metal studs. Wire mesh is then tied to the framework with wire or attached to it using clips and other fasteners. Lathers cut, join, and fasten materials using a variety of hand tools and portable power tools. They also use welding equipment or oxygen-acetylene torches for certain cutting and fastening tasks. Once the framework is built and in place, a plasterer completes the work by spreading plaster or another surfacing material onto the framework.

What's It Like at Work? Although some lathing is done on the inside of buildings, much of it is done on the exterior of buildings. This means that lathers often spend much of their workday outdoors. Since lathing can reach considerable heights on walls and may also be used on ceilings, lathers sometimes work from scaffolding, ladders, or lifts. For this reason and others, the work of lathers can be dangerous, so safety is always a vital consideration. Lathers may wear hard hats, eye protection, and gloves when they work.

CRITICAL THINKING Do you have a good sense of the shape of things? Do you like working with metal? How might a career as a lather be a good fit for you?

work of lathers is highly specialized

3 What Is a Millwright?

Have you ever gone bowling and wondered about the machine that picks up the pins, puts them back down in the correct spot, and then returns the ball? This machine makes bowling a lot of fun. Other buildings contain other types of machines. In fact, hidden within the walls or beneath the floors of most buildings are a wide variety of sophisticated machines that keep things running. These machines may generate electricity, pump water, compress air and other gases, process minerals, refine chemicals, and manufacture the materials, parts, or any number of the finished products that we use every day. The skilled workers who install much of this machinery and keep it in efficient operating condition are called millwrights.

A **millwright** installs and maintains compressors, pumps, conveyors, monorails, mining equipment, and many other kinds of machinery. Millwrights not only set up machinery and get it running, but are also often called upon to diagnose problems and make repairs. Millwrights work on the giant turbines that generate electricity in coal, hydroelectric, wind turbine, and nuclear power plants. They also work on machinery at automobile plants, steel mills, oil refineries, chemical companies, and at factories or facilities of every sort in just about every major industry. Millwrights even work on roller coasters. If you have ever enjoyed a safe ride at Disneyland or at a Six Flags amusement park, you can thank a millwright.

Millwrights have a great curiosity for how machines work.

They often develop keen insights into the workings of heavy machinery, and this makes them valuable for diagnosing problems when heavy machinery breaks down. The diagnostic capabilities of millwrights are not altogether unlike those of medical doctors. Millwrights look, listen, probe, diagnose the problem, and then devise a solution.

framing your future

Hope Harp knew millwrighting was in her future when she first stepped into a millwright shop as a young woman with few job skills. "It was full of lathes, milling machines, and welding equipment, and I knew immediately it was what I was supposed to do with my life," Harp recalled. She dedicated herself to learning all she could and soon won a millwright apprenticeship contest and embarked on a career at car plants and paper mills. She now shares her skills with new generations of millwrights as an instructor at the 112,000-square-foot training center of the Indiana/Kentucky Regional Council of Carpenters.

Is millwrighting in your future?

machines

How Millwrights Do Their Jobs Millwrights use a wide variety of hand and power tools, rigging, hoisting, and welding equipment, lasers, and precision measuring tools. It is very important that their work is precise. The sophisticated machinery they work on may have moving parts separated by spaces of no more than $^{1}/_{1000}$ of an inch, which is less than the thickness of a sheet of paper. Millwrights must make and use precise measurements to cut, join, and fasten a nearly endless variety of metal parts and construction materials. Also, the work of a millwright often involves testing and monitoring machinery to make sure it is running properly.

Millwrights must understand how large machines work and how their individual parts fit together. They must also understand how one part affects the performance of the whole machine. When necessary, a millwright must also be able to take entire machines apart and then reassemble them. The ability to recognize and fix broken parts and solve other problems with machinery is essential.

As in the other trades, the millwright's tasks require skill in the use of many different types of hand tools, power tools, and equipment. However, the millwright's knowledge of equipment may include the skillful use of welding equipment and hoists, as well as precise measuring and surveying tools. Millwrights must know how to read prints, charts, and diagrams. They also need to know how to use sophisticated electronic or computer-driven monitoring devices. Above all, a millwright needs the ability to size up a mechanical problem and provide a solution.

What's It Like at Work? Millwrights may travel long distances on short notice to fix problems in faraway plants. The work itself may be indoors or outdoors in conditions that may be wet or desert-like, freezing or steamy, clean or dirty. Millwrights work hard in conditions that may be difficult and on problems that often must be fixed quickly.

Millwrights often work with machinery that may have razor sharp blades or parts that move at tremendous speeds or may be extremely hot or cold. Some machines may contain toxic chemicals. The places where millwrights work may pose other safety risks as well. For instance, millwrights may have to work on scaffolding or deep underground. For all these reasons, health and safety are especially important considerations. Millwrights wear hard hats and, depending on the conditions, often wear eye protection, ear protection, gloves, work boots, and protective clothing.

...millwrights size up a mechanical problem and provide a solution.

CRITICAL THINKING Do you have a good sense of what makes machines run? Do you like working with engines and keeping them in running condition? Could you take a machine apart and then reassemble the pieces in the proper order? How might a career as a millwright be right for you?

4 What Is a Pile Driver?

Have you ever gone boating, tied the boat to a dock, and wondered what the dock was connected to under the water? Maybe you have looked at a tall skyscraper and wondered why it doesn't sink into the ground. Or perhaps you wondered what could possibly hold up a large bridge that supports hundreds of cars and trucks. The answer to all these questions lies with the pile driver.

Skyscrapers, sports stadiums, bridges, dams, and other large structures don't just sit on the ground or on an unsupported concrete foundation. If they did, they would slowly settle into the earth and eventually topple over. Many types of structures and the foundations on which they rest must be supported by sturdy concrete, wood, or metal shafts, called **pile**, which are driven deep into the ground. The skilled worker who installs the pile is called a **pile driver**.

how i see myself

Brent McLain has been a commercial diver in San Francisco for five years. A day's work might include resisting a 5-knot current while dragging 200 feet of hose, using power tools underwater in total darkness, and fending off curious harbor seals. McLain helps maintain pier pile, salvages wrecks, and assists officers with homeland security. Are you up for the challenge and adventure of an underwater pile driver?

Pile drivers also make it possible to build bridges and causeways that span broad expanses of water.

Pile drivers install pile to hold back the earth during excavations, to stabilize the foundations of large buildings, bridges, and dams, and to build docks and wharfs. **Pile drivers work with the heavy machinery** used to drive pile into the earth. Some pile drivers are also commercial divers who do the underwater construction necessary to provide sound foundations for bridges and other structures that are supported over water.

Pile driving is a bold occupation. **Pile drivers work with heavy equipment** to provide foundations for some of the world's largest and most impressive structures. The work of pile drivers makes it possible to build the dams that hold back rivers to provide water for drinking, irrigation, and hydroelectric power. Pile drivers also make it possible to build bridges and causeways that span broad expanses of water.

pile driving is a bold occupation

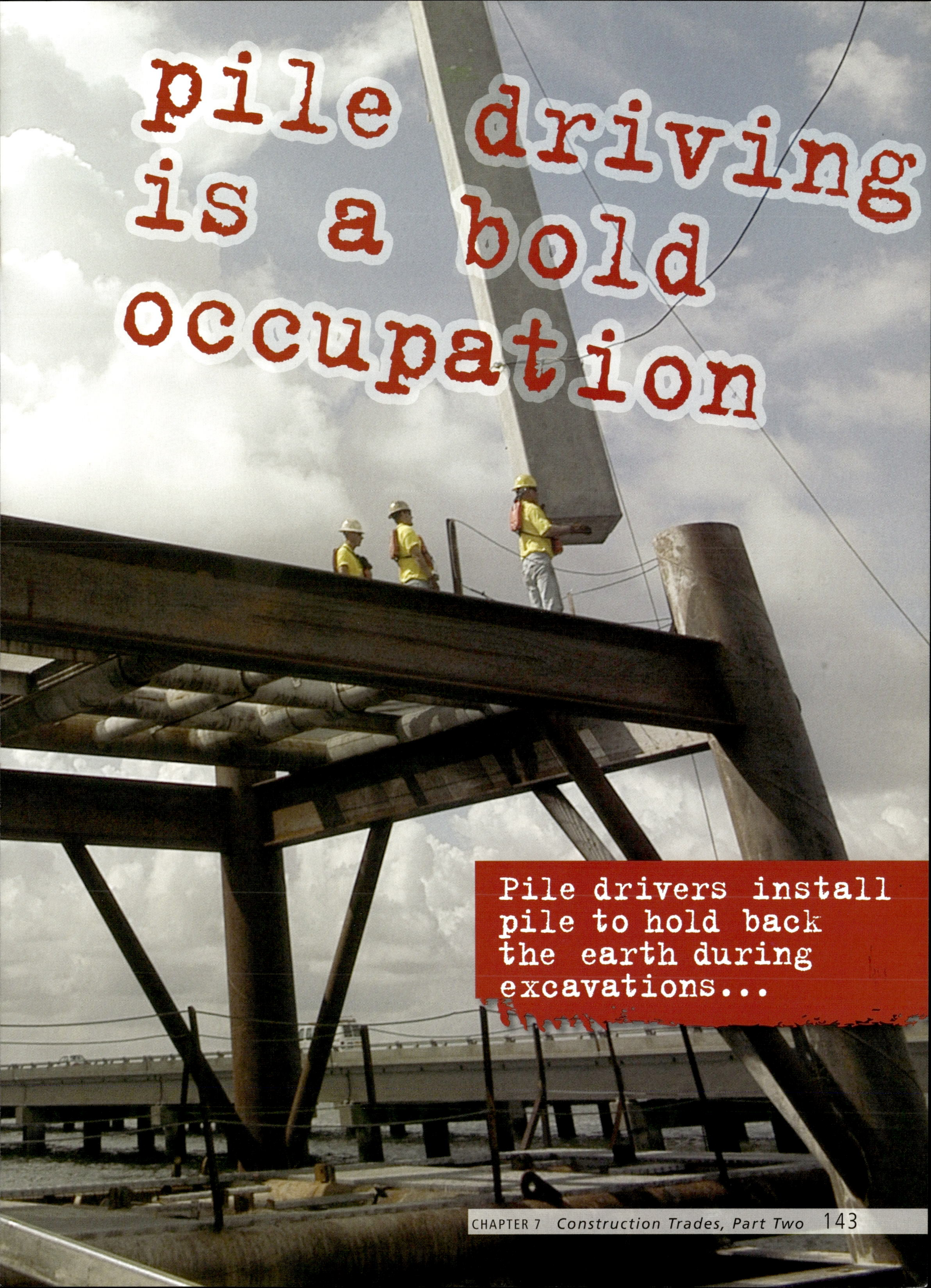

Pile drivers install pile to hold back the earth during excavations...

shout out!

Workers in Millbury, Massachusetts are immersed in training—in a 7,000-gallon underwater training tank. "One of the areas we knew was going to get bigger was the offshore gas pipeline industry," said Dave Borrus of the New England Regional Council of Carpenters. "We're teaching underwater welding, but there are a lot of underwater tasks that can be taught in it," Borrus said. Government contracts and regulations often specify that workers be certified in underwater skills, Borrus said. With energy security and road and highway investment becoming top 21st-century national priorities, the new training tank is going to make a big splash in providing skilled workers for construction and maintenance projects.

How Pile Drivers Do Their Jobs The work that pile drivers do is accurately described by the name of their occupation. Pile drivers operate heavy equipment to expertly and efficiently maneuver and drive pile into the earth during the early stages of a construction project. They also perform cutting and welding tasks both above and below water.

What's It Like at Work? Pile drivers are often the first workers to arrive on a construction site, and in most cases, their work must be completed before other types of construction work can begin. Pile drivers nearly always work outdoors and often work in every sort of weather. Their work is physically demanding and can be dangerous. Pile drivers wear hard hats, steel-toed work boots, eye protection, ear protection, and gloves. Personal flotation devices are also required when they work over water. Also, since docks, wharves, bridges, and piers frequently involve working on or around water from boats and barges, pile drivers need to know and follow the rules of seamanship.

CRITICAL THINKING

Would you like to play an important role in the construction of big, impressive structures such as skyscrapers and bridges? How do you think a career as a pile driver might be right for you?

5 Other Construction Occupations

The world of construction includes many other occupations. The rest of this chapter is devoted to describing some of these occupations, which range from boilermaker to sheet metal worker. One or more of these occupations may interest you as a career, and most can be entered through an apprenticeship program.

boilermaker

Electric power plants and many types of manufacturing facilities rely on steam boilers that must resist tremendous pressures. These boilers are assembled, installed, tested, maintained, and repaired by a **boilermaker**. The work done by boilermakers includes bolting and welding plate sections, tubes, drums, headers, pumps, and many other parts and pieces of equipment related to steam boilers. Boilermakers have a solid understanding of the techniques of steam power generation as well as geometry. They also are knowledgeable in the safe and efficient use of hand and power tools and equipment.

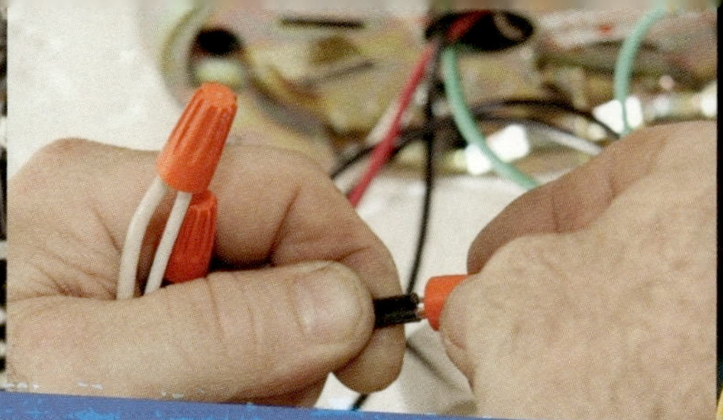

electrician

It is almost impossible to imagine a modern structure that has not been wired for electricity. Electricians safely install the electric wiring that provides light and power into nearly every room of every building. Today's electricians also install and maintain the wires and cables that bring computer and communication services to homes, businesses, schools, hospitals, factories, and government facilities. Electricians must be willing to work indoors and outdoors in all weather conditions. They need an aptitude for mathematics and physics and should be able to understand complex technical drawings.

bricklayer

Bricklaying is a very old and respected occupation. The work done by bricklayers not only enhances the structural integrity of buildings but often adds to their beauty as well. A **bricklayer** works with brick, stone, concrete block, adobe, and materials which may or may not be secured together with mortar. Bricklayers often work from scaffolding and must be able to handle heavy materials. The skills needed to properly place, point, and caulk building materials may take years to learn.

glazier

Glass makes houses and large buildings more livable by allowing natural light to reach their interiors. Glass also adds character and style to both ultramodern and more traditional architectural designs. A **glazier** is the highly skilled construction worker who handles, cuts, and installs glass in buildings and houses. Glaziers also construct frames for glass or work with products such as sliding glass doors that combine glass with metal frames, tracks, or rollers. They must be familiar with a variety of chemical sealants used to make installed glass panels airtight and watertight. Glaziers work both inside and outside buildings and sometimes work at considerable heights from scaffolding. Their work can be dangerous, and they must take great care to avoid breakage and cuts. Glaziers must have an aptitude for math and geometry and must be able to handle heavy materials.

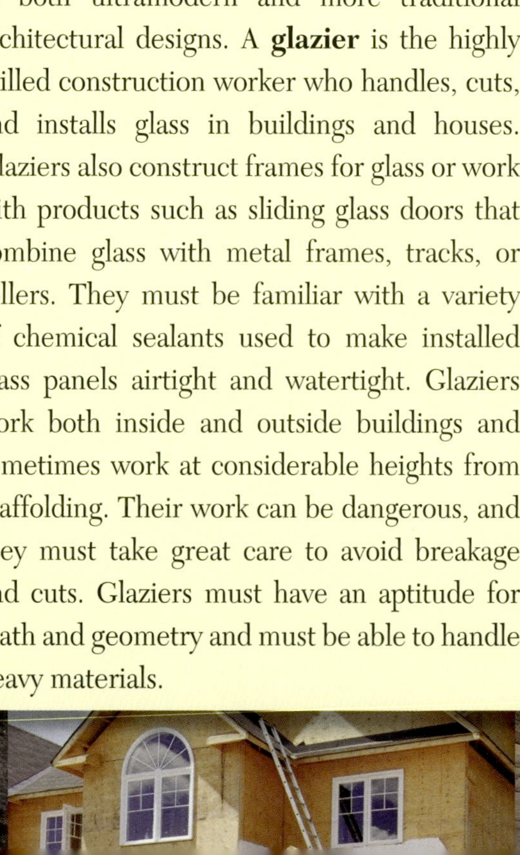

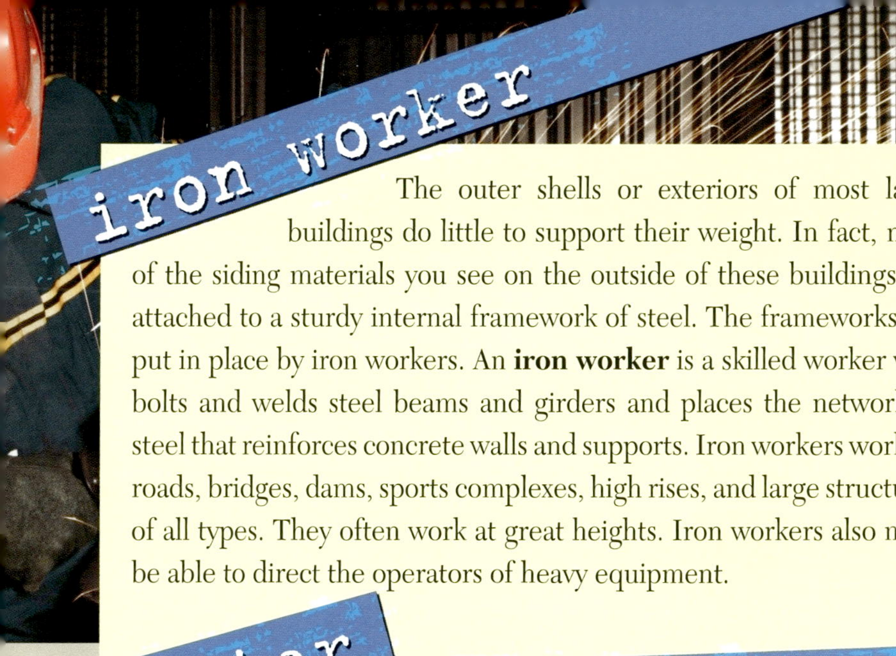

iron worker

The outer shells or exteriors of most large buildings do little to support their weight. In fact, most of the siding materials you see on the outside of these buildings are attached to a sturdy internal framework of steel. The frameworks are put in place by iron workers. An **iron worker** is a skilled worker who bolts and welds steel beams and girders and places the network of steel that reinforces concrete walls and supports. Iron workers work on roads, bridges, dams, sports complexes, high rises, and large structures of all types. They often work at great heights. Iron workers also must be able to direct the operators of heavy equipment.

painter
wallpaper hanger
drywall finisher

The interior walls of buildings and homes would look very plain and unattractive without the benefit of paint, wallpaper, and other finishes. The basic job of a painter and a wallpaper hanger is probably obvious without much further explanation. On the other hand, you may not be as familiar with the work of a **drywall finisher**. Once sheets of drywall have been attached to the interior walls and ceilings of a building or house, it is the job of drywall finishers to make all the individual sheets of drywall look like a continuous, smooth surface. Once this is done, drywall finishers often add decorative textures to make the surfaces more pleasing to the eye and also to hide surface imperfections. Most of the work of drywall finishers is done using paper tape and a plaster-like material called joint compound.

As for painters, they skillfully apply paint to the interiors of buildings and houses. They also paint the outside of certain buildings, homes, and structures such as bridges and water tanks. To do these jobs properly, painters must know the characteristics of a variety of paints and know how to apply each one. They must also be very detailed oriented and possess a strong sense of color and design. These characteristics also apply to wallpaper hangers, who must know how to select and apply a variety of adhesives and wallpapers.

building a better u

"Doing a great job is more than showing up and working a day's pay just to get better pay; it's when all the training and experience you've had falls into place. Pride in workmanship is also what many wish for and never achieve." Entrepreneur David A. Goldsmith points out that no matter what your occupation is, taking pride in what you do is what really counts.

pipefitter

In order for many industries to operate effectively, their facilities must have systems of pipes to deliver chemicals and various other products. These delivery systems may provide refrigeration to large buildings, move oil or gas to refineries, or supply hydraulic power to factories. A **pipefitter** installs and maintains these sturdy and often highly complex delivery systems of pipes. To do this, pipefitters must be skilled at cutting and bending metal pipes and connecting them to create leak-free joints that do not resist the flow of liquids and other materials. Pipefitters must be able to read and understand very complex drawings and be able to handle heavy materials. They must also be skilled at welding.

plumber

Plumbers have a hand in the construction and regular maintenance of just about every type of structure. They construct and repair the piping systems that deliver water to faucets, showers, toilets, washing machines, ice makers, and even swimming pools. They also provide the pipe systems and drains that carry away unwanted water and other wastes. To do this work, plumbers must know how to cut and make leak-free joints in steel, copper, and PVC pipes. Plumbers use torches to make solder joints and adhesives to make joints in PVC. Plumbers need an aptitude for mechanics and design and they must be able to read and understand complex drawings and technical data.

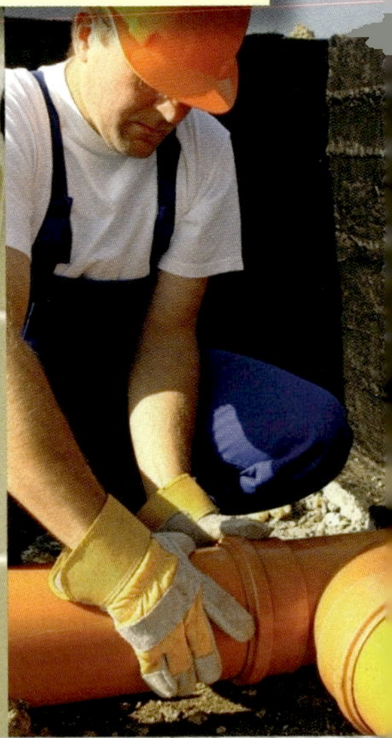

plasterer

Plasterers follow the lathers and add the artistic touches that turn the framework into a tree, rock, or decorative item. They do this by applying plaster once the lath has been installed. The interior and exterior surfaces of buildings and other structures are often covered with plaster, stucco, gypsum, and similar materials. Plasterers apply these materials with a trowel to cover the surfaces and create attractive designs. Plasterers are often required to do their work on scaffolding or lifts, where safety is a major consideration. Plasterers also need considerable manual dexterity and must pay close attention to detail.

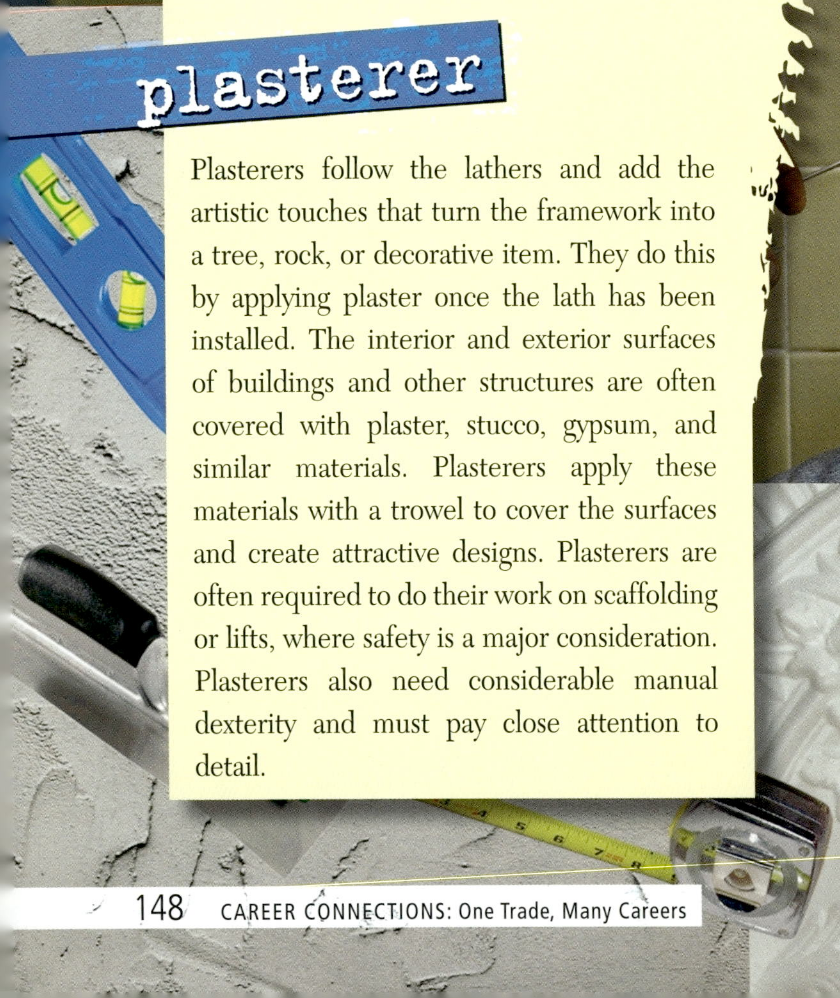

roofer

Nearly every building and home needs a roof to keep out the rain and weather. In fact, without a properly installed roof, most buildings would very soon become water damaged and begin to fall apart. Although roofers are not the workers who build the roof, they are the ones that make roofs waterproof. Roofers install and repair roofs with a wide variety of materials including rubber membranes, hot tar and gravel, slate, tile, and shingles. For obvious reasons, roofers usually work in high places and much of their work is done outdoors where they may be faced with all sorts of weather conditions. A roofer's work can be physically demanding and it requires strength as well as manual dexterity.

sheet metal worker

A **sheet metal worker** cuts, assembles, installs, and maintains a wide variety of sheet metal products that are used in the construction of most buildings and homes. For example, sheet metal workers install the duct work associated with heating, cooling, and ventilation systems. They also install metal walls, roofs, gutters, and architectural sheet metal that give buildings a modern appearance.

Sheet metal workers must be familiar with many different hand tools and specialized equipment designed to cut, bend, and roll sheet metal into various shapes. Sheet metal workers must also understand the characteristics of different kinds of metal, and they must know how to use a variety of fasteners and welding equipment. And, because they are making three-dimensional shapes with flat materials, sheet metal workers are also well served by their knowledge of geometry and math. They must also remain aware and take the necessary precautions when working with sharp pieces of sheet metal.

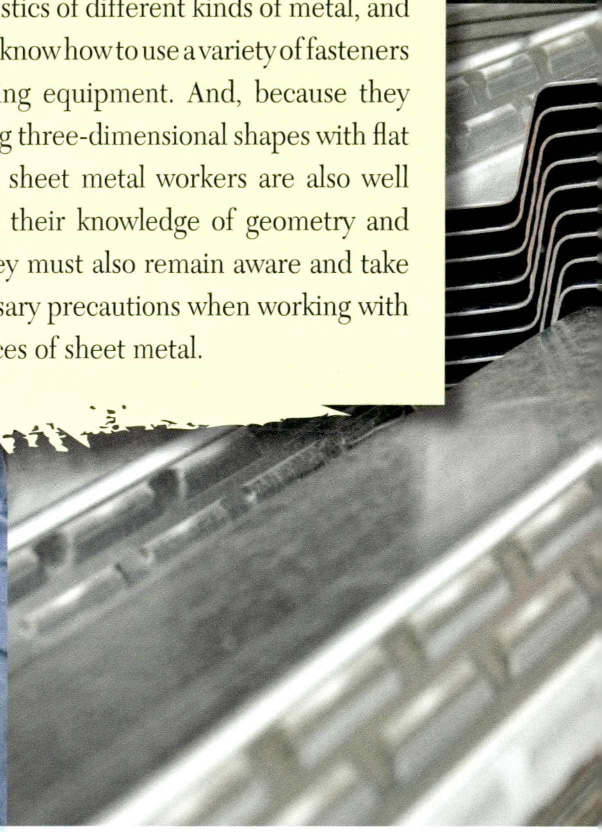

Chapter Check

On a separate piece of paper, write your answers to the following questions:

Multiple Choice

1. Which of the following would most likely work with adhesive materials?
   a) lather
   b) floor coverer
   c) bricklayer
   d) boilermaker

2. Which of the following occupations would most likely involve welding?
   a) glazier
   b) roofer
   c) electrician
   d) pile driver

3. Which of the following occupations requires the most precise measuring, sometimes to $^{1}/_{1000}$ of an inch?
   a) floor coverer
   b) pile driver
   c) millwright
   d) lather

4. For which of the following is it most critical to match the pattern, color, and direction of materials?
   a) millwright
   b) glazier
   c) floor coverer
   d) sheet metal worker

Fill in the Blank

5. A(n) ________________ has the job of making a roller coaster safe.

6. An ornate, curved ceiling is the work of a (n) ________________.

7. When building a new sports stadium, the first workers on the scene to build the foundation are ________________.

True or False

8. Plasterers add the finishing touches to the frameworks created by lathers. *T or F*

9. The internal frameworks of tall buildings are put in place by pile drivers. *T or F*

10. The jobsite for a millwright could be a nuclear power plant. *T or F*

Important Words

Boilermaker Skilled worker who assembles, installs, tests, maintains, and repairs equipment at facilities that rely on steam power generation.

Bricklayer Skilled worker who installs brick, stone, concrete block, adobe, and other materials that are often secured together with mortar.

Floor coverer Skilled worker who installs a variety of floor covering materials and maintains, repairs, or replaces existing flooring.

Glazier Skilled worker who handles, cuts, and installs glass in large buildings and houses.

Iron worker Skilled worker who bolts and welds steel beams and girders and installs these frameworks to reinforce concrete walls and supports for roads, bridges, dams, high rises, and large structures of all types.

Lather Skilled worker who creates walls, ceilings, or objects by erecting metal structures and then covering them with plaster or other surfacing material.

Millwright Skilled worker who installs and maintains compressors, pumps, conveyors, mining equipment and many other kinds of machinery.

Pile driver Skilled worker who installs concrete, wood, or metal shafts into the ground to support the foundations of large structures, docks and wharfs, and to hold back the earth during excavations.

Pipefitter Skilled worker who installs and maintains the complex delivery systems of pipes by cutting, bending, and connecting them so they can provide such products as refrigeration, oil, or gas.

Sheet metal worker Skilled worker who cuts, assembles, installs, and maintains a wide variety of sheet metal products, such as duct work, metal walls, and gutters, that are used in the construction of most buildings.

On the Trail of . . .

One way to discover what your ideal career might be is to see if you are drawn to any particular materials. On a piece of paper, make a list of the following building materials: wood, tile, plaster, steel, cement, stone, glass, drywall, metal. Add additional materials or building parts that come to mind. Circle the items on your list that interest you most. Next to these items, write the trades that use them. If this doesn't help you narrow down your career options, try the same exercise by listing such activities as: welding, excavating, wiring, sculpting, plastering, fixing machinery, operating heavy machinery, cutting and fitting. Add additional activities that come to mind. Circle the activities that you might want to do and identify the trades that engage in them.

.com

Actions proposed by the federal government to improve our infrastructure will create jobs for people in the construction trades. What does "infrastructure" mean? What kinds of construction projects will be needed to improve it? Which trades will need workers? Use the internet to research the answers.

Being the First Choice

Apprenticeship programs for the occupations described in this chapter will teach you the required skills. But knowing your aptitudes is important—for choosing a job and for an employer choosing you. Take personal inventory. How do you rate in the following areas: manual dexterity, eye-hand coordination, physical fitness (including strength and agility), sense of balance, sense of color, mechanical aptitude, ability to solve basic math problems quickly and accurately, ability to work as part of a team, ability to effectively communicate instructions to others. Write down examples of your proven abilities in any of these areas that you might describe in an interview for an apprenticeship program.

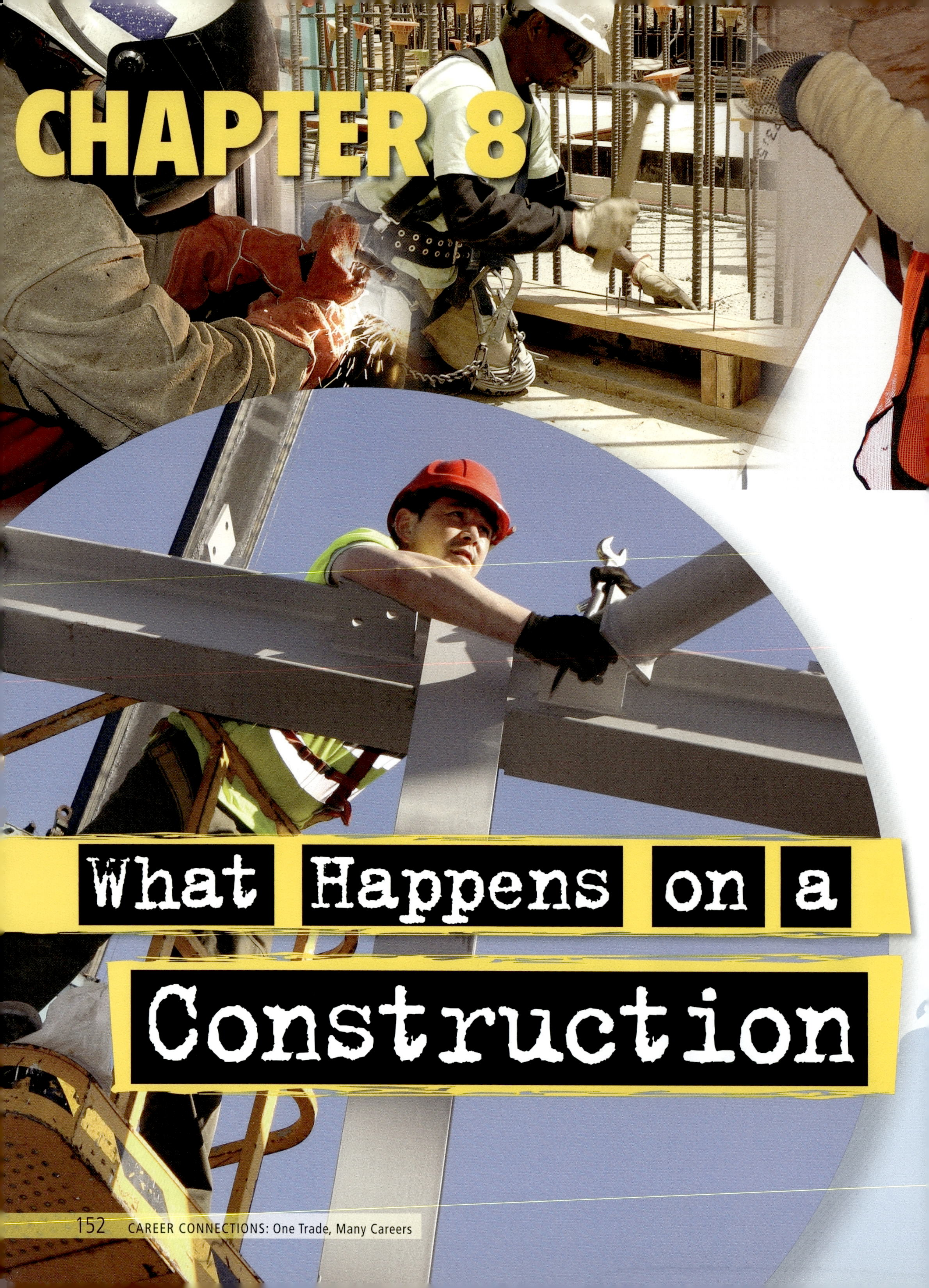

CHAPTER 8

What Happens on a Construction

If you have never had a job before, going to work will be a new experience. The workplace is a place where people work together to achieve a common purpose. Interesting and exciting things happen there, and it's a place where things get done. If the workplace is a construction site, then it is also a place where things get built.

On construction sites, just as in other workplaces, people are assigned roles and responsibilities.

These roles and responsibilities usually involve the use of tools and of special technical processes and procedures. Construction workers must be highly skilled in the safe and efficient use of their tools and know how to properly care for them. Clearly, all of the personal habits, skills, and attitudes necessary for a successful career are demonstrated on the job site. Workers also must be committed to following the rules and standards established by their company, their occupation, and federal and local agencies. Especially important are rules that affect safety.

What You Now Know

- That there are many choices of career paths
- That one or more of these choices interest you

What You Will Know

- How a construction site is operated
- The roles and responsibilities of the people working on a construction site
- The skills necessary to be successful in construction
- The critical role safety plays on the jobsite

Site?

exciting things happen

1 What Is a Construction Site?

A construction site is any place where a structure is being built or remodeled. It may begin as an empty field, a vacant lot on a city or suburban block, a few acres of forest, or someday even in outer space. A construction site may be alive with workers and crammed with materials and equipment, or it may be a relatively quiet and peaceful place. The sights and sounds of a construction site are determined by the type and size of the project, the stage of the construction process, and how much work is being done at the time.

Can you see yourself one day working on a construction site?

CRITICAL THINKING How would you recognize a construction site? What activities on a construction site do you find interesting? Can you see yourself one day working on a construction site?

STAGES OF CONSTRUCTION

A construction site may seem like a chaotic place with workers and machines coming and going. But actually, construction is an orderly process. **All structures are built in carefully planned stages.** Usually, one part of the process must be complete, or almost complete, before workers move to the next part of the process. The construction process will differ from project to project, but most structures are built in the following basic stages:

* **Site Preparation** Before construction can begin, the site must be properly prepared. Any trees, shrubs, or existing structures that may interfere with the construction process must be cleared away, and then the ground is prepared. This stage of the construction process is sometimes called **clearing and grading**.

* **Establishing the Foundation** The ground may seem hard if you trip and fall on it, but natural soils and rock formations are not firm enough to support modern buildings. To keep them from sinking into the ground and eventually toppling over, buildings are placed on top of a solid **footing** made of reinforced concrete. The footing is the part of the foundation that bears on the prepared soil. The foundation above the footing is also made of reinforced concrete, or concrete block, or a combination of these materials. In many cases the foundation is further supported by steel, wood, or concrete pile driven deep into the ground.

Erecting a Framework Just as the human body is supported by a skeleton of bone, buildings are supported by a framework of wood, reinforced concrete, or structural steel. Houses usually have a wooden framework. Tall commercial buildings and most other large structures are built around a framework of structural steel or reinforced concrete. Regardless of the material used, the framework must be in place before further construction can be done, such as the building of walls.

Installing Underground Utilities Pipes, wires, and cables that will bring water, natural gas, electricity, and various communications services to the building may be put in place either before or while the framework is being erected.

Enclosing the Building Once the framework is in place, walls, floors, roofs, and ceilings are added. Bulky components such as storage tanks, boilers, or large air conditioning compressors may also be installed at this time. When building skyscrapers or other tall structures, workers may enclose lower floors while the framework for the upper levels is still being erected.

Finishing the Exterior While the outer walls and face of a building add little or no support to the building, they do provide protection from the elements and give the building its architectural or decorative appearance. Finishing the exteriors of tall buildings usually requires working from scaffolding. Work on the exterior of a structure may continue right up until the building is put into service.

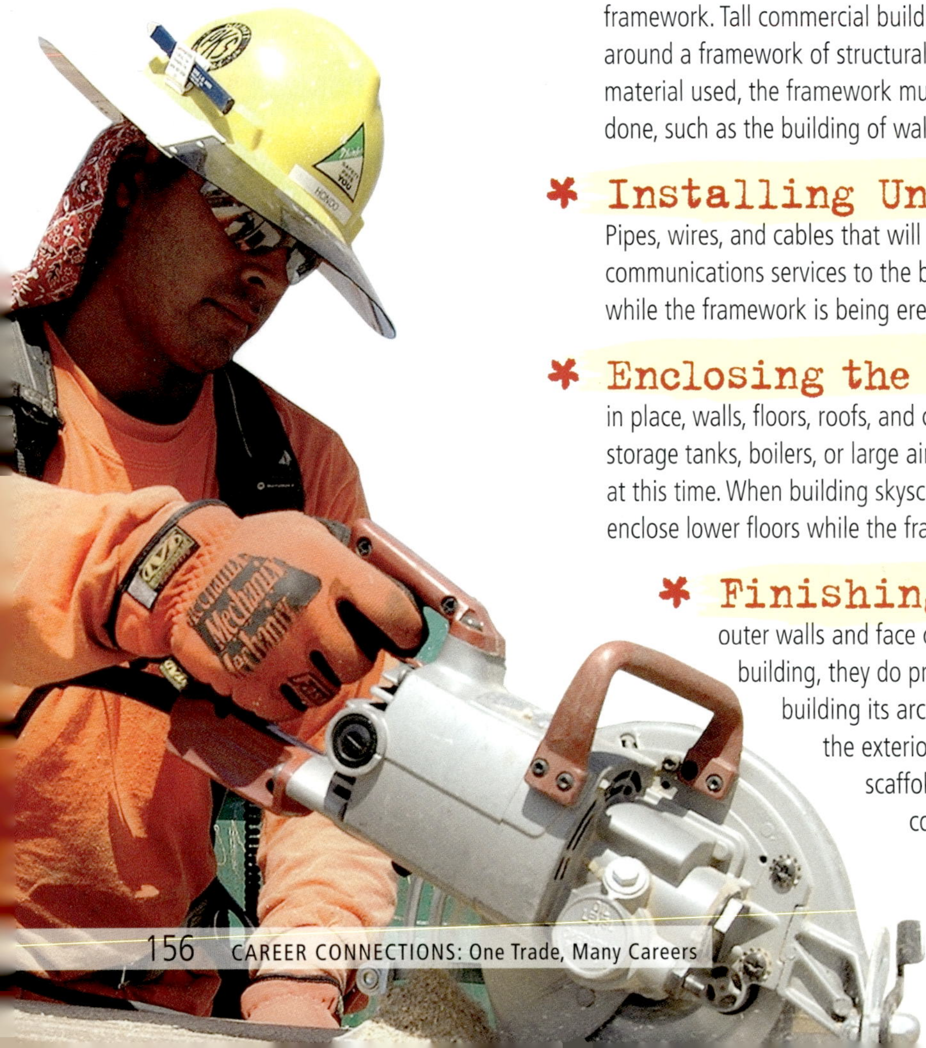

Finishing the Interior

Since the interior of a building is where people live or work, finishing that part of the structure is an extremely important and complicated process. Finishing the interiors of large commercial buildings usually involves the installation of complex systems and machinery that has been manufactured elsewhere and brought to the construction site. Once ventilation, heating, and air conditioning ducts are placed, wiring and plumbing must be installed. Rooms and hallways must be laid out, framed, and finished. Interior finishes such as wall and floor coverings must be installed. Then, cabinets are mounted and many other furnishings and decorative elements are added to make the interior complete.

Inspections Construction work is inspected at almost every stage by clients, architects, construction superintendents, and government inspectors. This is done to make sure the work is of high quality, meets the specifications of the project, and complies with safety codes and regulations. When a house or other building is complete, it will receive final inspections. Once the structure passes its inspections and is acceptable to the client, it is no longer a construction site. It is a finished building ready to be occupied.

Respecting Construction Sites A construction site is a place where many different types of work may be going on at the same time. It's a place where materials are being delivered and put to use, where power tools and heavy machinery are in operation, where open pits may have been excavated, and where unwary visitors would be exposed to all sorts of hazards. A construction site is a dangerous place and it is a place where workers must be able to do their jobs without distractions. For all these reasons, a construction site is a closed area. Only the workers and those who have official business to conduct should be allowed on the site.

Many construction sites are fenced and most are posted with signs that say KEEP OUT, CONSTRUCTION SITE, HARD HAT AREA, and so on. These fences and signs are put in place to keep members of the general public from accidently wandering onto a construction site where they may be injured. However, these signs and barriers may also serve to remind construction workers that a construction site is a special place where certain rules of safety and behavior must be followed. For instance, hard hats and other required safety gear are worn at all times on a construction site. When on a construction site, it is also important for workers to be constantly alert to their surroundings, and to avoid distracting other workers because this may interfere with their efficiency and may even place them in danger.

shout out!

A hundred years ago, the hard hat didn't exist. Miners used to protect their heads by wearing what resembled a baseball cap with a leather brim. In 1915, the E.D. Bullard Company, looking for ways to improve industrial safety, developed a hat that resembled a helmet worn by soldiers in World War I. The new hat was made out of steamed canvas, glue, and black paint. It was called the "Hard-Boiled Hat" because of the steam used in the manufacturing process. The first construction site in history that required hard hats was in San Francisco, when construction began on the Golden Gate Bridge in 1933.

CRITICAL THINKING Are the construction sites in your community fenced off and posted with warning signs? Does the public respect these construction sites?

2 Construction Roles and Responsibilities

Each worker involved in a construction project is assigned a function which, in some cases, may overlap with the functions of other workers. This section lists and describes various types of workers who contribute to a construction project. Some of the careers, such as architect and engineer, require four or more years of post-secondary education.

Architect Every structure that gets built is planned or designed by someone. Usually, this person is an **architect**. Architects apply their knowledge of art, engineering, materials, and the way people use structures when they draw plans for a building. Eventually, the architect will produce prints, which are scale drawings of the building. These indicate the dimensions of rooms, walls, ceilings, and floors. The architect may even produce a scale model of the structure to give clients and project managers a better idea of how the finished structure will look. In many cases, the architect will help supervise construction of the building.

Designer The tasks handled by architects and designers often overlap. A **designer** provides plans, sketches, scale drawings, prints, and scale models of buildings or significant portions of them. Designers may be more focused on the appearance and functional aspects of a structure than on the engineering necessary to build it.

Engineer Schooled in math, physics, and the structural sciences, an **engineer** is concerned with the structural integrity of a building and the materials used to build it. For instance, it is an engineer's responsibility to know whether a particular type of foundation or roof support can hold the weight that it must support. It's the engineer's job to make sure the structure is safe and functions as intended.

designer sketches plans draws scale models

General Contractor A **general contractor** is responsible for building and completing an individual project such as a house, a large commercial structure, or a housing complex development. The general contractor is accountable to the owner of the project.

General Superintendent A **general superintendent** is an employee of the general contractor. General superintendents oversee one or several construction projects and supervise one or more project superintendents. They also work with project managers, sub-contractors, and suppliers. A general superintendent has overall responsibility for completing projects on schedule and within a fixed budget. General superintendents may visit construction sites to make sure that the work is being done efficiently and that safety rules are being followed.

> ...work is being done efficiently and safety rules are being followed.

Project Manager While a project manager may seem similar to a general superintendent, the work of a project manager focuses more on schedules, cost estimation and control, timely payments, and completion, than on hands-on construction.

Project Superintendent A **project superintendent** manages the workers on a given project or group of projects. Project superintendents assign tasks to foremen, who in turn supervise individual workers or teams of workers. Superintendents schedule the delivery of materials and equipment, and they also handle personnel problems and safety issues. They are also responsible for the quality of the finished structure and for the safety of the workers who build it.

Subcontractor Usually, a general contractor hires a number of subcontractors. A **subcontractor** is a skilled worker who handles various aspects of construction such as painting walls or installing plumbing. Subcontractors may also be companies that provide the skilled workers needed to complete the project, such as insulators, roofers, electricians or plumbers.

how i see myself

Can you see yourself working on a construction site? Job opportunities in the construction trade are expected to be excellent over the next decade, according to the Bureau of Labor Statistics. Contractors in many areas are already reporting difficulty finding skilled workers, and there will be a need to replace the large number of workers who will be retiring. Employment is expected to grow in nonresidential construction. Many industrial plants will have to be replaced or remodeled. Construction of nursing homes and all types of healthcare facilities will be needed for the growing elderly population. Construction of new schools as well as replacement and renovation of older schools will also be needed.

...what kind of a career path can you envision for yourself?

Foreperson Individuals or crews handling a particular kind of work on a construction site may be supervised by a **foreperson** (formerly called foreman). In addition to supervising, a foreperson may even do some of the work. A foreperson assigns individual tasks and makes sure the work gets done properly.

Journey Worker A journey worker, (formerly called a journeyman), is a highly experienced and skilled construction worker from any of the construction trades who handles assigned tasks. It's the journey workers and apprentices on the construction site who actually build the structure.

Apprentice Apprentices are less experienced workers who are learning their trade while working alongside experienced journey workers. At first they may be assigned to handle materials and to do other tasks that do not require much skill. As they become more experienced, they are given jobs that require more skill and know-how. In time, worthy apprentices will handle jobs at the same level of responsibility as the journey worker and will earn the right to be called journey workers themselves.

CRITICAL THINKING When you read these job descriptions, what kind of a career path can you envision for yourself? Which of the jobs described here can you see yourself doing?

3 Skills Needed on a Construction Site

Construction work requires a wide range of skills. The personal skills needed on a construction site are the same as those required for any other type of employment. **Construction workers** must be able to listen carefully and speak clearly. They must be able to respond well to supervision and work with others as part of an effective team. They **must be able to manage time, make decisions, and solve problems.** They must be reliable, on time, and ready to do their best work every day. They should know how to think critically, that is, to ask the right questions and to recognize meaningful answers. Every worker should also have well developed basic skills such as reading, writing, and math.

Construction workers must have the hands-on skills needed to use tools that are required for the job. Reading and interpreting prints, using a computer, and executing a complex construction process are required technical skills. When workers step onto a construction site, they must bring all of these skills with them.

Experienced construction workers know how to safely and efficiently use many different hand tools and power tools. They know how to safely and efficiently use wood, metal, drywall, concrete, and many other materials. And they know how to make proper use of technical processes such as forming a level foundation, installing a staircase, or stretching a carpet.

nailing it!

Using the right tools for the job is critical on a construction site. And knowing how to identify tools and materials is equally important. Skilled tradespeople know which power tool or hand tool is needed and when. They can recognize one grade of material from another. They know one drill bit from another. They know the difference between a nut, bolt, screw, spacer, rivet, and clip and the tools needed for driving them. Do you know the nuts and bolts of building materials and tools, and is it something you want to learn?

CRITICAL THINKING What are the three kinds of skills needed by a construction worker?

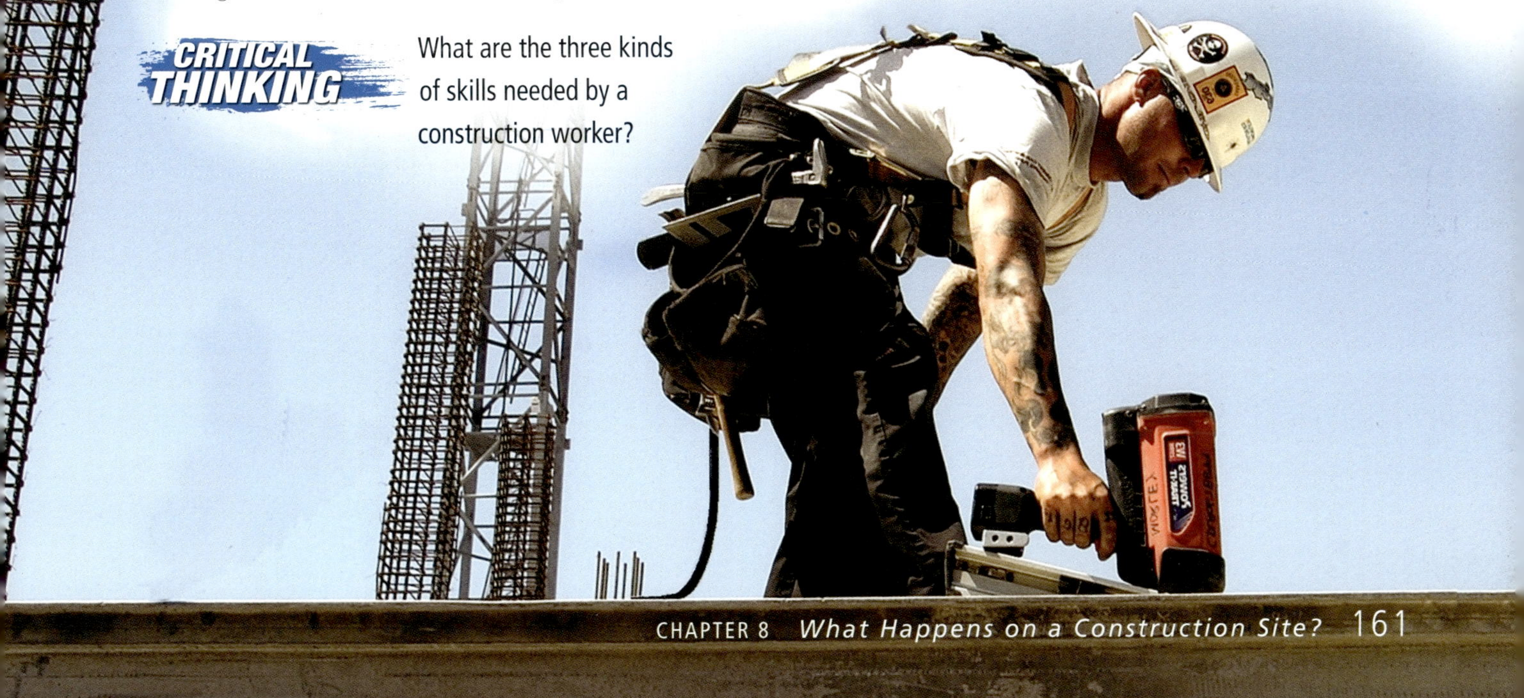

4 The Critical Importance of Safety

You may be wondering why safety is addressed in a book that deals with making a career choice. Actually, there are a couple of good reasons. Probably the most important reason is the fact that safety is essential on every construction project. While a career in construction can be very rewarding, it can also be dangerous if safety isn't followed at all times.

The human costs of work-related injuries are obvious. No one wants a worker to be injured or for the worker's family to share the burden of that injury. However, accidents and injuries that happen on the job have other costs as well. They cause production delays, and all too often they cause the loss of talented and highly trained workers. The government or an injured worker's union may have to provide supplemental income and pay for rehabilitation costs. When a worker is injured on the job, nobody wins. However, the ones who lose the most are the injured workers themselves.

...prevention is typically the key to staying safe.

Even small accidents can cause lasting harm to you, your career, your family, your union, your employer, or your community. Depending on the severity of the injury, you may lose the ability to do certain tasks. You may lose a finger, an arm, a toe, or a leg. You may lose the ability to see or hear. You may even lose your life. So, it is easy to understand why safety must be the first thing you consider when you go to work in the morning and throughout the work day. Many rules and regulations have been established to keep workers safe while on the job and these rules and regulations have been very effective in reducing the number of job-related injuries.

Another reason to discuss safety is that many of you will decide that you have an interest in a career in construction, and you may build some of the projects included in the Career Connections project books. Understanding the important role that safety plays in the workplace is beneficial before any project is started. As with almost anything in life, prevention is typically the key to staying safe.

Accidents Waiting to Happen

What causes accidents? Generally speaking, accidents are caused by a failure to be observant and to make safety the first priority. No job is safe if workers don't pay attention to what's around them and to what they are doing. No job is safe if workers don't put safety first. However, accidents often have more specific causes such as the following.

* **Failure to Follow the Rules** Work rules and regulations are put in place by companies and by federal, state, and local governments to protect lives and property. Workers who don't follow the rules put themselves and others in danger.
* **Lack of Communication** Workers arriving on a construction site for the first time may not be aware of the work rules and hazards associated with that particular project. They should be told about these rules and risks immediately. Clear communication with other workers on a construction site is vital. Everyone on the site should be warned when a worker is about to do something that may be hazardous to others, such as digging a new trench or connecting an electric power cable.
* **Failure to Observe Warning Signs** Construction site hazards should be clearly marked by warning signs. For example, a sign may say DANGER: HIGH VOLTAGE or EAR PROTECTION REQUIRED BEYOND THIS POINT. Workers must observe these signs and take the proper precautions.
* **Unsafe Work Habits** Workers with well organized work habits are less likely to be injured. Tools should be kept clean and in good working order. When tools and materials are not in use, they should be properly stored.
* **Lack of Skill** Even the simplest tools can be dangerous if they are not respected and used properly. For example, the sharp edges of cutting tools must be kept away from the hands and body at all times. Power tools can be especially dangerous and should not be used by anyone who lacks the necessary skill. Workers should never attempt to use an unfamiliar tool without supervision.
* **Alcohol and Substance Abuse** Intoxicating substances have no place on a construction site. Workers under the influence of these substances threaten the safety of everyone around them, and they are likely to be dismissed and lose the respect of their coworkers. Even when intoxicants are used away from the construction site during off duty hours, they may prove hazardous to work safety. That is because workers who have used alcohol or other intoxicating substances are likely to come to work the next day with slower reaction times and less efficient work habits.

CRITICAL THINKING How much importance do you put on safety? Do you know anyone who has been injured on the job? Do you know anyone who has been permanently disabled by a job-related accident?

framing your future

If you choose a career in construction, you should know that there are federal regulations in place to ensure the safety and health of construction workers. These regulations are enforced by the Occupational Safety and Health Administration (OSHA), an agency of the U.S. Department of Labor. OSHA has specific regulations that require contractors to identify, eliminate, and control hazards on a construction site. OSHA provides training, outreach, and education. A network of 1,100 inspectors and over 200 OSHA offices monitor and encourage workplace safety and health throughout the country.

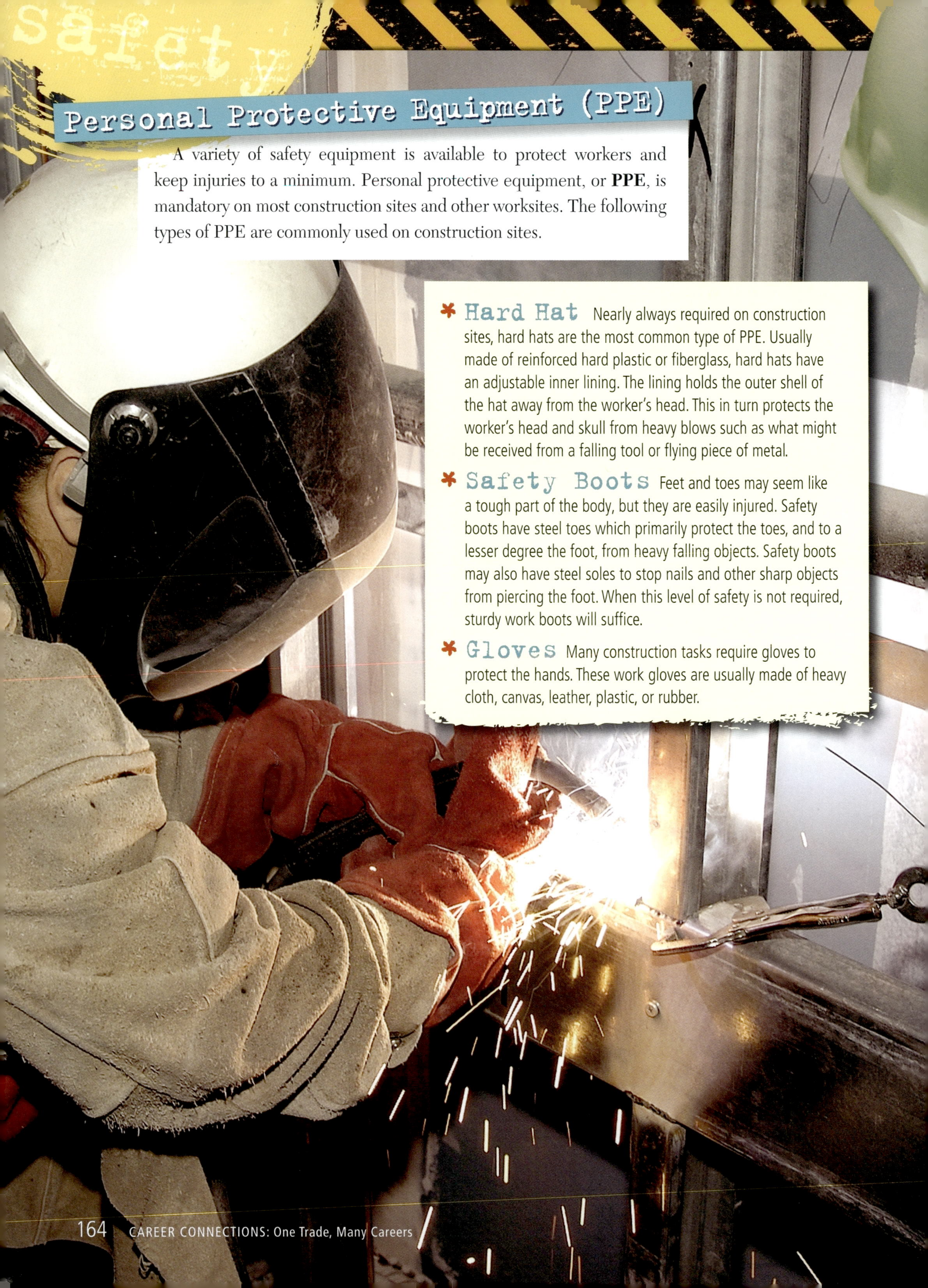

Personal Protective Equipment (PPE)

A variety of safety equipment is available to protect workers and keep injuries to a minimum. Personal protective equipment, or **PPE**, is mandatory on most construction sites and other worksites. The following types of PPE are commonly used on construction sites.

- **Hard Hat** Nearly always required on construction sites, hard hats are the most common type of PPE. Usually made of reinforced hard plastic or fiberglass, hard hats have an adjustable inner lining. The lining holds the outer shell of the hat away from the worker's head. This in turn protects the worker's head and skull from heavy blows such as what might be received from a falling tool or flying piece of metal.
- **Safety Boots** Feet and toes may seem like a tough part of the body, but they are easily injured. Safety boots have steel toes which primarily protect the toes, and to a lesser degree the foot, from heavy falling objects. Safety boots may also have steel soles to stop nails and other sharp objects from piercing the foot. When this level of safety is not required, sturdy work boots will suffice.
- **Gloves** Many construction tasks require gloves to protect the hands. These work gloves are usually made of heavy cloth, canvas, leather, plastic, or rubber.

* **Hearing Protection** Noises can damage the ears even if they are not loud enough to cause pain. Listening to loud noises, such as those caused by power tools, over a long period of time will almost certainly cause hearing loss. For this reason, workers exposed to loud noise should wear hearing protection. This usually consists of specially designed ear plugs or earmuffs that cup the ear and block out most noise.
* **Eye Protection** Eyes are the most easily injured part of the body, and eye damage is often difficult or impossible for doctors to repair. Safety glasses with side shields or wraparound lenses must be worn whenever there is the slightest danger of eyes being struck.
* **Face Shield or Hood** In some cases, a worker may need to protect the entire face as well as the eyes. A face shield or hood will prevent sparks and flying objects from striking the face. Welders use a tinted hood which protects the face and eyes not only from sparks but also from the intense brightness of the welding flash.
* **Respirator** Dangerous gases, dust, and other contaminants in the air may require the use of respirators. Respirators cover the mouth and nose and most are equipped with filters that remove contaminants. In some cases respirators are linked by hoses to tanks of compressed air or to external air supplies.
* **Safety Harness** When properly used, safety harnesses can prevent crippling or fatal falls. Safety harnesses typically consist of a series of straps that loop around the shoulders, legs, and pelvic area. Once the worker puts on the harness, it is attached to a secure anchor point with a lanyard, which is a short safety line. The lanyard is long enough to allow the worker to handle an assigned task, but short enough to prevent a disastrous fall.

building a better u

A safety harness is called a personal fall-arrest system. It is designed to arrest (stop) falls. Extensive fall-arrest training is provided to men and women who use these systems to make sure they fit properly and are comfortable. Workers using them come to regard them as a tool of the trade. As with other tools, workers learn how to properly adjust, maintain, and store them.

CRITICAL THINKING

Are you familiar with any of the PPE mentioned in this section? How would you respond to someone who sees hard hats, work gloves, or harnesses as trivial or "uncool"?

SAFETY practices

Safety practices such as wearing **a hard hat must become second nature**, like the daily habit of putting on shoes before you go outside. Construction workers learn about and develop good safety habits in much the same way they learn any other skill. In fact, well developed safety practices are just as important as work skills. That is because workers who are properly attentive to safety are most likely to make good employees and enjoy long and successful careers. The following tips will help you develop the skills you will need to function safely on a construction site.

Be observant at all times Keep your eyes and ears open to look and listen for potential safety hazards.

Know your tools Show respect for all hand tools and power tools. Even a simple tool such as a chisel can cause serious injury when not used or stored properly. Never use a tool with which you are unfamiliar. If you lack the skill needed to use a particular tool, don't attempt to use it without supervision and until you have developed the necessary skill.

Follow the rules Know all government and company safety regulations and never violate them for any reason. Keep up to date on changes in these regulations. If you have doubts about whether something you are doing will violate one of these rules, check with your supervisor.

Never rush an assignment When deadlines tighten, workers tend to get in a hurry. Studies show that workers are much more likely to be injured when a project is rushed. Work hard, but don't rush your work.

Make sure the work environment is safe Employers are required by law to maintain safe working conditions. If you are aware of safety violations or of unnoticed hazards where you work, point this out to your supervisor immediately.

Use personal protective gear Always use the PPE required by your assigned task or the conditions at the worksite. For instance, never work without wearing a properly anchored safety harness at heights where one is required. Be sure all your PPE is clean and in proper working condition, and make sure you know how to use it properly.

Know your task
Never try to do a job that you don't know how to do. If you know what you are doing, then you are more likely to do it safely. More than a few accidents and injuries have been caused by workers attempting to complete a process that they didn't understand. If you are assigned to do a task that you don't understand, point this out to your foreperson or supervisor so that you may be reassigned to a job that better fits your experience and training.

Know your limits
Do not attempt to handle a task that is too hard for you physically. For instance, don't try to lift or carry an object that is too heavy. If you are not strong enough or otherwise physically suited to a work assignment, enlist the help of a coworker.

Consider the safety of others
Never do anything that is likely to put others in danger. If you see a coworker approaching a hazard or about to do something dangerous, warn them. Watch out for your coworkers and they will watch out for you.

CRITICAL THINKING How do you think the habit of practicing safety first is acquired? Is practicing good safety habits just a matter of common sense? Do you think safety hazards remain the same throughout the job?

Chapter Check

On a separate piece of paper, write your answers to the following questions:

Multiple Choice

1. The construction process begins with which of the following stages?
   a) establishing the foundation
   b) enclosing the building
   c) site preparation
   d) installing underground utilities

2. Which building stage takes place after erecting a framework?
   a) installing underground utilities
   b) establishing the foundation
   c) enclosing the building
   d) finishing the exterior

3. Which of the following workers typically does hands-on work as well as supervising on a construction site?
   a) general contractor
   b) project superintendent
   c) journey worker
   d) foreperson

Fill in the Blank

4. Skilled workers such as insulators, electricians, and roofers are all examples of ____________________ that a general contractor hires to complete a construction project.

5. Workers wear ____________________ to protect against dangerous gases and dust in the air.

6. Safety boots are made with ____________________ to protect feet from sharp or heavy falling objects.

True or False

7. Clearing and grading is a process associated with finishing the exterior of a building. *T or F*

8. The person on a construction site who is directly accountable to the owner of the building project is the project manager. *T or F*

9. A safety harness is a belt that straps around the waist to prevent falls. *T or F*

10. Employers are legally required to maintain safe working conditions. *T or F*

Important Words

Architect On a construction project, the person who plans the structure to be built by creating scale drawings of the building and dimensions of all the elements.

Clearing and grading Activities associated with preparing a site for construction, including removing existing structures or plantings and shaping the surface of the ground.

Designer On a construction project, the person focused on the appearance and functional aspects of a structure.

Engineer On a construction project, the person focused on the structural integrity of a building and the materials used to build it.

Footing Solid concrete that is part of a building's foundation.

Foreperson On a construction project, a person who supervises individuals or crews, assigns tasks, and may also do some of the work.

General contractor On a construction project, the person responsible for building and completing the house or building, and who is accountable to the owner of the project.

General superintendent On a construction project, the person who works for the general contractor, supervises one or more project superintendents, and is responsible for making sure the project is completed on schedule and within budget.

PPE Personal Protective Equipment. Safety equipment, such as hard hats, safety boots, and gloves, required on a construction worksite.

Project manager On a construction project, the person focused on schedules, cost estimation and control, timely payments, and completion.

Project superintendent On a construction project, the person who manages the workers and their safety, assigns tasks to the foreperson, and is responsible for the quality of the finished structure.

Subcontractor On a construction project, a skilled worker or company of workers who handle various aspects of the project, including painting, plumbing, and roofing.

On the Trail of . . .

As you continue to narrow down your career choices in the construction industry, analyze the safety issues for three construction jobs that interest you. On a piece of paper, list what you would need to practice or learn to develop good safety habits for each job. Include in your list the types of PPE used for each job. Does the completed analysis increase your interest in one of the three jobs?

.com

Using the internet, locate the OSHA website, "Young Workers in Construction." Browse the areas of the website that interest you. Then go to the regular OSHA website and search for "Quick Cards." Print one of the quick cards that relates to one of your top three possible construction careers. If you can't print the card, write a summary of its points.

Being the First Choice

Knowing how to allocate resources—such as time, money, and materials—makes someone an important member of a construction team. If you can demonstrate these abilities, you can prove your value to a potential employer. Assume the position of project manager for a small building or renovating project. It can be something in your home, at school, or related to a hobby. Write an informal proposal for the project that describes the time, money, and materials needed for completion. You can use a project that you would like to complete or one that you have already completed. If you use one you have already completed, describe how well you managed your resources. For example, were you over or under budget? Did you buy too little or too much material? How much time did it actually take?

CHAPTER 9

Is a Career in Construction Right for You?

This is an exciting time in your life. Soon you will choose a career and enter the world of work. The career you select may be one that you will stick with for many years and maybe even until you retire. Or, it may be a starting point on your path to becoming an architect, building inspector, or teacher. Since you will be spending almost a third of your life at work, the occupation you choose ought to be something that you enjoy and that gives you a sense of purpose and personal pride.

The career decision you are about to make will determine the relative size of your paycheck, the type of benefits you will receive, where and how you will live, and what sort of lifestyle you will be able to afford. Your career decision can influence your life in many other ways as well. Your career may help you organize your life and give you a sense of purpose. It may change the way others think of you and the way you think of yourself. And, your career may be the source of many lasting friendships and good experiences.

For all of these reasons, choosing a career is an important step. You should make this decision carefully and thoughtfully while considering all of your reasonable options.

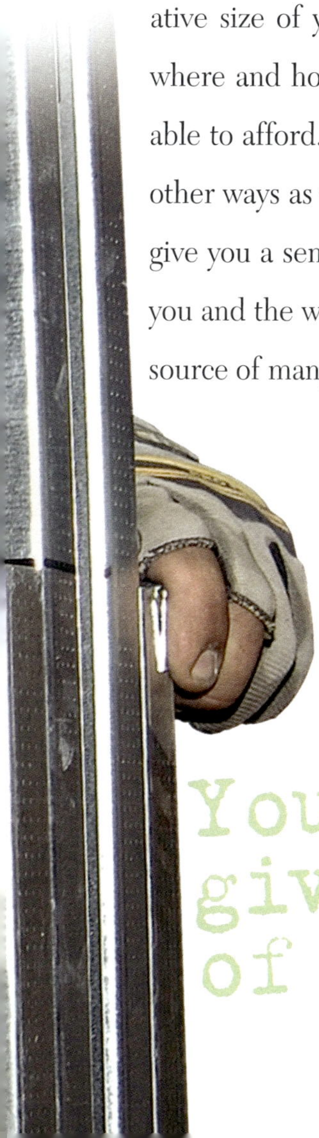

Your career may give you a sense of purpose.

What You Now Know

- That you have an interest in construction
- That the field of construction holds many opportunities
- The educational and training requirements to be successful

What You Will Know

- How to decide if construction is right for you
- How to narrow your choices

shout out!

Jan and Kim Nicosia of Detroit, Michigan, found a career that works perfectly for them: "Being husband and wife millwrights allows us to be together as we see much of the country while working at generating stations, automobile plants, and other factories. While this might not be the lifestyle for everyone, it makes us happy." After a recent training course to upgrade their skills, they said that "training allows us to keep living the dream as we have for more than a decade and a half of being together in a business that often keeps husband and wife apart."

1 Construction as a Career Choice

Your career options are as varied as the world of work itself. However, because you are reading this book, you may already be leaning toward a career in construction. To check this out, ask yourself the following questions:

Do you like...

* working with your hands?
* Are physical objects more interesting to you than words and numbers?
* Do you like the idea of doing physical work rather than working at a desk?
* Do you think you would like outdoor work?
* Do you like to build things?
* When you enter a building, do you ever wonder how it was built?
* When you step into a house, do you ask yourself how it could be made more functional or attractive?
* Do you like tools and machinery?
* Do you have a knack for fixing machines and making them run?

If you answered yes to most of these questions, then a career in construction may be a good choice for you.

There is a great deal of worthwhile information available on the internet or through libraries or government agencies such as the U.S. Department of Labor. However, you may get the most useful information from people who actually do the sort of work that interests you. Ask your friends and relatives if they know anyone who works in the construction industry. Even if this person does not have the exact occupation you are considering, he or she may be able to recommend someone who does. Experienced workers are almost always proud of their jobs, and are usually happy to tell you about their work life. They may even be willing to show you around a construction site.

Do you like tools and machinery?

Do you like the idea of doing physical work rather than working at a desk?

nailing it!

Chad Drake of Phoenix, Arizona, a carpenter for 12 years and now a superintendent, got inspiration about what to do with his life from someone close to him: "I remember my dad taking me to his jobsite when I was a kid. I knew he had a good job and that we were always taken care of, but it wasn't until I saw my father down in the earth, building a dam, that my eyes were opened to how amazing his work was." Is there someone in your life who is an inspiration? How has that inspiration affected you?

2 Deciding on an Occupation in Construction

If you have already decided that construction work is right for you, then your next step will be to decide which construction occupation to pursue. Evaluating the various construction occupations is partly just a matter of asking and answering questions such as the following:

- Does the idea of building structures with wood or concrete interest you? If so, then you might want to be a **commercial carpenter.**
- Do you like houses and finding ways to make them more attractive and functional? If so, then you might enjoy being a **residential carpenter.**
- Do you think you would like working with fine wood and veneer? Have you ever been interested in the elaborate exhibits used in conventions? If so, then you might enjoy **mill-cabinetmaking.**
- Do you appreciate attractive carpets and wood or tile floors? If so then you might enjoy being a **floor coverer.**
- Do you enjoy a wide variety of tasks when you are working? If so, then you might enjoy being an **interior systems carpenter.**
- Are you artistic? Does the thought of creating a metal framework for imaginative plaster structures interest you? If so, then you might enjoy being a **lather.**
- Do you like machinery and do you wonder how it is put together? If so, then you might enjoy being a **millwright.**
- Do you think you would like working outdoors creating foundations for large structures using concrete, steel, or wood? Or, if you are drawn to water, would you enjoy building piers or docks? If so, then you might enjoy being a **pile driver.**

Asking and answering questions such as these may help you narrow the list of likely construction occupations to a few or perhaps even to one.

building a better u

"School shop programs give us more qualified manpower coming into the workforce," says Bill White of K&W Construction in Hebron, Indiana. White has been in the business for 30 years, and employs graduates of a building trades training program. He feels that they tend to be more responsible and ambitious than average, and, because they know what they're doing, they don't face the frustration that a lot of new hires might experience. "It's a competitive market and they're a little more productive. The more productive your employees are, the more efficient you are, and you can pay them more if they know what they're doing."

answering

Do You Have What It Takes?

Construction occupations require a high level of skill in working with tools and materials. Do you have the patience and manual dexterity necessary to learn those skills? Are you willing to do the hard work it takes to learn them? To have a successful career in construction, you also need the following:

- Well-developed communication and math skills
- Ability to master technical processes and procedures
- Willingness to follow work and safety rules
- Ability to work as part of a team
- Ability to take direction from a supervisor
- Ability to accept criticism and take responsibility
- Willingness to work hard and stick to a job until it is done
- Ability to make sound decisions
- Ability to do quality work and take pride in a job well done

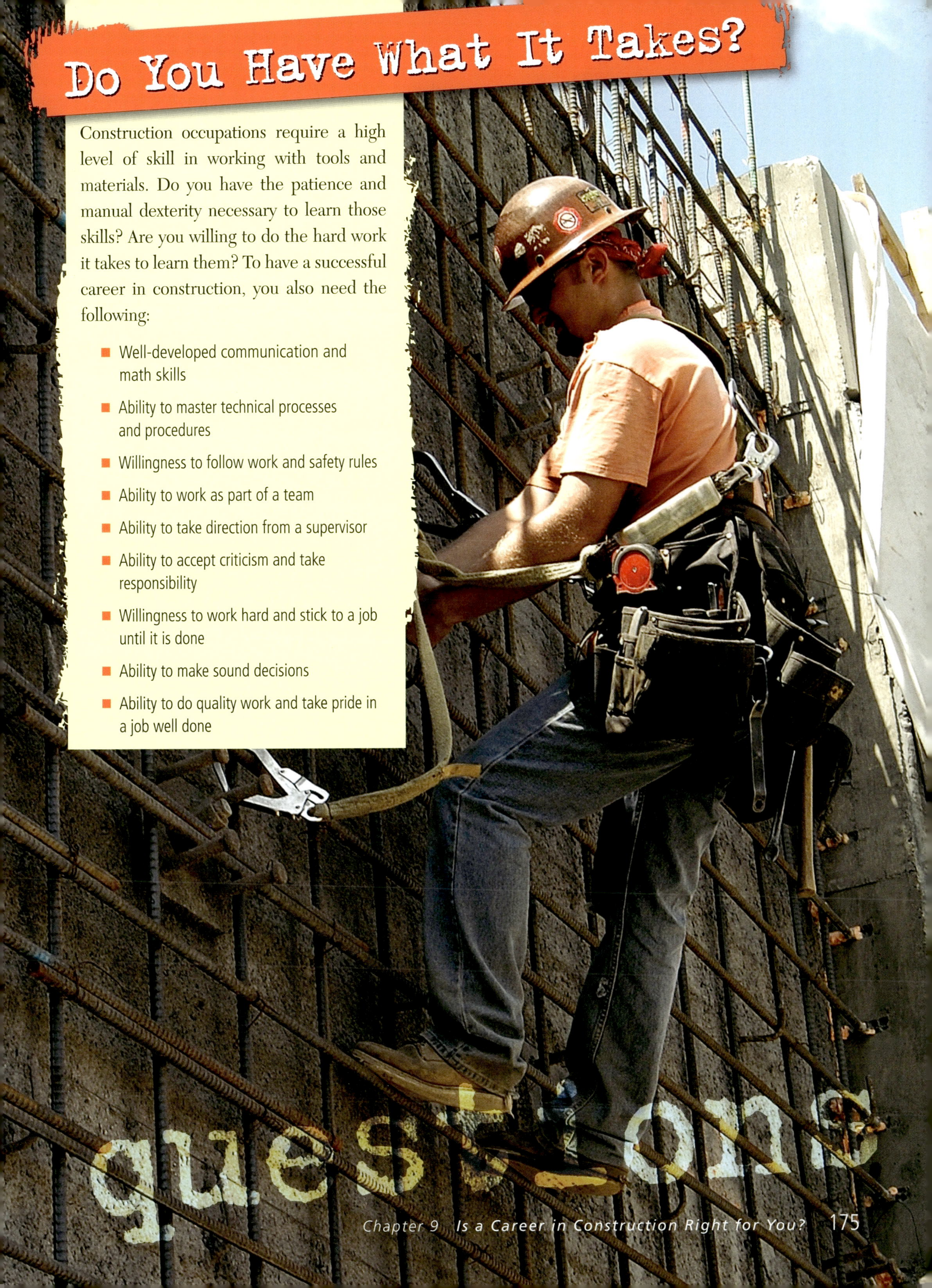

getting started

Getting Started So you want to do construction work? Then what's the best way to get started? If you are in high school now, you should enroll in classes that prepare you for your chosen occupation. Perhaps the best way to learn a construction occupation is to gain acceptance into a state or registered building trades apprenticeship program. Apprenticeships combine classroom study with paid practical experience in the workplace.

So you want to do construction work?

Your Career

The following checklist may help you measure your progress toward choosing an occupation.

- ☑ Recognize the need to make a career decision
- ☑ List your interests, values, goals, and personal strengths
- ☑ Evaluate career clusters
- ☑ Select the career cluster that best matches your interests, values, goals, and personal strengths

build the

Your Career and Your Life At your age, you have a lot of options. One of those options is a career in construction. If you develop a solid foundation of knowledge and skill, a construction career is more likely to provide you with satisfying employment than many other career choices. Construction workers can expect to be paid well and to receive some of the best benefits of any industry. Since people are always going to build things, construction occupations will always be in demand. Perhaps the best thing about a career in construction is that you can take pride in it. Construction workers can actually see and take satisfaction in what they have built, even many years after they completed the construction.

More than most career choices, a construction occupation offers you a strong sense of identity. You can tell people what you do and be proud of it. A career in construction offers you the opportunity not only to build impressive structures but also to build the life you want.

> Perhaps the best thing about a career in construction is that you can take pride in it.

Checklist

- Evaluate the occupations within the career cluster that appeal to you
- Select the occupation that is the best fit
- Enroll in classes that will help prepare you for your occupation
- Take community college or trade school classes
- Seek on-the-job training
- Join an apprenticeship program
- Become a journey worker

set goals and
motivate
yourself
www.careervoyages.gov

Chapter Check

On the Trail of . . .

Every industry has its celebrity professionals who inspire, motivate, or serve as role models. The construction industry is no exception—it has famous architects like Frank Gehry and Julia Morgan; high-profile developers like Steve Wynn and Donald Trump; and engaging carpenters like Ty Pennington, Paul DiMeo, Mike Holmes, and Norm Abram, to name a few. Research someone in the construction industry who can serve as a role model for you. It can be someone in the public eye or someone in your own backyard. It doesn't have to be someone with the exact job you want, but someone with the personal and professional qualities you want. Make a list of all qualities and skills this person has that have made him or her successful in the construction industry. Check off the qualities and skills you feel you already have and circle the ones you want to develop in yourself as you pursue your career. How has this person's work contributed to society? How might the work you choose contribute to society? Write your answers to these questions.

.com

Go to the website www.careervoyages.gov. Search "Construction." View the "In-Demand Occupations." Print the descriptions of the jobs that interest you. For each of these jobs, print a state report which shows local vs. national wage comparisons and employment trends. Add notes on your printed pages about the education and training required for each of the jobs. Explore the website further. Sample some of the career videos. Go to the page with construction career links. Explore some of those websites. Add to your notes the web addresses for at least three websites that you plan to revisit.

Being the First Choice

Self-management is the ability to assess your own knowledge and skills, set goals, and motivate yourself. It is a personal quality that employers value and that is necessary for you to make progress on your career path. Take the next step. Find out where you can get the education and training needed for the job you want. Use the website www.careervoyages.gov to find apprenticeships, community colleges, and career centers in your area. Choose three possible programs. How can you get into these programs? What are the requirements? When can you apply? Summarize your options. Discuss them with your family, teacher, and guidance counselor.

search **Construction**

view **In-Demand Occupations**

photo credits

The following are credited and their material used in the creation of *Career Connections: One Trade, Many Careers.* Permission requested where required.

Front Cover

Jupiterimages Corporation (tl), (tr), (cl), (cr); Blend Images / Jupiterimages (tc); Image Source / Jupiterimages (c); Brand X Pictures / Jupiter Images / Getty (bl); Blend Images / Punchstock (bc); Corbis / Punchstock (br); Bittbox (bkg)

Front Matter

Pages ii–iii, Bittbox; page iv, Bittbox; page v, Image Source / Jupiter Images (tr); Jupiterimages Corporation (tc), (tr), (tr), (bl); Shutterstock Images (cr); page vi, Bittbox (tl); Getty Images / Christopher Robbins (tr); Jupiterimages Corporation (cl), (bl); page vii, Jupiterimages Corporation (t), (b); Bittbox, (tc); Southwest Regional Council of Carpenters (lc); Blend Images / Jupiter Images / Jose Luis Pelaez, Inc. (br); page viii, Bittbox; page ix, Jupiterimages Corporation (cl), (cr), (bl), (bc),(bc), (bc), (bl); Getty Images / Foodpix (cr); Creatas / Jupiter Images (cr); Shutterstock Images; page x, Southwest Regional Council of Carpenters (tc),(tc), (tc), (tc), (tc), (c), (c); Jupiterimages Corporation; page xi, Jupiterimages Corporation (c); Southwest Regional Council of Carpenters (c), (c), (c), (c), (c), (bc); page xii, Jupiterimages Corporation (tl), (tr), (cr), (cl), (bl), (bc), (br); Southwest Regional Council of Carpenters (cl); Southwest Regional Council of Carpenters (cl), (cl); Istockphoto (cl); Jon Wire - Local Philadelphia 1906 (bl); Norbert McLaughlin (b); page xiii, Jupiterimages Corporation; page xiv, Bittbox (t); Jupiterimages Corporation (tl); page xv, Shutterstock Images

Part 1 Opener

Page 2, Jupiterimages Corporation; page 3, Getty Images / Foodpix (tl); Jupiterimages Corporation (tc), (cr); Creatas / Jupiter Images (tr); Shutterstock Images, (cl)

Chapter 1

Page 4, Jupiterimages Corporation, (tl), (tr), (c); page 5, Jupiterimages Corporation, (tl), (tr); page 6, Brand X Pictures / Jupiter Images, (tl); Jupiterimages Corporation, (tc), (tc); Image Source / Jupiter Images, (tr); page 7, Image Source / Jupiter Images; pages 8–9, Jupiterimages Corporation; page 10, Image Source / Jupiter Images, (tr); Image 100 / Punchstock, (tc); Jupiterimages Corporation, (tc); Creatas / Jupiter Images, (cl); page 11, Jupiterimages Corporation, (tr); Shutterstock Images, (br); page 12, Jupiterimages Corporation, (tl), (tc), (tc), (cl); Image 100 / Puchstock, (tr); page 13, Shutterstock Images (tc); Jupiterimages Corporation, (c), (bl); page 14, Shutterstock Images, (cl); Jupiterimages Corporation, (bl); page 15, Jupiterimages Corporation; page 16, Punchstock / Corbis (tl); Jupiterimages Corporation, (tc), (cl); Brand X Pictures / Jupiter Images (tc); Score by Aflo / Jupiter Images, (tr); page 17, Jupiterimages Corporation; pages 18–19, Rubberball / Jupiter Images; page 20, Polka Dot / Jupiter Images, (tl); Jupiterimages Corporation, (tc), (lc); Shutterstock Images, (tc); Corbis / Punchstock, (tr); Comstock / Jupiter Images, (bc); page 21, Jupiterimages Corporation; pages 22–23, Jupiterimages Corporation,(bkg)

Chapter 2

Page 24, Jupiterimages Corporation, (tl), (cl), (tc), (bkg); page 25, Jupiterimages Corporation, (tl), (tr); page 26, Jupiterimages Corporation, (tl), (tc), (tc), (tr), (lc), (bl); page 27, Image Source / Jupiter Images, (tr); page 28, Jupiterimages Corporation; page 29, Jupiterimages Corporation, (tl), (tc), (tc), (cr); Inspirestock / Jupiter Images, (tr); page 30, Jupiterimages Corporation, (tl), (bl); page 31, Jupiterimages Corporation, (tl), (tc), (tr), (cl); pages 32–33, Jupiterimages Corporation; page 34, Blend Images / Punchstock; page 35, Jupiterimages Corporation; page 36, Blend Images / Punchstock; page 37, Jupiterimages Corporation (bkg), (bc); pages 38–39, Jupiterimages Corporation (bkg)

Part 2 Opener

Page 40, Punchstock / Blend Images; page 41, Jupiterimages Corporation, (tl), (tc), (cr); Corbis / Punchstock (tr); Comstock Images / Jupiter Images (cl)

Chapter 3

Page 42, Jupiterimages Corporation (c), (tr); page 43, Jupiterimages Corporation (tl), (c); Inspirestock / Punchstock (tc); Brand X Pictures / Getty Images (tr); page 44, Jupiterimages Corporation (tl), (tr); Southwest Regional Council of Carpenters (tc); Istockphoto (cl); page 45, Jupiterimages Corporation, (t); Istockphoto, (cr); page 46, Jupiterimages Corporation (tl), (cl); Southwest Regional Council of Carpenters (tc); Bigstock Photo (tc); Istock Photo; Shutterstock Images (bl); page 47, Bigstock Photo, (tl); Southwest Regional Council of Carpenters (tr); Jupiterimages Corporation, (cl), (br); page 48, Bigstock Photo; Bigstock Photo; Istockphoto; page 49, Getty Images / Christopher Robbins (c), (br); Shutterstock Images (bc); page 50, Jupiterimages Corporation (tl), (tc), (tr); Blend Images / Jupiter Images / Jose Luis Pelaez, Inc (tc); Shutterstock Images (cl); Shutterstock Images / Diego Cervo, (bl); page 51, Jupiterimages Corporation (tr); Getty Images / Yellow Dog Productions (b); page 52, Jupiterimages Corporation (tl); page 53, Southwest Regional Council of Carpenters; page 54, Jupiterimages Corporation (tl), (tc), (bl); Southwest Regional Council of Carpenters (tr); page 55, Blend Images / Jupiter Images; page 56, Cultura / Jupiter Images; page 57, Istockphoto / Lise Gagne; page 58, Jupiter Images / Getty Images; page 59, Shutterstock Images (tc), (tc); Jupiterimages Corporation; Jupiterimages Corporation; page 60, Shutterstock Images; page 61, Shutterstock Images; page 62, Shutterstock Images; page 63, Jupiterimages Corporation; pages 64–65, Jupiterimages Corporation

Chapter 4

Page 66, Jupiterimages Corporation (tl), (tc), (tr); Blend Images / Jupiter Images (bl); page 67, Jupiterimages Corporation (tl), (tr); page 68, Jupiterimages Corporation (tl), (tc), (tc), (tr); Shutterstock Images / Gelpi; page 69, Jupiterimages Corporation (cl), (cr); pages 70–71, Jupiterimages Corporation; page 72, Shutterstock Images (bkg); page 73, Shutterstock Images; page 74, Shutterstock Images (bl), (tl); Southwest

Regional Council of Carpenters (cl); page 75, Shutterstock Images, (bkg); Southwest Regional Council of Carpenters; page 76, Shutterstock Images (tl), (tc), (tc); Jupiterimages Corporation (tr), (tl), (cl), (cl), (c); page 77, Design Pics RF / Jupiter Images; Jupiterimages Corporation; page 78, Jupiterimages Corporation; page 79, Shutterstock Images; page 80, Istockphoto (tl), (tc); Shutterstock Images (tr), (tl); Jupiterimages Corporation (bl); page 81, Jupiterimages Corporation; pages 82–83 Jupiterimages Corporation (bkg); page 83, Blend Images / Jupiter Images / Jose Luis Pelaez, Inc.; pages 84–85, Jupiterimages Corporation (bkg)

Chapter 5

Page 86, Jupiterimages Corporation (tl), (c), (cl); Ron Olson, (tr); page 87, Jupiterimages Corporation (tl), (tr); page 88, Jupiterimages Corporation (tl), (tc), (tc), (tr), (lc), (br); Page 89, Jupiterimages Corporation; page 90, Jupiterimages Corporation (tl), (lc), (bl), (bc), (br), (bl); page 91, Jupiterimages Corporation (tl), (tc), (tc), (tr), (bl), (bc), (br); pages 92–93, Shutterstock Images; page 94, Jupiterimages Corporation; page 95, Jupiterimages Corporation; page 96, Jupiterimages Corporation (bl); page 97, Jupiterimages Corporation (tl), (c), (tr), (cl), (cr), (b); Shutterstock Images (tc); page 98, Jupiterimages Corporation; page 99, Jupiterimages Corporation; page 100, Jupiterimages Corporation (tl), (tc), (tc), (tc), (tr); Shutterstock Images (tl); John Lund/Drew Kelly / Blend Images / Jupiterimages (cl); page 101, Jupiterimages Corporation; pages 102–103, PhotoAlto / Punchstock; page 104, Jupiterimages Corporation; page 105, Jupiterimages Corporation (tl), (tc), (tr), (br); pages 106–107, Corbis / Jupiter Images; pages 108–109, Jupiterimages Corporation

Part 3 Opener

Page 110, Dreamstime (bc); 123RF (bkg); page 111, Jupiterimages Corporation (tl), (tc); Shutterstock Images (tr), (tr), (cr)

Chapter 6

Page 112, Jupiterimages Corporation (bl), (tc); Shutterstock Images (tl); page 113, Punchstock (tl); Jupiterimages Corporation (tr); page 114, Jupiterimages Corporation (bl); Southwest Regional Council of Carpenters (tl); 123RF (tc), (tc), (tr); page 115, Jupiterimages Corporation (cr); page 116, Shutterstock Images (bkg); page 117, 123RF (tl); Shutterstock Images (tc), (tc), (tc), (tr), (cl), (cr); page 118, Dreamstime (tl); page 119, 123RF (tr); page 120, Southwest Regional Council of Carpenters (tl); page 121, Jupiterimages Corporation (bc); Dreamstime (tl), (cl), (cr); Shutterstock Images (tc), (tr); page 122, Shutterstock Images (bkg); page 123, Southwest Regional Council of Carpenters (b), (tc); Shutterstock Images (tl), (cl), (cr); Dreamstime (tc), (tr); page 124, Dreamstime (bkg); Shutterstock Images (bl); page 125, Southwest Regional Council of Carpenters (bl); Jupiterimages Corporation (tc), (cl), (cr); 123RF (tc); page 126, Southwest Regional Council of Carpenters (cl); page 127, 123RF (bl); Jupiterimages Corporation (br),(tl), (tc); Shutterstock Images (tc), (tr); Southwest Regional Council of Carpenters (cr); page 128, Jupiterimages Corporation (tl); pages 128–129, Jupiterimages Corporation (bkg); page 129, Jupiterimages Corporation (br); pages 130–131, Jupiterimages Corporation (bkg)

Chapter 7

Page 132, Southwest Regional Council of Carpenters (c); Shutterstock Images (tl); Jupiterimages Coporation (tr); page 133, Ray Heaton (tl); Southwest Regional Council of Carpenters (tr); istockphoto (br); page 134, Jupiterimages Corporation (tl); Jupiterimages Corporation (cl), (cr), (tr); Shutterstock Images (b); page 135, Southwest Regional Council of Carpenters (tr); page 139, Southwest Regional Council of Carpenters (tl), (tc), (tr); Jupiterimages Corporation (b); page 140,Southwest Regional Council of Carpenters (l); page 141, Southwest Regional Council of Carpenters (tl), (tlc), (tr); Dick Quinn (tc); istockphoto (tc); Jon Wire, Local Philadelphia 1906 (cl); Norbert McLaughlin SME (b); page 142, Southwest Regional Council of Carpenters (l); page 143, Mike Bennie; page 144, Southwest Regional Council of Carpenters; page 145, Shutterstock Images (tl); Shutterstock Images (tc); Jupiterimages Corporation (tc), (tr), (cl), (bl), (bl); page 146, Jupiterimages Corporation (tl), (tl), (cl), (cr), (bl), (bc), (cr), (br); Shutterstock Images (tc); page 147, Jupiterimages Corporation (tr), (cr), (bc), (br); page 148, Jupiterimages Corporation (tl), (tc), (tr), (cl), (bkg), (c); Shutterstock Images (br); page 149, Jupiterimages Corporation (tr), (cr), (bl), (br); page 150, Southwest Regional Council of Carpenters (tc), (tr); Jupiterimages Corporation (c); page 151, Southwest Regional Council of Carpenters (tc), (tr)

Chapter 8

Page 152, Southwest Regional Council of Carpenters (tl), (tc), (tc), (tc), (tr); pages 152–153, Southwest Regional Council of Carpenters (b); page 154, Southwest Regional Council of Carpenters (t), (bl); Jupiterimages Corporation (br); page 155, Jupiterimages Corporation (tr); page 156, Southwest Regional Council of Carpenters (tl); Dick Quinn (tc); Jupiterimages Corporation (bl); page 157, Southwest Regional Council of Carpenters (tr); Jupiterimages Corporation (b); page 158, Jupiterimages Corporation; page 159, Southwest Regional Council of Carpenters (tc), (tr), (cl), (b); page 160, Southwest Regional Council of Carpenters (tl), (tc), (tc), (tr), (bl); Jupiterimages Corporation (b); page 161, Jupiterimages Corporation (tc), (tr), (br); page 162, Southwest Regional Council of Carpenters; page 163, Jupiterimages Corporation (cr), (bl), (bl); page 164, Jupiterimages Corporation (tc); Southwest Regional Council of Carpenters (bl); pages 164–165, Jupiterimages Corporation (bkg); page 165, Southwest Regional Council of Carpenters (tr); pages 166–167, Jupiterimages Corporation (bkg)

Chapter 9

Page 170, Southwest Regional Council of Carpenters (tr), (c); page 172, Southwest Regional Council of Carpenters (tl), (tc), (tc), (tc), (tr), (bl); page 173, Southwest Regional Council of Carpenters (tr); page 174, Dick Quinn (tl); Southwest Regional Council of Carpenters (tc), (tc), (tr); Ron Olson (cl); page 175, Southwest Regional Council of Carpenters; page 176, Southwest Regional Council of Carpenters; page 177, Southwest Regional Council of Carpenters; page 178, Southwest Regional Council of Carpenters; page 179, Jupiterimages Corporation (bkg)